China's Cinema of Class

China's commercial film industry can be used as a map to understand how class is interwoven into the imaginations that inform and influence social change in Chinese society. Film consumption is important in this process, particularly for young adult urbanites that are China's primary commercial cinema patrons.

This book investigates the web between the representation of class themes in Chinese film narratives, local audience reception to these films, and the socialisation of China's contemporary class society. Bringing together textual analyses of narratives from five commercially exhibited films: *Let the Bullets Fly* (Jiang: 2010), *Lost on Journey* (Yip: 2011), *Go Lala Go!* (Xu: 2011), *House Mania* (Sun: 2011) and *The Piano in the Factory* (Zheng: 2011); and the reception of 179 Chinese audiences from varying class positions, it investigates the extent to which fictional narratives inform and reflect current class identities in present-day China. Through group discussions in Beijing, Hangzhou, Nanjing, Lanzhou and Taiyuan, the author searches for audiences beyond major cities that are typically the focus of film consumption studies in China. As such, the book reveals not only how deeply and widespread the socialisation of China's class society has become in the imaginations of Chinese audiences, but also what appears to be a preference of both audiences and filmmakers for the continuation of China's new class society.

Revealing the extent to which cinema continues to play a key role in the socialisation of class structures in contemporary Chinese society, this book will be important for students and scholars of Chinese Studies, Film Studies, Communication Studies, as well as observers of China's film industry.

Nicole Talmacs is a Lecturer in Media and Communication at Xi'an Jiaotong-Liverpool University, China.

Routledge Studies on China in Transition
Series Editor: David S. G. Goodman

42 Young Chinese in Urban China
Alex Cockain

43 Prostitution Scandals in China
Policing, media and society
Elaine Jeffreys

44 Unequal China
The political economy and cultural politics of inequality
Edited by Wanning Sun and Yingjie Guo

45 Elites and Governance in China
Edited by Xiaowei Zang and Chien-Wen Kou

46 Choosing China's Leaders
Edited by Chien-Wen Kou and Xiaowei Zang

47 Rural Policy Implementation in Contemporary China
New socialist countryside
Anna L. Ahlers

48 NGO Governance and Management in China
Edited by Reza Hasmath and Jennifer Y. J. Hsu

49 Dams, Migration and Authoritarianism in China
The Local State in Yunnan
Sabrina Habich

50 New Mentalities of Government in China
Edited by David Bray and Elaine Jeffreys

51 China's Cinema of Class
Audiences and Narratives
Nicole Talmacs

China's Cinema of Class
Audiences and Narratives

Nicole Talmacs

LONDON AND NEW YORK

First published 2017
by Routledge
2 Park Square, Milton Park, Abingdon, Oxon OX14 4RN

and by Routledge
711 Third Avenue, New York, NY 10017

Routledge is an imprint of the Taylor & Francis Group, an informa business

© 2017 Nicole Talmacs

The right of Nicole Talmacs to be identified as author of this work has been asserted by her in accordance with sections 77 and 78 of the Copyright, Designs and Patents Act 1988.

All rights reserved. No part of this book may be reprinted or reproduced or utilised in any form or by any electronic, mechanical, or other means, now known or hereafter invented, including photocopying and recording, or in any information storage or retrieval system, without permission in writing from the publishers.

Trademark notice: Product or corporate names may be trademarks or registered trademarks, and are used only for identification and explanation without intent to infringe.

Every effort has been made to contact copyright holders. Please advise the publisher of any errors or omissions, and these will be corrected in subsequent editions.

British Library Cataloguing-in-Publication Data
A catalogue record for this book is available from the British Library

Library of Congress Cataloging-in-Publication Data
Names: Talmacs, Nicole, author.
Title: China's cinema of class : audiences and narratives / Nicole Talmacs.
Description: Milton Park, Abingdon, Oxon ; New York, NY :
   Routledge, 2017. | Series: Routledge studies on China in transition ; 51 |
   Includes bibliographical references and index.
Identifiers: LCCN 2016040135 | ISBN 9781138228009 (hardback) |
   ISBN 9781315393988 (ebook)
Subjects: LCSH: Social classes in motion pictures. | Motion pictures—
   Social aspects—China. | China—In motion pictures.
Classification: LCC PN1995.9.S6 T35 2017 | DDC 791.43/6552—dc23
LC record available at https://lccn.loc.gov/2016040135

ISBN: 978-1-138-22800-9 (hbk)
ISBN: 978-1-315-39398-8 (ebk)

Typeset in Times New Roman
by Apex CoVantage, LLC

Printed and bound in Great Britain by
TJ International Ltd, Padstow, Cornwall

For my parents

Contents

List of figures and tables		viii
List of abbreviations		ix
Acknowledgements		x
1	Chinese audiences and the cinema of class	1
2	Class on screen and in reality: pre-conditioning audiences	22
3	*Let the Bullets Fly*: the socialisation of assumptions	27
4	*Lost on Journey*: prejudice in class relations	49
5	*Go Lala Go!*: secretaries, shopping and spinsterhood	73
6	*House Mania*: homeownership, marriageability and masculinity	99
7	*The Piano in a Factory*: *suzhi*, industrial heroes and the spectacle of poverty	127
8	Conclusion: class, the film and the filmmaker	146
	Films list	153
	Appendix: group discussants	154
	Let the Bullets Fly 154	
	Lost on Journey 160	
	Go Lala Go! 167	
	House Mania 173	
	The Piano in a Factory 179	
	Index	187

Figures and tables

Figures

3.1	Promotional film poster: *Let the Bullets Fly*	27
3.2	Overthrowing landlords in the *Red Detachment of Women*	41
3.3	The peasantry listen intently to Qionghua	41
3.4	Zhang Mazi yells over his shoulder to mobilise the poor	42
4.1	Promotional film poster: *Lost on Journey*	49
4.2	Industrial juxtapositions in *Lost on Journey*	55
4.3	All beggars are liars	65
5.1	Promotional film poster: *Go Lala Go!*	73
5.2	Cuteness has its rewards	80
5.3	Shoes as power in *Go Lala Go!*	92
6.1	Promotional film poster: *House Mania*	99
6.2	"Many film directors live in this building"	112
6.3	Xiao Hei is "cured"	113
6.4	"All companies that have rented this space have made it to the Fortune 500 list"	113
6.5	Yingming announces an evacuation due to the H1N1 virus	113
6.6	Yingming as an aging university entrance examiner	114
6.7	"Baldy" arrives with his cash to buy property	120
7.1	Promotional film poster: *The Piano in a Factory*	127
7.2	Chen Guilin seeks collective solutions	141

Table

5.1	Product placement count for *Go Lala Go!*	91

Abbreviations

CCP	Chinese Communist Party
CCTV	China Central Television
CFGC	China Film Group Corporation
CGI	Computer Graphics Imaging
CHIP	Chinese Household Inequality Project
KTV	Karaoke Television
PRC	People's Republic of China
RMB	*Renminbi* [人民币]: Chinese dollar
SAPPRFT	State Administration of Press, Publication, Radio, Film and Television
SARFT	State Administration of Radio, Film and Television
SOE	State-Owned Enterprise
USD	United States dollar

Acknowledgements

This book would not have been possible without the assistance and support of a great many people. I would like to first and foremost extend my deepest gratitude to Professor David Goodman for his guidance and support throughout this project, and for the invitation to include the volume in Routledge's studies on *China in Transition*. I would furthermore like to extend my gratitude to Professor Wanning Sun for her insightful observations and suggestions as the project progressed.

To carry out the fieldwork required for this project, a great many people extended their assistance to ensure that everything ran smoothly. My sincerest appreciation goes to Professor Li (Northwest Normal University), Professor Yao (Shanxi Finance and Economics University), Professor Zhou (Nanjing University), Dr Li (Shanghai International Studies University), Dr Hao (Tsinghua University), Dr. Lü (Chinese Academy of Social Sciences), Jiang Zheng, Lucy Dean, Chen Long and Fern Huey Tan, for their efforts in coordinating willing discussants, and in some occasions, ensuring that film screenings went ahead despite adversity. Thanks also to my friends Nate Jones, Chen Long and Sveta Peshina, who generously opened their homes to me during the fieldwork.

The support my friends and family have shown me throughout this project has likewise been overwhelming. The discussions I had with my father Rudi on issues pertaining to the content in this book I will cherish well into my future, while special mention goes to my uncle, Peter, who advised me on earlier drafts, and finally the relentless encouragement Bede Payne gave to make sure this book went to print. My thanks also to my many friends, not all of whom can be listed here, who provided me necessary coffee breaks to get across the line.

Last, and most certainly not least, a warm thank you is extended to the 217 (of which 179 feature in this book) discussants who gave up their time to attend these film screenings and share with me their thoughts and opinions across China. Likewise, to producer Jessica Kam, who took the time out of her busy schedule to discuss with me the production of *The Piano in a Factory*. It goes without saying that I take full responsibility for the manner in which conversations have been framed in the following pages.

1 Chinese audiences and the cinema of class

What is often discussed is a nation's cinema, but very seldom do we speak of a nation's cinema of class. Namely, how a national cinema socialises the class structures that inform the nation's broader narrative of social organisation. Studies of Chinese cinema to date are not excluded from this predicament. While one can draw general assumptions in hindsight about the role that Chinese cinema played in socialising class in the founding of the People's Republic of China (PRC, hereafter referred to as "China") during 1949–1976, in part because class rhetoric was so prominent in the establishment of the modern Chinese nation state, the relationship between film consumption and the socialisation of class among Chinese audiences in contemporary China has been largely overlooked – not only in terms of how filmmakers portray narratives about class for the big screen, but how one film narrative may take on unique meanings when consumed by audiences through different class lenses, and what implications this may have for everyday life in socially stratified China. China's cinema of class emerges in this book through textual analyses of five commercially distributed and exhibited films across the country during 2010–2011: *Let the Bullets Fly* 《让子弹飞》 (Jiang: 2011), *Lost on Journey* 《人在囧途》 (Yip: 2010), *Go Lala Go!* 《杜拉拉升职记》 (Xu: 2010), *House Mania* 《房不剩防》 (Sun: 2011) and *The Piano in a Factory* 《钢的琴》 (Zhang: 2011); and their receptions gathered through discussion groups with Chinese audiences of varying classes in Beijing, Hangzhou, Lanzhou, Nanjing and Taiyuan.

Class in contemporary China is ubiquitous, though the previously favoured peasant-worker-soldier narratives are notably absent from the current Chinese commercial film circuit. The absence of socialist narratives for commercial consumption provides cinema-goers a clear indication that class struggles are no longer matters of concern for China's big-screen characters, and by extension should not be for their audiences. A glance at the domestic films exhibited in China's rapidly expanding cinema circuit would lead one to believe that Chinese society is full of optimism and opportunities for all to contribute to the nation's development – and stem from the dominant Han Chinese ethnicity. For characters that *do* struggle, they are shown to understand that their hardship or class subordination is for the nation's and their own interests. In contrast to the language of the "masses" (*qunzhong*, 群众) that glossed over the very likely inequalities of film

2 The cinema of class

consumption during Mao Zedong's leadership from 1949 to 1976 (Clark 2011; Hemelryk Donald 2014), today's commercial cinema programming overseen by the State Administration of Press, Publications, Film, Radio and Television (SAP-PRFT) appears to favour urban lifestyles and middle class audiences over any others. Not a class that prefers to watch films more so than any other, merely a class that will ideally characterise and lead China's harmonious development to an olive-shaped (*ganlanxing shehui*, 橄榄型社会) consumer society.

It is difficult in hindsight to draw conclusions with certainty about how propaganda films exhibited during Mao's leadership aided the socialisation of class, particularly as box office information from this era is sketchy at best (Zhang 2004: 192; Clark 2011). Paul Clark's (2012: 42) comment that film spectatorship was a "combination of pleasure at the images of socialist heroes of this era and pain at the limited choices available" does provide some indication of the film consumer's experience. The replication of production values and authoritative moral voice of propaganda films from this period in Chinese film history (so much so Yomi Braester [2008] calls for the political campaign to be understood as a genre) does seem to suggest that Chinese filmmakers during the socialist era produced films from the position that Chinese audiences were or had to be uniform in how they were socialised, even if this was in rhetoric only. Likewise, Chinese audiences possessed a willingness and commitment to the communist class narrative onscreen, or at a minimum were required to appear to do so. As such, scholarship to date has generally accepted that the communist narratives and film production qualities during Mao's reign were unapologetically instructional and broadly targeted. The Chinese audience's engagement was, in turn, appropriately pedagogical.

Now facing one of the world's greatest degrees of social and economic inequality, maintaining social harmony while pursuing China's economic reform agenda requires new approaches to the stories people tell, consume and share about what China's current socio-economic status quo is. Contemporary mainstream cinema in China thus produces class narratives that inform new class identities, legitimises prejudice towards class others, affirms assumptions about the permanence of these inequalities and advocates a pragmatic acquiescence to the politico-economic structure as it is currently organised. Chinese audiences in turn are far from uniform in their film consumption practices, and class position quite explicitly informs the sense-making processes they employ when watching these very films.

As film consumers, Chinese audiences actively seek out commercial films that appeal to their entertainment sensibilities to watch (if they have the opportunity to do so at all), or act upon recommendations of their peers. These entertainment sensibilities are informed by their experiences of Chinese society, which is more frequently being informed by their experiences with China's now politically acceptable class differentiation, vis-à-vis historically, when film production and consumption were exercises in propagating Mao's discourse of a class*less* society. A range of factors can inform class positioning and thus experience in contemporary China: income, education, access to social welfare and infrastructure, political membership or association, household registration (*hukou* 户口), geographical location, gender and ethnicity. Often, the variances in these factors are informed

The cinema of class 3

directly or indirectly by social planning policies initiated by the Party-state. In a country rapidly increasing its number of cinema projection screens, Chinese audiences are in turn becoming finely attuned to commercial films that were not intended for their consumption. In other words, Chinese audiences are resoundingly conscious of which class films are targeted to. As a result, class ideals in film narratives can be tailored to appeal to either privileged or underprivileged audiences, or a combination of both; ultimately informing the moral and entertainment value that audiences gain from being active (or potentially active) cinema-goers. A narrowing diversity of commercial films produced that are attractive, however, or accessible to all Chinese audiences, has meant that the tastes of a great majority of Chinese audiences are not being catered to within the commercial cinema space, creating inequalities in cinema consumption across China.

Regardless of whether film production directly or indirectly relies on the Party-state institutionally through SAPPRFT for production assistance and distribution endorsement, the films that *do* receive commercial exhibition across China can only be understood as very real (and sometimes lucrative) proponents of social change in China. This book does not attempt to determine whether the film narrative or the audience is of greater importance in socialising class, though it does argue that the class of an audience plays a significant role in determining how a film's narrative is comprehended and what elements of a narrative attract an audience's focus when watching these very films. It is furthermore not explicitly concerned with critiquing the artistic practice of commercial filmmaking in contemporary China. It is about the narratives, the audiences, and how they *both* relate to the socialisation of class taking place on the periphery of what is typically discussed and examined by scholars of Chinese cinema and society.

New directions

Scholarship to date has typically focused on addressing Chinese films attractive to the Western academe's curiosities and opportunities in the Chinese film industry, while the domestic film industry's social relevance to Chinese audiences has been little explored (Berry 2012: 494). With local blockbusters becoming legitimate commercial competition to Hollywood imports, the time is ripe for examination of the domestically produced films that Chinese filmgoers are willingly paying to consume. As Yomi Braester (2005: 552) says, contemporary commercial Chinese films "aim not only at box office success, but also at shaping economic agendas and visual experience, social networks and [the] aesthetic environment" of its Chinese audiences. But while Braester stops short of including class identities and class relations to this list, one could argue that socialising new class identities and relations is in fact the crux of each of the agendas that Braester lists.

Since the commercial reform of the Chinese film industry, the argument has been made by Ying Zhu (2003: 2) that "[t]he arrival of a Hollywood-influenced popular entertainment wave has taken Chinese cinema back to its commercial roots, undermining cinema's pedagogical/ideological value promoted by the state and its aesthetic value advocated by film artists." Zhu's position, though, overlooks

4 *The cinema of class*

the continued prerogative that the Party-state maintains over the control of cinema and cultural production through its censorship approval processes, and media broadcasting more broadly. As Matthew Johnson (2012: 173) warns, "it is easy to overestimate the degree to which these reforms represent an actual challenge to the propaganda state model." What may seem like a retreat from official control over the Chinese commercial film industry could arguably have as much to do with a socialised consensus among Chinese filmmakers of the necessity for China's broader reform agenda than a loosening of intense interest in the film industry by the Party-state. Indeed, SAPPRFT's duty is to be the Chinese Party-state's institutional cultural gatekeeper, and the Party-state does not answer to the film industry – the film industry requires SAPPRFT and the Party-state's approval for its viability and expansion; like any other industry that operates on the financial and ideological scale that the film industry does in China. Commercial filmmaking in China can only be understood as a mutually beneficial activity for all involved: the Party-state, filmmakers, commercial film exhibitors and film consumers. This said, Chinese audiences do continue to be aware of the authority the Party-state has through SAPPRFT in officially sanctioning film exhibition in China, while also recognising the quantity of non-official interests involved in a film's production. As such, the dynamic between commercial film production and consumption in China is unique to film industries and audiences around the world.

The commercialisation of China's film industry is not solely responsible for China's present degrees of class consciousness; nor is the Party-state solely responsible for the narratives commercial films relay. The Chinese commercial film industry with its potential for mass production and distribution and ongoing need for state approval, though, is simply one forum within which class and class consciousness in Chinese society is manifest and can, and should, be investigated as imaginary, politically and economically driven phenomena. As the following chapters reveal, filmmakers' narratives and audiences alike appear to be in agreement about the inability to reverse China's class society, some audiences even indicating a preference *for* a class society after watching the films that are the focus of this study. If this is the case, then China's popular cinema's contribution to legitimising the inequalities that China faces as acceptable, particularly among a privileged and educated audience who are most inclined to visit a mainstream cinema, should be keenly investigated and contemplated for how we may understand social change and the responsibilities of creative work in contemporary China.

Audiences and sense making

Suggesting that class influences media consumption is not new. A recent study by Shanghai's Fudan University's Research Centre for Information and Communication Studies (复旦大学信息与传播研究中心 2010: 1–3) for example found that the adoption and utilisation of new media in a Shanghai context is influenced by a user's economic capacities, gender and age, which results in differences in residents' understandings of their *citizenship, identities and attitudes towards social integration and class awareness*. Similarly, audience research in England has revealed the extent to which class lenses can, and do, influence television consumption and identity formation among English audiences (Morely and Brunsdon 1999; Skeggs 2009; Wood and Skeggs 2011). Despite China's and the UK's contrasting social histories and contemporary systems of political organisation, scholarship suggests that where class exists, social inequalities can and do influence how media is consumed, and by extension social behaviour. While Guiquan Xu (2014: 151) argues that Chinese communications scholars have yet to develop terminology in Chinese that captures the notion of sense making implied by the English term "audiences", this book argues that sense making is, nonetheless, what Chinese audiences do when they watch *cinema*, and that the present-day socialisation of class directly informs this sense-making process. Arguably, this has always been the case, and it is from this standpoint that this book takes its point of departure. Simply put, understanding the sense making of contemporary Chinese commercial films by Chinese audiences requires an understanding of the pre-conditioning audiences bring to their sense-making processes: whether class privilege has pre-conditioned an audience member to engage in spectatorship-as-citizen and agent, or class subordination has encouraged spectatorship-as-state subject; albeit these are not always mutually exclusive. China's cinema of class is a dynamic site by which variances in pre-conditioning create variances in sense making among Chinese audiences. As such, China requires a diversified film industry to meet these audience needs, as the films featured in these following pages reveal.

Commercial filmmakers rely on engaging narratives for their audiences to be convincingly transported and ensure a film's commercial success. In turn, audiences pitch their own realities and experiences against the experiences of the fictitious characters to make sense of the circumstances presented by the filmmakers. In the viewing process, audiences respond consciously or not to internal questions such as, *what would I do if I were in this situation? Do I believe this story? Do I agree with how the narrative was resolved? What in this story attracts or repels me? Which characters do I like or dislike?* Often the result of this process is summed up in a simple question we ask each other as we leave the cinema: *"so, what did you think of the film?"* Although a seemingly superficial question, built into the provision of such a value judgement are a variety of indicators of moral conditioning, aesthetic preference and political ideology that audience members have brought to their viewing experience (Kahn 2013). What makes Chinese audiences unique is that both historical and contemporary notions of pre-conditioning prior to film consumption can influence contemporary film comprehension. On the one hand, Chinese audiences may have critical skills borne out of privilege from the past and of the present (Hemelryk Donald 2014) or engage sense-making paradigms that draw on learned behaviours of film consumption-as-state subject from the recent past – for example, Sara Friedman's (2006: 618–623) ethnographic study of female Chinese audiences' spectatorship of the Hong Kong–Taiwanese co-production *Twin Bracelets* (Huang: 1991), which turned their film watching "into a pedagogical project" as if watching a documentary. Chinese audiences are sense makers no doubt, but class, social histories and privilege within China's

6 *The cinema of class*

reform agenda informs the pre-conditions for how sense making is articulated. Analysing mainstream cinema to gauge social change in China must therefore be a combination of how film narratives are constructed and chosen for exhibition, how Chinese audiences given the opportunity for sense making explain their comprehension of these same narratives, and how class, and inter-generational experiences of class, pre-condition audiences in their sense making of fictional narratives in the present; sense making, it should be noted, that has real implications for the social lives of these film audiences.

It would be neglectful of me as the author to not take a moment to reflect on my own role in this process. Sense making is not simply confined to the Chinese audiences of these films. Indeed, I, as a foreign researcher, am similarly placed in this sense-making process as both a non-Chinese audience member of these films offering textual analyses, drawing associations between audience responses and film content for the benefit of you, my audience. As my reader, you will also reach your own sense making about the propositions I propose based on your own pre-conditioning: the Chinese films that you have already watched, your own class position within the society in which you reside and your own experiences with Chinese society. With this in mind, this book's aim is not to be a definitive text on China's film audiences, but to act as a departure point for a new conversation about how the web of performance, consumption and sense making informs the imagination and storytelling that legitimises class formation in contemporary China. At minimum, it is an attempt to scratch the surface of the mystery of who in fact are China's audiences.

The need for social harmony

Hu Jintao's presidential term (2003–2013) was hallmarked by his "harmonious society" (*shehui hexie*, 社会和谐) vision for China, a response to the growing social inequalities that were the result of the first two decades of economic reforms. Arguably, one way to achieve social harmony has been to subtly manipulate how Chinese people understand the inequalities they endure. Wanning Sun (2013) believes this has been achieved by shifting the perceived responsibility of social wellbeing away from the Party-state and onto the individual, while Xiaobu Su (2011: 314) explains:

> [China's] leaders have to formulate ideologies to shape mass consciousness and equate the Party's interests with the popular interests of society at large. The ultimate goal is to render these ideologies – the Party's beliefs and values – natural and self-evident in people's minds and in their daily practice so that the Party can win the consent of the masses.

One way to achieve this has been the introduction of the rhetoric of China's aspirational middle classes (Goodman 2008; Rocca 2008; Ren 2013). Hai Ren (2013: 143) believes the language of a Chinese middle-income stratum has acted as an "insurance measure" to manage the risks of the disenfranchised in China's modern society. In doing so, the language of a middle class has acted as a "dispositive" to disseminate "practices, knowledge, measures, and institutions that aim to manage, govern, and orient Chinese citizens' behaviors, gestures, and thoughts". For David Goodman (2008: 37), the language of the middle class is "more egalitarian" than talking about "the super-wealthy or the new bourgeoisie" in a political system that ideologically should abstain from encouraging wealth creation associated with bourgeois morality. Although the definition of what constitutes the middle class has been contentious, through China's mass media the language of a middle class has been brought into everyday mainstream discourse (He 2012). Similarly, the confirmation of the existence of a middle class identity, perceived of as a political privilege, wealth and lifestyle has been vigorously propagated through Chinese advertising and consumer behaviour (Davis 2000; Davis 2005; Hanser 2008; Kharas and Gertz 2011; Li 2011); education (Kraus 1989; Lin and Sun 2011; Tsang 2013); an urban real estate market (Fleischer 2007, 2010; Pow 2009; Li Zhang 2010); and the rhetoric of a "*suzhi renkou*" (素质人口), or a "quality population" (Woronov 2003; Anagnost 2004; Kipnis 2006).

Suzhi (素质) is a central concept in much of what is discussed in the following chapters. *Suzhi* does not refer to any particular quality per se, but to broad moral judgements of a person's core human "quality" or "value" that is placed within an abstract spectrum of civility. These human qualities and values can seemingly be drawn out and nurtured into existence by varying forms of education such as scholarship, cultural pedigree and moral conditioning (Woronov 2003; Anagnost 2004; Kipnis 2006). Since the term *suzhi jiaoyu* (素质教育, "education for quality") entered China's education policy in 1999, China's youth have been institutionally directed to judge *suzhi* in themselves and in others within the classroom environment (Woronov 2003: 77–78), while the symbol of a family's *suzhi*, particularly among the aspirational classes depends on the family's ability to invest in their children's extra-curricular education, including lessons in music, swimming, dancing, calligraphy and rollerblading. *Suzhi* ensures that Chinese considered to have "high" *suzhi* gain "more income, power and status" (Kipnis 2006: 295), and Chinese perceived to have low *suzhi* become the site for "extraction of surplus value enabling capital accumulation" – in other words, become the subjects of a form of "labour discipline" (Anagnost 2004: 193). *Suzhi* is convenient rhetoric that invites prejudicial imaginations about class others to take shape and the industrial subordination of the lower classes to be easily enforced.

Although the discourse of China's emerging middle class and their *suzhi* has attracted much conjecture on the part of Chinese observers, as Phillip Huang (2009: 426) points out, the promised olive-shaped ideal of China's society currently looks more "flask shaped". At the top of Huang's metaphorical flask are the wealthy gentry (Lu 2014). These privileged Chinese are either direct benefactors of political affiliation or became so subsequent to their economic rise (Dickson 2008; Chen and Dickson 2010; Guo 2013). The Party-state's loosening of CCP membership regulations to include capitalist entrepreneurs has, as Hans Hendrischke (2013) argues, functioned to subdue the emergence of a bourgeois consciousness that may push for greater political influence, while Bruce Dickson (2003) calls them

8 The cinema of class

China's "red capitalists". The consequence has been public antagonism towards corruption and nepotism, which is generally understood to be the reason for the emergence of an immensely wealthy class in China (Zang 2008: 54–60). To placate this antagonism, wealthy entrepreneurs have made efforts to improve their public reputations through charitable philanthropy (Carillo 2008), with questionable success. The base of Huang's "flask", though, refers to the excessively disproportionate number of Chinese disadvantaged by the current social and economic structure. Goodman (2014: 124) claims that the subordinate classes constitute 85 per cent of China's population, making them in numbers by far the dominant classes in contemporary China.

China's subordinate classes broadly speaking consist of, firstly, retrenched workers of the former State-Owned Enterprise (SOE) sector that historically provided universal welfare to its employees. These include workers reassumed into the manual labour economy, or those in labour limbo, "temporarily" without work. A great proportion of SOE retrenched workers have now become sole traders (*getihu*, 个体户) in China's informal economy (Rocca 2003; Appelton et al. 2006; Huang 2009, 2013; Andreas 2012). Next, the subordinate classes include China's new urban poor (Li and Sato 2006; Solinger 2010, 2013) and the transitory rural migrant workers who are denied access to public welfare services in urban areas where they work because of their rural household registrations, thus living as "second class citizens" (Solinger 1999: 3–7; Huang 2009: 408). Reforms have also created new class structures in rural China (Jacka 1997; Unger 2002). While these class structures are often tied to economic concerns, they also have social implications, such as the "cultural authority" that rural migrant workers acquire within their home communities due to their capacity to disseminate new impressions they adopt while working in urban areas of hygiene, law, civilised culture and modern society (Nyíri 2010: 81).

This melting pot of disadvantage has resulted in an increase in protests in China. Li and O'Brien (2010: 86) report that statistics reveal "collective incidents" increased in China from "8,706 in 1993 to 87,000 in 2005 with about 40 percent of them occurring in the countryside". The international media's attention was drawn to the issue of labour unrest in China when reputable Western corporations were implicated in a series of industrial protests that took place in 2010, including strikes at Foxconn, Honda and Toyota plants. Despite this, scholars are sceptical that these incidents indicate the emergence of a working class consciousness. Instead, as Chan and Siu (2012: 84) argue, these "protests and strikes have almost always been spontaneous and have involved very specific issues of discontent within a factory", not cohesive class action. Without a union movement independent from the Party-state (Feng 2009), cohesive industrial class action is an unlikely progression. Finally, the most under-developed area of research into class in contemporary China is how China's ethnic minority groups experience class. Xiaowei Zang's (2012) argument that social unrest involving Uyghur groups in the Xinjiang region, for example, may in fact be the result of class-based disadvantages more so than ethnically motivated, provides us only a glimpse into this social complexity still to be further explored.

The dynamism and depth of the issue that is "class" in contemporary China can only be of immense concern to the Party-state. In saying this, the necessity to examine the means of cultural and knowledge mediation that Xiaobu Su (2011) believes is so crucial to creating China's class hegemony based on a complacency in and acquiescence to the status quo, is worthy of immediate attention – particularly how this cultural and knowledge mediation engages the next generation of China's middle class urbanites and the nation's multibillion-dollar commercial film industry. For not only are China's future middle classes anticipated to act as moral and economic gatekeepers between the two spectrums of China's deeply stratified "flask-shaped" society, but are anticipated to do so in social conditions that are arguably unpredictable and unsustainable.

Examining China's cinema of class: from narratives to access

Socialising class is not only a pragmatic re-education of what is "the new order", but one that requires the reshaping of visual and emotional responses to presentations of inequality, corruption, power abuse, sexism, exploitation and notions of the individual – especially to explain the new value system placed on individuals in terms of their *suzhi*, or "human quality", that underscores much of how these circumstances are justified. Such cultural conditioning often crudely determines how the privileged and underprivileged classes in Chinese society conceive of (if at all) their access to, their right to engage in, and in which context they can engage with, the opportunities modern China offers.

Let the Bullets Fly, *Lost on Journey*, *Go Lala Go!*, *House Mania* and *The Piano in a Factory* have a range of commercial attributes that advocate for their inclusion in this book. These attributes include: the scale of box office revenue from that of a multimillion-dollar blockbuster to revenues of a modest scale, as well as how the films were financed (co-productions, state investment, foreign investment); all five films were located in the pirated DVD economies in Beijing, Hangzhou and Nanjing, where group discussions were held, and were also available for torrent download and online streaming from a variety of Chinese websites. Exhibition timing within the year and the length of time exhibited was also considered (from nine weeks for *Let the Bullets Fly* during the New Year's Festival peak filmgoing season to two weeks for *House Mania* out of peak season), and whether a film had particular marketing attributes. These included industry recognition (*The Piano in a Factory*), breaking box office records (*Go Lala Go!* and *Let the Bullets Fly*), initiating a series of similarly themed and highly popular films (*Lost on Journey*) or containing overt product placement that arguably assisted in the film's exhibition approval (*House Mania* and *Go Lala Go!*).

The varying production values also advocated for each film's selection. As studies by both Bourdieu (1984) and Barnett and Allen (2000) show, tastes in film aesthetics, and film consumption practices are often reflected along class lines. Accordingly, these five films have been consciously chosen for their differing production values, including two films that relied on computer graphic imagery (CGI) similar to that

10　*The cinema of class*

of Hollywood blockbusters (*Let the Bullets Fly* and *Go Lala Go!*), two films with minimal post-production (*Lost on Journey* and *House Mania)*, and one film with more niche "artistic" production values (*The Piano in a Factory*), but nonetheless commercially exhibited throughout mainstream cinemas. The Chinese film industry does lean heavily towards the genres of comedy and romance, yet these five films cover a variety of genres (as generously as five films can allow), including: romance (*Go Lala Go!* and *House Mania*), comedy (*Lost on Journey, House Mania* and *Let the Bullets Fly*), drama (*The Piano in a Factory*) and action (*Let the Bullets Fly*).

The narratives selected are also far from an exhaustive selection of cinematic interpretations of the class-related issues in contemporary China. Yet, they have been chosen in light of the extensive literature on class in China already published, including: narratives about the powerful and the ruling elites (*Let the Bullets Fly*); class relations (*Lost on Journey*); white collar labour, femininity and consumption (*Go Lala Go!*); homeownership and masculinity (*House Mania*); retrenched workers in the informal economy and *suzhi* (*The Piano in a Factory*). The five films not only reflect the challenging nature of class within contemporary China, but the sheer dynamism and variety of class narratives available within the Chinese film industry since its commercialising reforms over a decade ago.

Despite the supposed freedom to consume what one wants in a commercial film market, Chinese audiences consciously confine their preferences for films with narratives that are produced (both narrative-wise and cinematographically) to complement their class-based sensibilities and media literacy capacities. This includes narratives that feature their own class in a positive moral light, or narratives that are about class others that pander to their class-based feelings of superiority – for either spectrum of the class structure. Chinese audiences are also acutely attuned to what their peers will enjoy watching. As the Chinese audiences featured in this book confirm, they will also only ever recommend films to friends and peers *if* they believe their peers will enjoy the film based on their own enjoyment. While marketing practitioners have long understood this to be the principle of word-of-mouth marketing, this can also be understood as the containment or the spread of ideas among similarly classed audiences and social networks attracted to particular films and practices of film consumption. Varying approaches to film production, therefore, through genre, cinematography and even casting of popularly known actors whose real life reputations project certain qualities of the class that their performances are typecast, subsequently target audiences for institutional messages produced specifically for their consumption.

Group discussions

The decision to conduct and observe group discussions about class narratives in popular films served two purposes. Firstly, to see if, and how, interpretations of class narratives differed from class to class, and secondly, to gauge how groups segregated by class may have differed in their approaches to negotiating opinions in a group environment.

The cinema of class 11

A total of 179 Chinese nationals participated in twenty-nine discussion groups for the five different films across five Chinese cities. These participants are categorised as: "peasants"; "rural migrant workers"; "factory workers"; "factory team supervisors"; "university students"; "low-level administrators"; "white collar workers"; "professionals" and "professors". The distinction between peasant and rural migrant workers requires some clarification. Goodman (2014) categorises China's "twenty-first century" peasants by their relationship to the land along with where their household registration is tied. As audiences in Lanzhou, for example, were employed primarily in agrarian peasant labour, they are referred to in-text as "peasants", despite the off-season casual labour (known as *dagong*, 打工) they may undertake in urban areas. Audiences in Hangzhou and Nanjing, however, are referred to in-text as "rural migrant workers" because despite having household registrations in rural areas and access to family allocated rural land, their primary, and in the majority of cases, only, form of employment and/or paid labour they have undertaken in their young lives has been and still is exclusively performed in urban areas.

Groups consisted of:

- **Beijing** (Beijing)
  - 23 participants
  - Average age of participant: 27 years old
  - Four groups: *Let the Bullets Fly*; *Go Lala Go!*; *House Mania*; *The Piano in a Factory*; all with white collar workers and professionals.
- **Hangzhou** (Zhejiang Province)
  - 12 participants
  - Average age of participant: 27 years old
  - Three groups: *Go Lala Go!*; *House Mania*; *The Piano in a Factory*; all with rural migrant workers.
- **Lanzhou** (Gansu Province)
  - 53 participants
  - Average age of participant: 28 years old
  - Nine groups: *Go Lala Go!* (Master students/factory managers); *House Mania* (Bachelor students/professors); *The Piano in a Factory* (Master students/factory workers); *Lost on Journey* (Master students/peasants); *Let the Bullets Fly* (Master students).
- **Nanjing** (Jiangsu Province)
  - 20 participants
  - Average age of participant: 31 years old
  - Four groups: *Let the Bullets Fly*; *Go Lala Go!*; *House Mania*; *The Piano in a Factory*; all with rural migrant workers.
- **Taiyuan** (Shanxi Province)
  - 71 participants
  - Average age of participant: 39 years old
  - Nine groups: *Let the Bullets Fly* (low-mid level administrators/mixed/ Master students); *Lost on Journey* (professionals (2 groups)/white

12 *The cinema of class*

collar workers); *Go Lala Go!* (Bachelor students); *House Mania* (white collar workers and professionals); *The Piano in a Factory* (professionals).

Further details may be found in the appendix.

Participants were assured at the beginning of each group discussion that their identities would remain anonymous. Audience members are each therefore referred to in-text by the initials of the film they discussed and a number to which they are assigned in the appendix. A set of standardised questions were asked of each group as a means of unearthing points of distinction from group to group, and class to class in film comprehension, including: what the audience liked and disliked about the film; their favourite and least favourite characters; their interpretations of crucial scenes and comprehension of plot resolutions. Audiences were obliged to have watched the entire film in order to participate in the group discussion and were only allowed to participate in one group. This was so that the format of the group discussion did not become habitual for audiences and maintained a degree of spontaneity in the discussion environment.

The socialised understanding of class

Some overarching themes can be drawn about how China's big-screen storytelling contributes to the socialisation of class. Firstly, characters are quite blatantly portrayed as having differing degrees of *suzhi* (素质), or "quality" and audiences are provided with clear visual cues to determine characters as either "poor" or "rich". Secondly, class is presented as the distinction between being the projector, or recipient, of prejudice in everyday life. Thirdly, class consciousness is presented as the compatibility of shared histories between characters and the audiences, and the ability or inability for collective writing of *new* social histories. Lastly, the socialisation of class, in a practical sense, is determined by an audience's engagement in the storytelling at all, both physically and intellectually. Having access to "film conversations" and by extension broader sociocultural conversations that film consumption engenders is a privilege that not all Chinese are entitled to. This is not only in terms of how a film is comprehended, but in a potential audience member's capacity and probability to patronise a cinema at all.

Class as *suzhi* and gendered performances of the individual

As noted above, *suzhi* is central to the analysis presented here and to the performance of class on China's big screens. Little discussed is that *suzhi* is deeply intertwined with newly defined performances of gender. Indeed, the most intimate attribute of an individuals' identity is their gender, so while man's *suzhi* is judged by his homeownership (and location thereof), his masculinity, occupation and wealth provision for the support of his family unit, woman's *suzhi* is judged by her pedigree, education, consumption, femininity and cuteness and the ability to

The cinema of class   13

fulfil domestic obligations of cultivating *suzhi* in her children. And if need be, retreating from the workforce to achieve these goals. By aligning issues of class with the individual's human quality and gender, China's cinema of class aligns inequalities between homeowners, labouring women, even children, as indisputable, justifiable and "naturally" explained by the "quality" of the individuals in question. The inequalities and corruption of the housing market are not an issue of class, *man's* quality is. Woman's professional and economic social mobility is not her problem, her *unmarried and childless* qualities are. Equality of education and access to education is not the problem, *fathers* who cannot earn to support their *wife's* requests for their children's advantageous education and *suzhi* cultivation are. The esoteric language of fashion and luxury commodities that communicate personal *suzhi* to the outside world are not indicators of an unjust commodities market (to say nothing of the exploited labour that goes into the production of the commodities), *women* who lack brand recognition are, and by extension so are the *men* who cannot afford these commodities for their female counterparts.

Class experience is negotiated in China's commercial cinema through the redefinition of the relations between men and women as issues of individual human quality. Although this does not deny the importance of gender to class struggle during China's socialist era, or the argument that women were never truly emancipated during the socialist period, in contemporary times the propagation of these gendered ideals of "quality" most certainly do not hide behind discourses of women's emancipation or gender equality anymore. Not only does China's new cinema of class issue an invitation for the proliferation of sexism and chauvinism as an attribute of legitimately placed prejudices within China's class society, but through the conceptualisation of sexism and chauvinism as *the* natural order, places the capacity for women's and men's liberation alike in China in an even more difficult position for generations of Chinese to come. The unapologetic manner in which notions of *suzhi* and *suzhi*'s gendered overtones are layered on top of one another for audiences of China's cinema of class leaves in no uncertain terms how life trajectories will be determined for audience members, and the experiences of class they can predict to have, as determined by their ability to obtain and project *suzhi*.

Class as the projector of prejudice

To determine *suzhi* is to prejudge. It is a privilege and act of power when one may prejudge a class other in a manner that results in one's own social and economic capital gain. Particularly if prejudging another as having a lower *suzhi* justifies the suppression of the other industrially, economically and politically. The creation of natural lines between in-groups and out-groups that allows these seemingly comprehensible lines of class distinction in Chinese society is very much the feature of how class is brought to life in the nation's commercial film industry. In some cases, the invitation to prejudge the class other is explicit, whereas in other films it is implicit – and smuggled into the unfolding events of the film. The most explicit encouragement for prejudice in China's cinema of class is the stereotypical representations of China's poor and rural peoples. Cinematically portrayed as culturally

14   *The cinema of class*

and politically ignorant, economically unstable, uneducated and physically dirty, the stereotypes of China's labouring classes that China's privileged classes recognise of their disadvantaged class other serves not to educate China's aspirational classes about the hardships of China's lower classes or to engender sympathy in the viewer – but to socialise privileged audiences on how to manage their prejudices towards hardship within the mainstream contexts that constitute their daily lives. Commercial cinema teaches privileged cinema-goers how to recognise rural migrants in urban spaces, how to behave in response to their proximity, and how to recognise and uphold their performances of *superiority* to rural migrants through their dress, behaviour, life ambitions, and *suzhi*. Furthermore, in China's unpredictable state of flux during the nation's transition to a market economy, projecting prejudices can in fact be helpful and *affirmative* for self-preservation and broader social harmony.

This is not to say that China's subordinate classes are immune to projecting prejudices of their own towards their class other. But it is an acknowledgement that the projected prejudices of the subordinate classes often have far less social, political and economic clout in their application than the prejudices of the aspirational classes. As it is, the socialisation of prejudice is how social, political and cultural power works to legitimise class structures that subordinate one group of people to another. In terms of film consumption and audiences, the point of critique then becomes how the lower classes respond to the fictional prejudices projected towards their in-group in an on-screen context. What subordinate classed audiences of China's cinema of class suggest is that their responses are far from antagonistic when faced with these narratives and visual cues. Produced for the big screen in the most accessible film genre, namely comedy, China's subordinate classes find as much enjoyment in their in-group's depiction on the big screen as their more privileged counterparts. Unable to perceive that these depictions of their class as ignorant, unfashionable, and lacking *suzhi* on the big screen may in fact work against their in-group's class empowerment, let alone express this opinion within a group discussion forum, leaves little room to negate the impressions that China's cinema of class propagates of underprivileged Chinese – and particularly Chinese from rural origins. Without doubt, China's cinema of class allows prejudice to flourish, and China's privileged classes are the benefactors of these narrative devices to the detriment of Chinese lacking social distinction.

Class consciousness as shared histories

In a society in flux, class consciousness relies not only on shared economic class interests in the present, but also on the narrative of shared past histories. Histories locate commonalities among people and are crucial for recognising one's in-group, and furthermore, for establishing foundations upon which collective futures can be built. In a transient urban environment where it is difficult to identify superficially who is who, sharing histories is particularly important. If one considers the intensity of internal migration China has experienced, China's cinema of class should in theory function to propagate narratives of old and new class histories among

Chinese audiences for the ultimate goal of social cohesion. In a contemporary context, this may refer to narratives about shared values between urban and rural folk, poor and wealthy Chinese, or China's ethnic minority groups, who do not fit neatly into the Han-dominated paradigm of contemporary Chinese society, and by extension, histories between the women and men within each of these paradigms. Contemporary film consumption in China, though, affords little opportunity for shared social histories to be cultivated and written in the present. China's cinema of class functions not to educate audiences about the inequalities faced by a class other, but to educate audiences on how they may understand their own social status within a newly defined urban mainstream context, and how they should behave accordingly. Film consumption in this case is the socialisation of the individual audience member's perception of personal history – not the facilitation of shared histories with the characters representative of class others projected on the big screen.

This phenomenon is most typically seen in narratives that address the lack of historical familiarity between rural and urban Chinese. What underscores most of the humour in these films lies in the protagonists' unfamiliarity with each other's socio-cultural histories and, accordingly their present writings of their own class identities within China's urban environments. Urban and rural, privileged and underprivileged audiences alike are encouraged to laugh at the peculiarities of the class other and accept their own anomalies as their in-group's status quo, ensuring that differences in histories are reinforced for watching audiences.

In the case where a history does not exist, Western histories have been adopted to inform new class identities and labour expectations, particularly in the service and white collar sectors that formed with the presence of foreign capital along China's eastern coastline. The adoption of Western histories to write present histories for Chinese white collar workers, however, raises a point for serious deliberation. For while the rural and urban, wealthy and poor and Han and minority dichotomies operate on one level, the adoption of Western histories for the purpose of writing the present history for Chinese white collar workers places a proportion of privileged Chinese closer to their Western counterparts historically than it does to their own labouring or agrarian population. Not only does this become then an issue of discordant rural and urban histories, or histories of wealth and disadvantage, but Chinese and Western histories among Chinese workers. Consequently, film narratives that feature a shared class history and future between China's privileged white collar workers and, say, manual labourers are rendered unimaginable.

Class as access and exclusion of particular audiences

It is a privilege first and foremost to be able to attend a mainstream cinema in China. China's primary film audience is the nation's educated, young adult, urbanite population. The demanding work schedules and wages earned by both China's urban poor and rural-urban migrant workers hinder these classes from becoming active cinema patrons. Similarly, film marketers do not engage the subordinate classes as potential patrons of their films on the big screen. Worker audiences are

16 *The cinema of class*

accordingly excluded from the broader conversation that commercial film consumption can offer – a conversation about the acceptability of prejudice, consumption, gender, taste, labour, wealth and, importantly, politics. This exclusion from the broader conversation not only leads to perceptions that China's lower classes lack *suzhi* within the labour market, but also ensures that the lower classes are denied familiarity with the cultural etiquettes required of respectable society, and the awareness of how to control how they are perceived by their class others (as the middle classes arguably aspire to do). None of the 43 labourers of the subordinate classes who feature in the following chapters had been to a mainstream cinema in the cities that they lived and laboured in. Entertainment for these workers gravitated around free-to-air tele-series on state-run television channels or online streaming platforms very late in the evening after working arduous hours, or whatever might be available in their local pirate DVD market. This does not mean that these workers were disinterested in film consumption, but mere "cinema attendance" as a leisure time activity has yet to permeate China's young adult labouring classes in the way that the normalcy of the activity has for privileged urbanites in the same age bracket. Furthermore, two- to three-hour-long films that require emotional and intellectual investment are cumbersome entertainment products when consumed after a hard day's labour, therefore engendering a preference for expedient entertainment in the form of reduced one-hour TV programmes with less complicated narratives. This also includes the likelihood of encountering marketing materials that might direct them towards film consumption practices similar to those of the more privileged classes. Again, such a discussion cannot even enter into the realities of young adult rural populations who can only imagine visits to an urban commercial cinema in abstract notions.

For Chinese who do, and can, access China's commercial film industry, being engaged in the "filmic conversation" is likewise not guaranteed or encouraged for all audiences alike. Production values such as genre, computer graphics and narrative theme and content can function to attract or deter specific audiences. For example, *Let the Bullets Fly* indicated that audiences with Party membership engaged more comfortably and optimistically with the film's content than audiences without membership. The film *Go Lala Go!* spoke exclusively to privileged female audiences, while their privileged male counterparts found little meaning in the narrative for themselves – and the rural migrant workers of either gender were alienated by the portrayal of white collar labour alike. *House Mania*'s jab at low-income males from Beijing unable to afford real estate and "old" production qualities deterred the very social group it was portraying, while appealing to their similarly aged counterparts outside of Beijing living in more favourable housing markets. And *The Piano in a Factory*'s artistic production values were disliked by the greater majority of audiences found in each class, aside from a handful of university students and notably privileged mothers for whom the theme of a young girl's piano education confirmed their priorities as nurturers of their child's *suzhi*. Each of the conversations generated by the five films in this book are in fact important for Chinese of all classes to engage in discussions about. Yet, China's cinema of class ensures variances in socio-cultural identities and aesthetic tastes, which results in inclusion and exclusion of particular audiences in the storytelling process. Accordingly, China's cinema of class socialises not only conflicting class understandings between audiences of different classes, but can do so within audiences of similar classes too.

Narrative resolutions in China's cinema of class

Narrative resolutions are crucial to the power and political application of China's cinema of class. The decision to be ambiguous or clear in a narrative resolution indicates the moral lesson that the filmmaker is trying to convey. Ideally, as a filmgoer, a Chinese audience member who "chooses" to watch a film commercially should have the media literacy skills required to critique a film's narrative resolution. This "choice" to consume, though, is never borne out of a disposition separate from the lived experience a filmgoer has of Chinese society. Indeed, the narratives that bring audiences to their plot interpretations and the broader socio-economic structure that brings them *to the cinema at all*, is anything but a self-professing process detached from the interests of China's economic reform agenda. The skills to critique plot resolutions, therefore, requires a powerful extension of the imagination on the part of Chinese audiences to perceive possibilities not provided to them by the filmmaker or their everyday experiences of Chinese life. China's cinema of class reflects, therefore, the extent to which China's class society has become a normalised fixture in China's everyday life, as well as the cultural imagining that validates the necessity and inevitability of China's class society in its efforts to modernise. If this were not the case, audiences of these five films would not have so eloquently reinforced what could easily be argued as attitudes and sentiments that support the Party-state's reform agenda at the conclusion of each film as they did – particularly for films that left the narrative resolutions ambiguous and encouraged audiences to feel they had reached the conclusions they did of their own accord, reading truths into a film's representation of life experiences of contemporary China.

Films and audiences

The following chapters provide a filmic map of how the socialisation process takes place on China's big screens as both a collective and individual process. Chapter 2 provides "behind the scenes" observations and details of organising and conducting group discussions with Chinese audiences. Then in Chapters 3 and 4 the book examines narratives focused on the collective: Party-state-society relations and inter-class relations. Chapter 3 examines the blockbuster *Let the Bullets Fly*, and how the film normalises assumptions about power abuses in China and the impenetrable nature of China's leadership. Without providing an alternative system of governance to that present in the narrative or the narrative resolution, *Let the Bullets Fly* is shown to engender a pragmatic acquiescence to the continuation of China's current leadership and power structure among Chinese audiences. Chapter 4 features the film *Lost on Journey* and explores how Chinese cinema

18 *The cinema of class*

portrays prejudices in class relations between social groups as "affirmative" and desirable. Narrative juxtaposition to the Hollywood original *Planes, Trains and Automobiles* (Hughes: 1987) is used to illustrate the divergences that the Chinese filmmakers took from the Hollywood original to capture class relations with "Chinese characteristics". In Chapters 5, 6 and 7, the focus shifts to the notion of the individual through narratives of the woman, man and child. Chapter 5 analyses the commercial blockbuster *Go Lala Go!*'s effort to negate the perceived threat of social instability that China's *shengnü* (leftover women) – successful, professional and unmarried white collar women – may cause to China's ambition for social harmony. In Chapter 6 the focus turns to China's "crisis of masculinity", as in young men being unable to invest in the urban property market, in *House Mania*. And finally, in Chapter 7, the cultivation of *suzhi* in China's next generation comes to life in the artistic film *The Piano in a Factory*. The concluding chapter deliberates on how we may understand the role of the filmmaker within China's cinema of class; in particular, the inherent and unavoidable privilege that filmmakers possess as producers of these very narratives of class.

For filmmakers hoping to capitalise on co-producing opportunities with Chinese filmmakers or to exhibit within China's potentially lucrative commercial film circuit, understanding the ideological function of China's commercial film industry and its relationship to its audiences in a time of intense social change is critical to achieving success. Although this book is a modest introduction to China's expansive commercial film industry and audiences, its discussion is not without significance. As the global film industry shifts its focus to China's growing audience base and profit potential, understanding China's audiences and the commercial films they consume is but a timely task.

References

Anagnost, Ann. 2004. The Corporeal Politics of Quality (*Suzhi*). *Public Culture* 16 (2): 189–208.

Andreas, Joel. 2012. Industrial Restructuring and Class Transformation in China. In *China's Peasants and Workers: Changing Class Identities*, edited by Beatriz Carrillo and David S. G. Goodman, 102–123. Cheltenham and Massachusetts: Edward Elgar.

Appelton, Simon, John Knight, Lina Song, and Qingjie Xia. 2006. Labour Retrenchment in China: Determinants and Consequences. In *Unemployment, Inequality and Poverty in Urban China*, edited by Li Shi and Hiroshi Sato, 19–42. London and New York: Routledge .

Barnett, Lisa A., and Michael Patrick Allen. 2000. Social Class, Cultural Repertoires, and Popular Culture: The Case of Film. *Sociological Forum* 15 (1): 145–163.

Berry, Chris. 2012. Chinese Film Scholarship in English. In *A Companion to Chinese Cinema*, edited by Yingjin Zhang, 484–498. Chichester, West Sussex: Wiley-Blackwell.

Bourdieu, Pierre. 1984. *Distinction: A Social Critique of the Judgment of Taste*. Translated by R. Nice. Cambridge. MA: Harvard University Press.

Braester, Yomi. 2005. Chinese Cinema in the Age of Advertisement: The Filmmaker as a Cultural Broker. *The China Quarterly* 183: 549–564.

——. 2008. The Political Campaign as Genre: Ideology and Iconography during the Seventeen Years Period. *Modern Language Quarterly* 69 (1): 119–140.

The cinema of class   19

Carillo, Beatriz. 2008. From Coal Black to Hospital White: New Welfare Entrepreneurs and the Pursuit of a Cleaner Status. In *The New Rich in China: Future Rulers, Present Lives*, edited by David S. G. Goodman, 99–111. Oxon and New York: Routledge.

Chan, Anita, and Kaxton Siu. 2012. Chinese Migrant Workers: Factors Constraining the Emergence of Class Consciousness. In *China's Peasants and Workers: Changing Class Identities*, edited by Beatriz Carrillo and David S. G. Goodman, 79–101. Cheltenham and Massachusetts: Edward Elgar.

Chen, Jie, and Bruce J. Dickson. 2010. *Allies of the State: China's Private Entrepreneurs and Democratic Change*. Cambridge, MA: Harvard University Press.

Clark, Paul. 2011. Closely Watched Viewers: A Taxonomy of Chinese Film Audiences from 1949 to the Cultural Revolution Seen from Hunan. *Journal of Chinese Cinemas* 5 (1): 73–89.

——. 2012. Artists, Cadres, and Audiences: Chinese Socialist Cinema, 1949–1978. In *A Companion to Chinese Cinema*, edited by Yingjin Zhang, 42–56. Chichester, West Sussex: Wiley-Blackwell.

Davis, Deborah, ed. 2000. *The Consumer Revolution in Urban China*. Berkeley: University of California Press.

——. 2005. Urban Consumer Culture. *The China Quarterly* 183: 692–709.

Dickson, Bruce J. 2003. *Red Capitalists in China: The Party, Private Entrepreneurs, and Prospects for Political Change*. Cambridge and New York: Cambridge University Press.

——. 2008. *Wealth in Power: The Communist Party's Embrace of China's Private Sector*. Cambridge and New York: Cambridge University Press.

Feng, Chen. 2009. Union Power in China: Source, Operation, and Constraints. *Modern China* 35 (6): 662–689.

Fleischer, Fredericke. 2007. "To Choose a House Means to Choose a Lifestyle." The Consumption of Housing and Class-Structuration in Urban China. *City & Society* 19 (2): 287–311.

——. 2010. *Suburban Beijing: Housing and Consumption in Contemporary China*. Minneapolis: University of Minnesota Press.

Friedman, Sara L. 2006. Watching Twin Bracelets in China: The Role of Spectatorship and Identification in an Ethnographic Analysis of Film Reception. *Cultural Anthropology* 21 (4): 603–632.

Goodman, David S. G. 2008. Why China Has no New Middle Class: Cadres, Managers and Entrepreneurs. In *The New Rich in China: Future Rulers, Present Lives*, edited by David S. G. Goodman, 23–37. Oxon and New York: Routledge.

——. 2014. *Class in Contemporary China*. Cambridge: Polity.

Guo, Yingjie. 2013. Political Power and Social Inequality: The Impact of the State. In *Unequal China: The Political Economy and Cultural Politics of Inequality*, edited by Wanning Sun and Yingjie Guo, 12–26. Oxon and New York: Routledge.

Hanser, Amy. 2008. *Service Encounters: Class, Gender, and the Market for Social Distinction in Urban China*. Stanford, CA: Stanford University Press.

He, Jin. 2012. The Transformation and Power of "Middle Class" Language in Chinese Media Publications. In *The Rising Middle Classes in China*, edited by Li Chunling. Reading: Paths International.

Hemelryk Donald, Stephanie. 2014. Senior Audiences and the Revolutionary's Subject in the People's Republic of China. In *Meanings of Audiences: Comparative Discourses*, edited by Richard Butsch and Sonia Livingstone, 135–150. London and New York: Taylor and Francis.

Hendrischke, Hans. 2013. Institutional Determinants of the Political Consciousness of Private Entrepreneurs. In *Middle Class China: Identity and Behaviour*, edited by

20 *The cinema of class*

Minglu Chen and David S. G. Goodman, 135–148. Cheltenham and Massachusetts: Edward Elgar.

Huang, Phillip C. C. 2009. China's Neglected Informal Economy: Reality and Theory. *Modern China* 35 (4): 405–438.

——. 2013. Misleading Chinese Legal and Statistical Categories: Labor, Individual Entities, and Private Enterprises. *Modern China* 39 (4): 347–379.

Jacka, Tamara. 1997. *Women's Work in Rural China: Change and Continuity in an Era of Reform*. Cambridge and Melbourne: Cambridge University Press.

Johnson, Matthew D. 2012. Propaganda and Censorship in Chinese Cinema. In *A Companion to Chinese Cinema*, edited by Yingjin Zhang, 153–178. Chichester, West Sussex: Wiley-Blackwell.

Kahn, Paul W. 2013. *Finding Ourselves at the Movies: Philosophy for a New Generation*. New York: Columbia University Press.

Kharas, Homi, and Geoffrey Gertz. 2011. The New Global Middle Class: A Crossover from West to East. In *China's Emerging Middle Class: Beyond Economic Transformation*, edited by Cheng Li, 32–51. Washington, DC: Brookings Institute Press.

Kipnis, Andrew. 2006. Suzhi: A Keyword Approach. *The China Quarterly* 186: 295–313.

Kraus, Richard C. 1989. *Pianos and Politics in China: Middle-class Ambitions and the Struggle over Western Music*. Oxford: Oxford University Press.

Li, Chunling. 2011. Characterizing China's Middle Class: Heterogeneous Composition and Multiple Identities. In *China's Emerging Middle Class: Beyond Economic Transformation*, edited by Cheng Li, 135–156. Washington, DC: Brookings Institute Press.

Li, Lianjiang, and Kevin J. O'Brien. 2010. Protest Leadership in Rural China. In *Chinese Politics: State, Society and the Market*, edited by Peter Hays Gries and Stanley Rosen, 85–108. Oxon and New York: Routledge.

Li, Shi, and Hiroshi Sato, eds. 2006. *Unemployment, Inequality and Poverty in Urban China*. Oxon and New York: Routledge.

Li, Shi, Hiroshi Sato, and Terry Sicular, eds. 2013. *Rising Inequality in China*. Cambridge: Cambridge University Press.

Li, Zhang. 2010. *In Search of Paradise: Middle-Class Living in a Chinese Metropolis*. Ithaca, NY: Cornell University Press.

Lin, Jing, and Xiaoyan Sun. 2011. Higher Education Expansion and China's Middle Class. In *China's Emerging Middle Class: Beyond Economic Transformation*, edited by Cheng Li, 217–242. Washington, DC: Brookings Institute Press.

Lu, Peng. 2014. Wealthy-gentry Politics: How are Capitalists in China Chosen for the 'Houses'? *Australian Journal of Political Science*, 40 (2): 157–173.

Morely, David, and Charlotte Brunsdon. 1999. *The Nationwide Television Studies*. London and New York: Routledge.

Nyíri, Pál. 2010. *Mobility and Cultural Authority in Contemporary China*. Seattle: University of Washington Press.

Pow, Choon-Piew. 2009. *Gated Communities in China: Class, Privilege and the Moral Politics of the Good Life*. London: Routledge.

Ren, Hai. 2013. *The Middle Class in Neoliberal China: Governing Risk, Life-building, and Themed Spaces*. New York: Routledge.

Research Centre for Communication and Information Research, Fudan University [复旦大学新闻学院,复旦大学信息与传播研究中心]. 2010. Introduction to the Project "New Media Technology Environment and Shanghai Audiences" [《新媒体技术环境下的上海受众》问卷调查项目简介]. *Journalism Quarterly* 2 (104): 1–3 [新闻大学 第2期, 总第104期].

Rocca, Jean-Louis. 2003. Old Working Class, New Working Class: Reforms, Labour Crisis and the Two Faces of Conflicts in Chinese Urban Areas. In *China Today: Economic Reforms, Social Cohesion and Collective Identities*, edited by Taciana Fisac and Leila Fernández-Stembridge, 77–104. London: RoutledgeCurzon.

——. 2008. Power of Knowledge: The Imaginary Formation of the Chinese Middle Stratum in an Era of Growth and Stability. In *Patterns of Middle Class Consumption in India and China*, edited by Christophe Jaffrelot and Peter van der Veer, 127–139. Los Angeles: SAGE.

Skeggs, Beverley. 2009. The Moral Economy of Person Production: The Class Relations of Self-Performance on 'Reality' Television. *The Sociological Review* 57 (4): 626–644.

Solinger, Dorothy J. 1999. *Contesting Citizenship in Urban China: Peasant Migrants, the State, and the Logic of the Market*. Berkeley, Los Angeles and London: University of California Press.

——. 2010. A Question of Confidence: State Legitimacy and the New Urban Poor. In *Chinese Politics: State, Society and the Market*, edited by Peter Hays Gries and Stanley Rosen, 243–257. Oxon and New York: Routledge.

——. 2013. Temporality as Trope in Delineating Inequality: Progress for the Prosperous, Time Warp for the Poor. In *Unequal China: The Political Economy and Cultural Politics of Inequality*, edited by Wanning Sun and Yingjie Guo, 59–76. Oxon and New York: Routledge.

Su, Xiaobu. 2011. Revolution and Reform: The Role of Ideology and Hegemony in Chinese Politics. *Journal of Contemporary China* 20 (69): 307–326.

Sun, Wanning. 2013. Inequality and Culture: A New Pathway to Understanding Social Inequality. In *Unequal China: The Political Economy and Cultural Politics of Inequality*, edited by Wanning Sun and Yingjie Guo, 27–42. Oxon and New York: Routledge.

Tsang, Eileen. 2013. The Quest for Higher Education by the Chinese Middle Class: Retrenching Social Mobility? *Higher Education* 66 (6): 653–668.

Unger, Jonathan. 2002. *The Transformation of Rural China*. Armonk, NY: M.E. Sharpe.

Wood, Helen, and Beverley Skeggs. 2011. *Reality Television and Class*. London: Palgrave Macmillan on behalf of the British Film Institute.

Woronov, Terry Ellen. August, 2003. *Transforming the Future: "Quality" Children in the Chinese Nation*. PhD, Department of Anthropology, The Faculty of the Division of Social Sciences, The University of Chicago.

Xu, Guiquan. 2014. The Articulation of Audience in Chinese Communication Research. In *Meanings of Audiences: Comparative Discourses*, edited by Richard Butsch and Sonia Livingstone, 151–169. London and New York: Taylor and Francis.

Zang, Xiaowei. 2008. Market Transition, Wealth and Status Claims. In *The New Rich in China: Future Rulers, Present Lives*, edited by David S. G. Goodman, 53–70. Oxon and New York: Routledge.

——. 2012. Scaling the Socioeconomic Ladder: Uyghur Perceptions of Class Status. *Journal of Contemporary China* 21 (78): 1029–1043.

Zhang, Yingjin. 2004. *Chinese National Cinema*. New York: Routledge.

Zhu, Ying. 2003. *Chinese Cinema during the Era of Reform: The Ingenuity of the System*. Westport and London: Praeger.

2 Class on screen and in reality
Pre-conditioning audiences

At the conclusion of a group discussion conducted with rural migrant workers in Nanjing, a postgraduate student present for the focus group commented, "I had no idea there were people like this in China." When asked what this student meant by her comment, she explained that she did not realise what "they", as in rural migrant workers, were like or that "they" thought like they did. This student admitted she had never spoken to a rural migrant worker before, despite having many preconceived notions about "them" from sightings in the street and learning about "their" struggles through her university studies. Although it might be expected that she was somewhat better informed considering her high degree of education in the social sciences, upon reflection, it was not altogether surprising. Up until this point, she had had no reason to engage with rural migrant workers as they were not part of her immediate social network, and had only crossed paths with "them" in a service provision context, such as at the university canteen where rural migrant workers are employed in food preparation and provision for university students.

Film screenings with rural migrant workers in Nanjing started at 7 pm, after participants had laboured a twelve-hour day in the university canteen or in other capacities within the university campus. In one case, a participant struggled to stay awake during the film screening, explaining that he had a second job and would start work again at 3 am, and would sleep only 3 hours after the focus group before his next shift. A 40 RMB[1] compensation for this participant's time would hardly seem worthwhile for such discomfort, but the opportunity to earn extra money and watch a feature film on a larger-than-usual screen convinced this worker to participate. It should also be noted that the elder who had been engaged to recruit participants was highly respected in this university's rural migrant worker community, having worked there consecutively for twelve years. Deference to his elder may have also played a role in this worker's willingness to participate.

In Hangzhou, the demanding work schedules for rural migrant worker participants mirrored those in Nanjing. These participants were employed in a karaoke centre. Film screenings were conducted at 3 am in the morning. These participants nominated their free time as between 2:30 am and 6 am, at which time they explained they would return home and sleep until 2 pm, in order to start their next shift at the karaoke centre at 4 pm the following afternoon. The local contact, a rural migrant worker employed at the karaoke centre in a team supervisory role, refused monetary compensation on behalf of his work colleagues, but was happy for soft drinks to be provided in return for their participation.

Both in Nanjing and Hangzhou, the time-intensive work schedules with reportedly only one day off per month fundamentally hampered any possibility for these 20- to 35-year-old workers to have "free time" during hours that were conducive to visiting a cinema. In theory, the cinema is open to anyone who can afford to buy a ticket to enter. In practice, the demanding labour expectations and minimal wages earned by lower classed Chinese, or by peasants in rural areas that due to the nature of agrarian labour have no distinct "weekend" or access to urban cinemas, mean that China's subordinate classes have been, and are, quite literally *physically* excluded from China's cinema economy, whether intentionally or not. As the time-intensive working conditions of these participants mirrored other investigations that found rural migrant workers consistently work approximately 10- to 12-hour days in urban areas, 7 days a week (Ma 2007: 248), it can be safely presumed that the rural migrant workers who participated in this project were not unique in their labouring predicament. It should be stressed that this lack of cinema attendance was by no means due to a lack of enthusiasm on the part of these participants to watch Chinese cinema.

After offering to compensate rural migrant worker participants 10 RMB per hour in Nanjing, the local contact assisting the negotiations with the community elder chastised me for offering 10 RMB per hour. This amount was deemed too generous. The contact believed compensation for rural migrant workers should have been capped at 5 RMB per hour and an unhealthy precedence had been set by me in offering more. Academics in Taiyuan and Lanzhou and privileged contacts in Hangzhou were likewise confused why focus groups with peasants, migrant and factory workers were included in this research. The comment that focus groups with China's lower classes would be "没有意思" (*meiyou yisi*), a phrase that implies a mixture of "will yield little results" and "be of no interest" was offered a number of times. These contacts believed that to achieve "good" results it would be wisest to restrict the screenings and discussions to university students and/or white collar workers in urban areas, as they were China's real film watchers. The language was clear from Chinese contacts in positions of moral authority: lower classed Chinese were not only prejudged as not having worthwhile opinions about the films that they would watch, but that seeking their opinions was a meaningless task.

The opinions these local contacts expressed were not altogether *inaccurate*; no rural migrant worker or peasant had visited a cinema complex, and none had seen in full any of the films screened as part of this project. In response to the questions regarding favourite genre, national cinema and nominating a favourite film in the demographic surveys audiences were required to complete prior to the film screening, these participants were observed to on occasion refer to each other's responses for guidance on their own surveys. A couple of middle-aged migrant workers in Nanjing lacked film and literacy skills to understand the film they watched. For peasants in rural Lanzhou, it was above all else an issue of access to a cinema. These audiences explained that a screen was sometimes erected in the

24 *Class on screen and in reality*

village square to broadcast China Central Television (CCTV) tele-series but that the probability of them visiting a cinema anytime soon was unlikely.

At no point, however, did these audiences express no curiosity in watching the films featured in this book, even if they did not understand or even like the film. Furthermore, among their own class, they could be seen to enjoy the discussion environment. Not having been to a cinema appeared to influence responses from peasants and migrant workers when they were asked to nominate an appropriate value of a ticket to see the film that they had just watched. The lowest amount nominated was 60 RMB and the highest amount was 180 RMB (although middle aged factory workers stated they would *not* choose to visit the cinema). Considering the average box office ticket price can be 20–30 RMB using online vouchers, and the wages that these workers earn, these were exceptionally high values placed on an abstract notion of a trip to the cinema.[2] A high value seemed to be given not only because of the value placed on the opportunity to visit the cinema and the consumption of cinema, but because such a leisure activity was perceived to be something that only wealthy urbanites would engage in doing. As a result, the migrant workers living in urban areas in particular had never even considered seeking out a cinema, and none of them were aware of online discount voucher options that would provide them affordable access to a cinema, *if* these young rural migrant workers had a work schedule that provided them the time to go. The working schedules of China's labourers are just one way that China's lower classes are obstructed from fully participating in China's commercial cinema industry. The comments made by privileged Chinese about the lower classes in the coordination of the discussion groups (and in multiple cities with unattached local contacts offering the same opinions) suggested, however, that class-based senses of superiority that are well entrenched in the language and thinking of China's privileged classes may too influence whether films are marketed at all to lower classed Chinese as cultural products designed for their consumption.

Group discussions with workers (peasants, rural migrants and factory workers) on a whole were 10–15 minutes shorter than with their educated, urban counterparts. This was due to acts of deference between participants that substantially shortened conversation times. When provided the opportunity to share their thoughts on a film's narrative, one participant, often more vocal than his or her peers, would typically respond. When fellow participants were asked if they agreed, there would be a chorus of "*tongyi*" (同意), translatable as, "agree". Regardless of whether these participants did or did not agree with the original speaker, or know or did not know how to respond, the practice was not to show disagreement within the discussion process. Lower classed participants treated responses as "group responses" and showed body language of confidence in this group unity, often giggling among themselves when agreeing with the confident speaker.

In the case of groups with varying levels of privilege, acts of what could only be described as social humiliation were observed from those of lesser privilege. Often less-privileged participants would become unsure of their answer in the presence of a seemingly more knowledgeable participant from a more privileged position (typically declared by this participant vocally). Less-privileged participants would noticeably retreat from the discussion. The collective enthusiasm of those in similarly classed worker groups to "agree" changed to the self-deprecating remark of "no idea" (*bu zhidao*, 不知道) and in some cases defensive body language such as a shoulder shrug to deflect the discussion away from them. This behaviour was not observed in groups of similarly lower classed workers. Not only did this behaviour suggest that those of lesser privilege are *aware* that they lack social capital in such situations, but that they are aware that their opinions are devalued by their more privileged counterparts. Degrees of privilege therefore should be understood as staggered and recognisable for participants with less privilege in their proximity to others of greater privilege. While lower classed participants displayed confidence in their group association, less-privileged participants in groups with varying degrees of privilege displayed tendencies to self-preserve and retreat from the general group discussion.

Cinema and China's privileged classes

In contrast, being privileged in China brings one not only advantages of education, access to social mobility, wealth and political association as the films in this book propose, but privilege also means that third parties will negotiate on your behalf with greater vigour. In stark contrast to the disappointment shown at not being able to get a lower price in negotiations made with rural migrant workers in Nanjing, expectations of compensation for those of the privileged classes (professors, white collar workers, university students, professionals) were quite clear. Negotiators for privileged participants ensured that an adequate compensation was provided so as not to embarrass the negotiator, the participant or the foreign researcher (and host) of the event. The local contact in Beijing advised that white collar workers would expect a minimum of 150 RMB compensation and food and drink provided during the film screening and discussion. The compensation was to be provided in an envelope and handed over in a relaxed fashion at the end of the group session. In Taiyuan, a banquet meal to thank participants for their time was recommended. In Beijing and Taiyuan there were no participants who turned down the envelope or invitation to dine. University students in Lanzhou and Taiyuan obediently attended the film screenings as instructed by their professors. Told it was part of their Bachelors and Masters studies, the students attended the group discussions in their free time and dutifully mopped the floors and wiped down benches as requested by their teachers.

Group discussions with the privileged classes ran for a minimum of an hour if not longer, depending on the breadth of opinions had by audiences. Participants were notably more confident in contradicting their peers' opinions and expressing their own opinions when the opportunity arose. Privileged audiences easily engaged with the narratives of each film and were able to draw lines between the film's content and the realities of Chinese society regardless of whether they enjoyed the film or not. Elderly cadres in Taiyuan and professors in Lanzhou stiffened their backs, sat forward in their chairs and spoke authoritatively about what they had understood the film to be about, often resulting in lengthy monologues, unaware that their peers were waiting to share their opinions too.

26 *Class on screen and in reality*

Although supportive of Chinese cinema, these audiences valued it as being of a lesser quality than that of Hollywood studio productions, or films from Japan and Europe. Students and professors in Lanzhou and white collar workers in Beijing and Taiyuan were far from enthusiastic in their evaluations of the commercial value of Chinese films in comparison to their lower classed counterparts. The highest price such a participant (LBF8) had paid was 60 RMB for an entrance ticket to see *Let the Bullets Fly*. LBF8's admission received surprised looks from his classmates, as the most common price paid for an entrance ticket to the cinema was 25 RMB using online discount vouchers and group ticket deals. In the case of *Go Lala Go!*, young females (Lanzhou and Taiyuan) explained they had seen the romantic comedy about white collar women at the cinema only because they were able to locate discount group vouchers on the internet. They were willing, however, to pay significantly more than 60 RMB for an entrance ticket if the film was imported. Mature participants (40 years and above) approximated the value of box office tickets for the films they watched as between 5 RMB and 20 RMB. These participants often prefaced their values with the assurance that in reality they would not go to the cinema, as it was perceived to be an activity only "young people" engaged in.

Regardless of whether one believes an audience informs a nation's cinema, or a nation's cinema informs its audience, the coordination and negotiations of these film screenings and discussion groups revealed that audiences of the five films featured in this book were pre-conditioned economically, socially and historically to engage with these film narratives from polarised and varying positions. The sense-making processes audiences revealed in the subsequent group discussions is evidence of this fact. China's new cinema of class confirms that China's audiences are not uniform, either in the pre-conditioning that they bring to their sense making of Chinese popular cinema or in their film consumption practices.

Notes

1 The exchange rate at the time of conducting the focus group was approximately 6 RMB to USD 1.
2 Workers in Hangzhou earned 1700 RMB per month (at the time, USD 283); university employees earned 1015 RMB per month (USD 169), including board; peasants earned approximately 80 RMB (USD 13) per day in the market depending on the season.

Reference

Ma, Chunhong [马纯红]. 2007. The Migrant Worker's Leisure Time and the Construction of Urban Areas [农民工闲暇生活现状与城市区建设]. In *Harmonious Society and Social Construction* [和谐社会与社会建设], edited by Fang Wenxin [方向新], 246–257. Beijing: Social Science Press [北京市: 社会科学文献出版社].

3 *Let the Bullets Fly*
The socialisation of assumptions

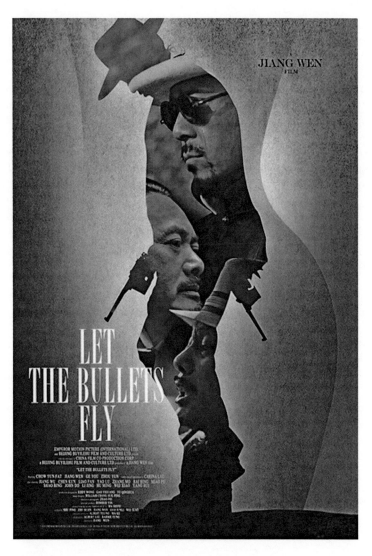

Figure 3.1 Promotional film poster: *Let the Bullets Fly*

28   *Let the Bullets Fly*

《让子弹飞》
(*rang zidan fei*)

Let the Bullets Fly

Director: Jiang Wen (姜文)
Starring: Ge You (葛优), Jiang Wen (姜文), Chow Yun-Fat
Box office: 636,875,000 RMB (USD 96,627,974)[1]
Exhibition period: Dec 2010–Feb 2011 (9 weeks)[2]

Synopsis

Let the Bullets Fly (Jiang: 2010) is set in fictional "Goose Town" sometime during the warring 1920s, in an unspecified area of southern China. Goose Town's despotic ruler, Huang Silang, has a bounty out for the military general-turned-bandit Zhang Mazi (nicknamed "Pockey"), who is notorious for his hijacking escapades that target the landed gentry's wealth. The bounty offered for Pockey's capture is, however, merely a means of masking Huang Silang's own money-making racket that his henchmen conduct under the guise of Pockey's reputation. Never did Huang suspect that the real Pockey would pay a visit to Goose Town. As fate would have it, Zhang Mazi (Pockey) hijacks conman Master Tang enroute to Goose Town, for which Master Tang has bought fake deeds to the title of Goose Town's Governor. Seizing the opportunity to target the despotic ruler's wealth, Zhang Mazi assumes the title of Governor for himself, and at gunpoint Master Tang agrees to the position of Zhang Mazi's "Counsel" in the scheme he had originally intended for himself. Begrudgingly, Master Tang also concedes his wife to play-act as Zhang Mazi's wife, and together they accompany Zhang Mazi and his gang, referred to as Brothers "Two", "Three", "Four", "Six" and "Seven", on to Goose Town.

Huang Silang is a powerful dictator who has accrued his wealth from human and opium trafficking. Housed in an impregnable citadel, Huang Silang has employed a decoy, because his own person has become so valuable. Wuhan and Master Wu (a martial arts scholar) are Huang Silang's henchmen. For the first time, both men have met their true match and their efforts to outwit each other under the veneer of dignified and courteous politeness are calculated, dangerous and unpredictable. Zhang Mazi's initial goal is to significantly deplete Huang Silang's wealth, but in achieving this, Master Tang, his wife, Brother Six and Brother Two all lose their lives. Zhang Mazi, incensed, resolves to not only obtain Huang's wealth, but also deliver the ultimate punishment: to unseat Haung Silang as Goose Town's leader and obliterate his power. To achieve this, Zhang Mazi must mobilise an uprising of Goose Town's townsfolk. Mobilising the poor of Goose Town turns out to be not an easy task, and only with the staged decapitation of Huang Silang's decoy do Goose Town's poor agree to storm Huang Silang's citadel, confident that repercussions for their support will not ensue. Understanding his imminent decline, Huang Silang ends his life fittingly from the top of his citadel where he was most comfortable ruling Goose Town. Zhang Mazi's clan also decide to disband and to relocate to Shanghai. Not interested in the life of a Governor, Zhang Mazi is shown leaving Goose Town on his lonesome. What happens to Goose Town and its leadership is left to speculation.

Introduction

The class structure of any capitalist society is not an organic process of social organisation; class structures are a result of economic management, the law, and the manner in which the law is policed. By this rationale, the contemporary extremities of China's class society must be understood as a result of the socio-economic planning of the powerful individuals who make up China's Party-state. Maintaining social harmony and negating class antagonisms towards the initiatives that have transformed China into one of the most unequal societies in the world, therefore, requires a normalisation of assumptions about what constitutes leadership in China, and the parameters by which the individuals involved lead. Assumptions that would not only encourage a pragmatic acquiescence by all classes to the Party-state's continued leadership, but moreover, the assumption there is in fact no other viable leadership alternative, even if change were possible.

China's growing commercial film industry is one avenue for socialising new assumptions about China's leadership. To use Yingjin Zhang's (2004: 223) words, it was not too long ago that socialist cinema presented "the history of modern China as a history of revolutions that, under the CCP leadership, have liberated China from the yoke of imperialism, feudalism and capitalism and will deliver the nation to a bright Communist future". While socialist narratives do still have a place in China's tele-series industry, in the commercial environment of popcorn, soft drink and competing Hollywood imports, portraying the nation's leadership on the big screen has required some readjustments. As the blockbuster *Let the Bullets Fly* highlighted, political narratives are highly popular in China, particularly if audiences can draw loose associations to China's contemporary leadership.

During the nine-week period that Jiang Wen's *Let the Bullets Fly* exhibited across Mainland China, the box office for the film took in revenues that were record-breaking for the time. From outside China, *Let the Bullets Fly* appeared to be a bold and risqué statement by director Jiang Wen, the China Film Group Corporation (CFGC – China's State-run and -owned film corporation), and SARFT (China's film censors) – the latter two being two institutions that typically err on the side of caution with entertainment that even tangentially criticises the Party-state's operations. What was in fact taking place, though, was an even greater occasion in China's popular film culture history. The commercial production and exhibition of *Let the Bullets Fly* indicated that CFGC and SARFT understood their filmgoing audiences' political fibre better than anyone else. The officially supported and sanctioned exhibition of *Let the Bullets Fly* revealed that the Party-state and the censorship bureau *knew* that China's audiences would not be mobilised or agitated after watching the film; that regardless of class, their response to the film's narrative would be to perceive acquiescence to maintaining the status quo

30 *Let the Bullets Fly*

as a reasonable solution to corrupt and unpredictable power structures like those portrayed in the film.

Let the Bullets Fly relies heavily on computer graphics imaging (CGI) and sophisticated post-production that make the *mise-en-scène* of the "Chinese Western" hyper-real – even surreal at times. The characters wear costumes that are indicative of 1920s China, when fashions were a combination of Chinese and imported influences. At 132 minutes, *Let the Bullets Fly* relies heavily on dialogue, wordplay and cultural innuendo, with intermittent high-intensity horse chases and gun battle scenes. Audiences require a high degree of concentration to follow the plot twists and the many uses of decoys by the protagonists, Zhang Mazi and Huang Silang, and their respective gang members. For an audience who can follow the film's narrative, *Let the Bullets Fly* is a deeply engaging and intellectually stimulating cinematic experience. In contrast, audiences with minimal comprehension are left with an unsatisfyingly lengthy film with inexplicable action, dialogue and visual contexts. Lower classed audiences with minimal media literacy found it difficult to project their life experiences and understandings onto the film's narrative in order to make sense of the plot's trajectory during the group discussions. *Let the Bullets Fly* should be understood, therefore, as a film for an educated audience with strong media literacy capacities.

Audiences and group discussions

The average age of an audience member for group discussions about *Let the Bullets Fly* was 26 years; seven (7) were male and 27 were female. As this is the primary age group of filmgoers in urban China and judging by the commercial success of *Let the Bullets Fly* in China, it was not altogether surprising that young educated urbanites had already seen *Let the Bullets Fly* prior to attending these film screenings – the overwhelming majority of this demographic had, in fact, seen the film multiple times. For other audiences, these screenings were their first viewing of *Let the Bullets Fly*. In Beijing the group that watched *Let the Bullets Fly* was chiefly educated white collar workers with political membership. In Lanzhou, the group consisted of postgraduate students from the social sciences. In Nanjing the group consisted of rural migrant workers with low levels of education and limited career mobility. In Taiyuan there were three groups: one of low level administrators largely with rural backgrounds; workers in mixed levels of administration and service work; and postgraduate students in business studies with majority CCP membership.

Film literacy is a skill often taken for granted in developed societies, but for two female migrant workers in Nanjing and some audience members in Taiyuan, lower levels of media literacy impeded their narrative comprehension and their capacities to discuss *Let the Bullets Fly*. This was despite attentively watching the entire 132 minutes of the film and laughing in a number of scenes. These scenes consisted of actors contorting their facial expressions or performing slapstick sequences. The workers in Nanjing believed *Let the Bullets Fly* was "too complicated"; they "did not understand" what had occurred in the film and confirmed they would not recommend *Let the Bullets Fly* to their friends for this reason. Another male worker in Nanjing (LBF15) stated that the scenes heavy in dialogue were "of little value" and "not interesting". LBF15 gave as an example the banquet scene in which the two protagonists, Huang Silang and Zhang Mazi, use wordplay to outwit the other. He believed that the two protagonists should "fight like men to resolve their problems". In contrast, a number of young professionals in Beijing and postgraduate students in Taiyuan and Lanzhou nominated this same scene as their favourite. LBF8 in Lanzhou, for example, appreciated the intellectual wit displayed by Zhang Mazi's wordplay because he had a personal interest in poetry. While there are scenes of action in *Let the Bullets Fly*, the emphasis on dialogue despite being an "action" film did prove unattractive to lower classed audiences and impeded the entertainment value and their ability to lose themselves in the film's narrative. The fact that *Let the Bullets Fly* is political in its thematic content is not only indicative of how political film narratives can exclude China's lower classed audiences, but reveals the shortcomings of how political life is experienced for the greater proportion of Chinese people. Not surprisingly, the audiences that agreed to recommend the film to their social network were young adult audiences, educated, privileged, with urban household registrations, and some political association.

The conclusion

This discussion is most effectively started by how the film's narrative concludes. *Let the Bullets Fly* concludes somewhat ambiguously. What becomes of Goose Town's people, its political system and Zhang Mazi is left to the audience's speculation. Audiences were asked what they believed might happen to Goose Town's political future. Regardless of class position, audiences of *Let the Bullets Fly* were unanimous that there was only one interpretation to the film's conclusion: an alternative system of political governance would *not* result from Huang Silang's demise. Audiences were initially provided two interpretations for the film's conclusion: whether the narrative of *Let the Bullets Fly* was the defeat of capitalism or the defeat of a dictator. When prompted with these two options, audiences rejected them both, as they assumed the two options referred to the removal of capitalism or the current leadership in today's China (as opposed to merely an abstract "dictator"). When the two proposals were provided to audiences in Beijing, LBF1 became quite agitated by the proposals and emphatically repeated three times "我爱 我家!" (*Wo ai wo jia*). The statement is translatable in the context of the discussion as "I love my country/countrymen!" LBF1's position seemed to be that an overthrow of the Party-state was an attack on her fellow countrymen, which the Party-state embodied. An overthrow of the Party-state was perceived as an affront to the Chinese people and the progress that the nation's people had made – progress that had relied on the introduction of capitalist market activities to achieve. In an effort to challenge the steadfast positions audiences expressed, a further alternative conclusion was provided that a local talent from within Goose Town's subordinate classes might rise up to lead Goose Town, or

32   *Let the Bullets Fly*

that "democracy", as in open elections for representational governance, might eventuate. Each group also steadfastly rejected these options, albeit audiences with little film comprehension passed on the question stating they "did not know". Only two conclusions were reached across the five discussion groups of what the ambiguity of *Let the Bullets Fly*'s plot resolution implied. The first option was that "Beijing", as the political centre, or the Party-state, which was often referred to as the illusive "they" (*tamen*, 它们), would send a replacement official to rule. It should be clarified that no reference to Beijing is actually made in the film's script, and during the 1920s, Beijing's position as a capital was contentious – Nanjing was in fact the capital for much of the 1930s and 1940s, so this reference to "Beijing" was unexpected. The second option was that another conman like Master Tang would once more buy the post of Governor (even cheaper) and rule in conjunction with Goose Town's landed gentry as Huang Silang is shown to do in the film. Postgraduate student LBF10 in Lanzhou joked, "until another similar challenge to *their* rule would take place". The strength of the first assumption and the multiple nominations this assumption received among differently classed audiences in varying cities suggested that regardless of degree of inclusion or exclusion to China's political life, audiences brought pre-conditioned assumptions from their own experiences of Chinese society to their sense making of Goose Town's leadership that the leadership would not change. It is also worthwhile noting that no audience member believed that the change of allegiance shown by Huang Silang's henchmen to Zhang Mazi at the turning point of Huang Silang's rule indicated a shift in ideological positions of these characters. "They will just follow whoever is in charge so they can benefit," commented LBF9 in Lanzhou.

As the film does not start with its conclusion however, the shaping of assumptions throughout *Let the Bullets Fly*'s narrative must be understood as being part and parcel of the 132 minutes that delivered these audiences to the conclusion of "Beijing's" invincibility. Understanding the purpose of *Let the Bullets Fly*'s narrative in terms of socially engineering its audiences should not be a question of what the film's conclusion means – Chinese audiences were very certain what the conclusion implied – but in fact what the assumptions are that the film encourages that brought these audiences so resolutely to their final conclusions – that is, understanding how abuses of power in Chinese society have been socialised as the assumed norm.

Socialising assumptions about power abuse

Power in *Let the Bullets Fly* is first and foremost expressed in wealth and wealth's relationship to political power. Huang Silang is a propertied man of immense proportions. The audience learns early on from Master Tang that Huang Silang has accrued his wealth through the exploits of human trafficking and the opium trade. Huang Silang's trades operate under the tutelage of General Liu of the prestigious Republican Army, and Goose Town's records show that Zhang Mazi's arrival as a fake Governor is not the first time Huang Silang has struck a deal to exploit his political relationships for capital gain, nor the first time Governors

Let the Bullets Fly 33

with bought deeds have visited Goose Town. Huang Silang's opponents, Master Tang and Zhang Mazi, are likewise aware of wealth's ability to gain and control power. Indeed, it is Master Tang who bought the deeds to the position of Governor in the first place, and even Zhang Mazi, the film's hero, has been living as an outlaw stealing other people's wealth, albeit his character is morally excused in that he only steals from the wealthy. This cannot overlook, however, that Zhang Mazi himself takes on the position of Governor without any ethical conflict and shows no qualms in letting the poor townspeople of Goose Town believe him to be Governor.

Arriving in Goose Town, Master Tang's first task is to survey Goose Town's administrative documents. It is in this scene that the benefits of political affiliation are revealed as opportunities for wealth accumulation. Discovering that the previous Governor had legislated a tax on the townspeople for a period of what added up to the next 90 years, Master Tang is significantly dismayed. At Zhang Mazi's confusion, Master Tang earnestly explains the documents to show that the already destitute townspeople have little more to offer them and their scam:

Zhang: [. . .] 老子从来就没想刮穷鬼的钱
But I never take money from the poor . . .

Tang: 不刮穷鬼的钱你收谁的呀？
If we don't take poor people's money, then whose money?

Zhang: 谁有钱挣谁的
Whoever has money, of course.

Tang: 当过县长吗？我告诉告诉你！县长上任，得巧立名目，拉拢豪绅，浇水捐款。他们交了，才能让百姓跟着交钱，得钱之后，豪绅的钱如数奉还，百姓的钱三十七分成
Ever been a Governor? I'll explain it to you. To take up the post of Governor, you have to think up strategies to rope in the gentry to pay a contribution to a tax. After they've paid, the townsmen will follow and also pay. After you've got the money, you reimburse the gentry with what they paid, and then you split the rest 30–70 . . .

Zhang: 怎么才七十成啊？
We only get 70?

Tang: 七十是人家的！能的三成还得看黄四郎的脸色
70 belongs to the rich! We only get 30 on Huang Silang's discretion!

The portrayal of collusion may seem exaggerated and farcical in *Let the Bullets Fly*. Yet the portrayal is unsettlingly reminiscent of what is already known about the political collusion to abuse positions of power for wealth accumulation that has characterised China's leadership since economic reforms. As *Let the Bullets Fly* is set during the 1920s, one could easily claim that the film's narrative simply reflects the buying into official ranks that was common practice in late imperial and Republican-era China, as Norman Stockman (2000) reports was the case. The historical situation of the film's script, though, appeared superfluous to

34   *Let the Bullets Fly*

the Chinese audiences; indeed, it is entirely possible that the producer's "sometime in the warring 1920s" tagline at the start of the film functioned precisely to encourage audiences to think that the era in which the film's narrative was set was open to interpretation. Accordingly, the assumption that wealth accumulation in China is a direct result of the abuse of political power (or "pulling connections", referred to as *la guanxi*, 拉关系) made the fictional implication of this abuse of power in *Let the Bullets Fly* far from shocking for Chinese audiences.[3] This was best captured in LBF28's (Taiyuan C) comment, that *Let the Bullets Fly* "clearly satirises corrupt officials in China, there is no clear boundary between people of integrity and evil". As Bruce Dickson (2008: 215) explains, the "sale of party and government offices" is post-reformed China's "peculiar form of bribery", and every class of Chinese audience appeared well informed of this fact. In fact, every audience member agreed at the conclusion of *Let the Bullets Fly* that the statement "money can buy political power and political power can make one rich in China" was true, although audiences in Nanjing were simply asked whether they agreed with the statement, as the issue of the Governor's deeds being illegally purchased was not entirely comprehended by all.

This overwhelmingly positive response to the statement was despite varying factors that may have impacted on responses of the audiences, including their class position, regional location and age group. And even though in Beijing and in the group Taiyuan C, audiences were observed to be somewhat wary about agreeing with the statement in front of their peers and a foreign researcher, no audience member refuted, or challenged, the statement. For the rest of the audiences who shared their opinions, particularly in Lanzhou and Taiyuan A and B and one male in Nanjing (LBF15), they were observably confident in their assumptions. As rural migrant worker LBF15 commented, "ah, they [officials] are all just looking after themselves," which he accompanied with a flick of his hand that appeared to speak on behalf of his peers who had far less narrative comprehension than he. LBF15's comment is important for two reasons: Yingjie Guo (2013: 18) describes the lines of power in China as those of "*exclusion* and *inclusion*" (author's emphasis). LBF15's comment captured Guo's "us and them" dichotomy, as not only a theoretical approach to understanding political power in China, but also as how it is experienced socially by China's lower classes. As LBF15's interpretation of the ambitions of the powerful came from a position of exclusion while watching *Let the Bullets Fly*'s depiction of those "included", as in the ruling elite, LBF15's assumptions about power abuse were confirmed by the film. That being said, what is also significant about LBF15's comment is his assumption that the corruption was a result of individual greed on the part of the officials who look after "themselves". LBF15's comment was not a concern for the Party-state's explicit relationship to both the planned and market economy, which undeniably creates and continues to create the environment in which such power abuse can take place. Returning to the original interest as to how assumptions about power abuse and wealth accumulation are normalised to benefit the Party-state's agenda, LBF15's comment is a perfect example of how challenges to the status quo may be deflected in the shaping of assumptions through cinema. The current system is not the problem: finding an effective way to weed out corrupt individuals from the system is.

Master Tang invests 200,000 RMB into the Governor's deed to Goose Town. He estimates his investment will double within a year. In reality, Chinese officials who have been charged with office-buying schemes have reaped returns well in excess of Master Tang's modest calculations. Despite the abuses of power for individual gain (so much so it is the feature of a commercial blockbuster), the Party-state continues to have an unchallenged legitimacy to rule. So far, public recognition of power abuses among China's ruling classes have not been the focus of mobilised class antagonism. While these audiences were not altogether satisfied with the corruption that they acknowledged characterises their country's leadership, the lack of antagonism may have to do with the fact that these audiences also firmly disagreed that the rule of law in China could solve or curtail the endemic abuses of power. The general belief was that only "force" executed by the Party-state could address the corruption of certain individuals.

The law and "policing" the law (or *being* the law)

The simple fact that the deeds for the position of Governor, the chief magistrate to Goose Town, could be bought establishes for audiences from the outset that the legal system in Goose Town is porous and unreliable. To symbolise this, Goose Town's magisterial drum, used to announce the request for a case to be brought before the magistrate, is shown neglected and consumed by vines at Goose Town's entrance. Huang Silang's preferred means of controlling the behaviour of Goose Town's people, i.e. evoking the townsfolk's obedience, has been through his henchmen's abusive and freely administered primordial policing tactics. His henchmen, led by Master Wu (a martial arts scholar) and Wuhan, are portrayed as irrational, unpredictable and fierce, and their acts of terror confirm that Huang Silang's wealth has allowed him to become a law unto himself. On a first viewing the law in Goose Town may appear to play a minor role in *Let the Bullets Fly*. Yet, the minor role that the law plays in *Let the Bullets Fly*'s narrative actually speaks volumes about how *Let the Bullets Fly* underplays the value of the rule of law in order to instil in its audiences scepticism about the feasibility of China's legal system.

Returning to Zhang Mazi and Master Tang surveying Goose Town's administrative documents, upon hearing that Zhang Mazi must sacrifice his earnings to Huang Silang at a 30/70 split, he exclaims:

Zhang: 我大老远的来一趟，就是为了看他的脸色？
  I came this far to serve his interests?
Tang: 那，你要怎么说，卖官当县长还真就是跪着要饭的，就这，多少人想跪还没这门子呢
  If you want to put it that way, many would love to be in your position, but few could afford to buy a post.

36   *Let the Bullets Fly*

[Zhang explains that he morally cannot justify the degrading act of kneeling before others like a beggar]

Tang: 百姓眼里，你是县长，可是黄四郎眼里，你就是跪着要饭的；挣钱嘛，生意，不寒碜

In the eyes of the townsmen, you are the Governor, but in the eyes of Huang Silang, you are a beggar; making money is just business, there is no shame!

Zhang: 寒碜！很他妈的寒碜！

To hell there isn't! This is shameful!

Tang: 那你是想站着还是挣钱呢？

Now, do you want to stand honourably, or make money?

Zhang: 我是想站着，还把挣钱了

I want to do both.

Tang: 挣不成！

Impossible!

[Camera close up of a gun that Zhang slams in front of Tang]

Zhang: 这个能不能挣钱？

Can I make money if I use this?

Tang: 能争，山里

Yes, as a bandit.

[Camera close-up of the courtroom's gavel that Zhang slams in front of Tang next to the gun]

Zhang: 这个能不能挣钱？

Can I make money if I use this?

Tang: 能争，跪着

Yes, as a beggar.

Zhang: 这个加上这个，能不能站着把钱挣了？

What if I used them both? Would I be able to stand honourably if I used them both?

[Hands clasped in a sign of awe at the brilliance of the proposal, Tang gushes, "Who really are you?"]

Zhang Mazi's "rule of law" in Goose Town is articulated in exactly the manner he proposes: a combination of the gavel and the gun, albeit the gavel is proved to be no match to Zhang Mazi's gun in engendering obedience. The first trial (and only trial) conducted in Goose Town's magistracy under Zhang Mazi's governorship features as defendant Master Wu, and the plaintiff (albeit unwillingly so) a small business operator only known as the "Noodle Vendor". Having collided with Master Wu, ironically while trying to escape Goose Town's magisterial drum rolling unrestrainedly through the High street, the Noodle Vendor is treated to extreme physical punishment at the hands of Master Wu. Zhang Mazi seizes the opportunity to bring Master Wu to court for his violent misdemeanour.

In the courtroom, Master Tang bangs his gavel, desperately trying to gain control of the court. The public cheer Master Wu as he wallops the Noodle Vendor in full view of Master Tang to flaunt his disregard for Master Tang's courtroom. The gavel brings Master Tang little power in his effort to control Master Wu's audacity. Only Zhang Mazi's entrance, bravado and cocking of his gun turn the trial serious. With gun cocked and pointed at Master Wu's head, Master Wu kneels and accepts his flogging from the Noodle Vendor, who in turn is (notably unwillingly so for fear of reprisal) forced to administer the punishment. Zhang Mazi walks out to address the townspeople gathered at the courtroom entrance, eager to hear the verdict of Master Wu's trial. Upon the sight of their new Governor the townspeople kowtow in deference. Zhang Mazi fires his gun pointedly into the air and demands the townspeople rise. He implores them never to kowtow before anyone in Goose Town again, and with gun cocked he defiantly declares that he has brought three things to Goose Town:

Zhang: 公平！公平！公平！
　　　　Justice! Fairness! Equity!

Enjoying the theatrics of his newfound moral authority and to punctuate his declaration, Zhang Mazi fires into the air once more. So ingrained is the response to kowtow in the face of force that the townspeople drop to their knees once more. Zhang Mazi reverts to the same system of social control as Huang Silang by overriding the judicial system to articulate that "justice" has arrived in Goose Town, and to enforce self-determination among the townspeople. In his desire to punish Master Wu and to antagonise Huang Silang, Zhang Mazi also interprets the crime and punishment as he sees fit, paying little regard to the trial Master Tang is trying to hold, to Master Tang's great frustration.

The inconsistencies and interpretation by *Let the Bullets Fly*'s hero, Zhang Mazi, of his application of the rule of law is not purely for humorous effect. As Colin Hawes (2013: 128) explains, China's legal "systems" are in actuality often fraught with inconsistencies of application by China's authorities:

> the problem arises when the CCP's own policies go against the laws promulgated by the state. There is no accepted procedure by which the courts can invalidate the Party policies that violate Chinese laws. Instead, what invariably happens is that courts 'interpret' the laws to fit Party policies, taking advantage of the kinds of vague general principles in the statutes.

In this vein, *Let the Bullets Fly* at no point provides an example of either Huang Silang or Zhang Mazi, applying the rule of law in a manner that is not to serve his own objectives. Rather, audiences are left to consider which of the two men are less bad in their violation and self-interpretation of Goose Town's laws.

In response to Zhang Mazi's brazen flogging of Master Wu, Huang Silang too stages his own version of a "trial". The trial involves Zhang Mazi's adopted

38 *Let the Bullets Fly*

son, Brother Six. Huang Silang directs his henchmen to set a trap for Brother Six to end up on trial for supposedly stealing from the same Noodle Vendor who was made to flog Master Wu. The Noodle Vendor, whose family's safety is threatened by Huang Silang, is terrorised into agreeing to the plot. The Noodle Vendor claims that Brother Six ate two bowls of noodles but only paid for one. Goose Town's landed gentry crowd around the plaintiff and the accused, some on chairs to improve their view. Wu Han and Master Wu sit at the top of the circle as self-proclaimed magistrates. At the scene's climax, a gun (similar to how Zhang Mazi's gun was pointed at Master Wu only scenes earlier) is held to the Noodle Vendor's head, and Wu Han claims that if Brother Six maintains his innocence, then the Noodle Vendor must be lying and therefore deserves to die. Horrified yet indignant, Brother Six desperately slices his gut open to draw out the value of a single bowl of noodles to prove his innocence. The teahouse falls silent as the contents of Brother Six's gut poignantly wobble in his bowl for dramatic effect. Wu Han starts to clap, pleased with his accomplishment. The gentry quietly scurry away, at which point Zhang Mazi bursts into the courtroom and takes aim at Wu Han and shoots – his bullet just scraping Wu Han's ear. The poignancy of the subsequent death of Brother Six is exacerbated by the audience's knowledge that Zhang Mazi and Master Tang were rushing to Brother Six's aid all the while.

Zhang: 讲茶大常？县衙不是断案的地方吗
          Why are they convening at the teahouse and not at the magistracy?
Tang: 你这个县衙是摆设，断案只有去讲茶大常，那才是真县衙！
          The magistracy is just a show! The teahouse is the real magistracy!

The irony of the teahouse being "the real magistracy" or the notion that courtroom trials are highly orchestrated and manipulated in China as *Let the Bullets Fly* suggests was not lost on Chinese audiences. When audiences were asked to give their opinions about this scene, the "Noodle trial" was overwhelmingly nominated as the most disliked scene in *Let the Bullets Fly*. The implied injustice of the trial in this scene, the poignancy of both Brother Six and the Noodle Vendor's situations and the scene's gore were all factors that unsettled audiences. Despite this, when audiences were asked which was the best way to rule China, the sentiment was resoundingly conclusive that the most effective way of ruling Chinese society would always be through force – not the law. Audiences understood that the law's inefficiency to protect either the Noodle Vendor or Brother Six was at the crux of this scene's action.

Although some female participants (Beijing, Taiyuan and Lanzhou) did preface their decisions with "ideally the law", males (all groups) unanimously agreed that "force" would always be the most effective way to govern and lead. In two discussion groups, females in Nanjing and Taiyuan (A and B) chose to pass on the discussion because they felt they "did not know". For the illiterate audience members in Nanjing, the legal system appeared to be an issue of power that was well beyond their immediate conceptual realities and they appeared uncertain how to engage with the conversation. All in all, *Let the Bullets Fly* appeared to shape or reinforce assumptions that the rule of law was ineffective in China among audiences that indicated their narrative comprehension, and baffled audiences who did not. Rather than interpreting audiences' opinions as a preference for force and violence though, or *Let the Bullets Fly*'s advocacy for vigilantism, these responses suggested that audiences had been desensitised towards the porous nature of China's rule of law long before participating in the film screening of *Let the Bullets Fly*. An example of this was LBF4's description of the scene:

> The townspeople [watching the staged courtroom trial] crowded in to see whether the new Governor brought "new law" to the town, or whether it was like the [Huang's] "old law"; they wanted to see how the new power struggle would fare, who would win. That is why they scattered after Brother Six sliced his stomach open: it was the same law – it was fake! Nothing had changed, and Huang won.

While very clearly able to interpret the fictional scene she had just seen in *Let the Bullets*, LBF4 also chose "force" as the best way to rule China only moments later. Drawing this conclusion shortly after describing the fictional scenario that supported a similar cynicism towards the law suggested that LBF4 was drawing parallels between what she saw in the film and her understanding of everyday China without the need to contemplate deeper on the issue. Like the townspeople of Goose Town, these audiences appeared to be attracted to the idea of the law, but were highly sceptical of the practicalities of a reliable judicial system ever being truly functional.

If the law's purpose is to restrain state power, the law's involvement (independently applied) in solving the corruption that is understood to be ripe within the Party-state would create havoc of a structural magnitude. Likewise, an independent rule of law may make moral judgements that contravene the agenda of the Party-state, particularly due to the complicit nature of so many officials and their abuses of power. A very plausible argument can be made, therefore, that the benefits to the Party-state of socialising assumptions that the rule of law is incapable of dealing with the corruption of officials like Huang Silang, Zhang Mazi and Master Tang and that "force" is the only way – "force" being the insurmountable leadership of the Party-state – is to socialise consensus among broader Chinese society to allow China's leadership to conduct the corruption purge "in house". The corrupt individuals who need to be weeded out should be provided *to* the courtrooms by the Party-state – not the other way around. Interestingly, audience assumptions regarding the abuses of power by China's elites were uniform across group discussions up to this point. Everyone had a similar understanding of the personalities of those in power. A deviation from uniform responses appeared during discussions about Goose Town's "poor" and their use as political pawns in Huang Silang and Zhang Mazi's power struggle.

40 *Let the Bullets Fly*

The poor as the masses: "穷鬼" (*qionggui*)

The poor of Goose Town are presented as a nameless, faceless, physical mass. Huang Silang requires the poor to acquiesce to his rule in order to consolidate and perpetually augment his personal economic power, and Zhang Mazi requires the punctuality of the poor to heed his call to provide physical mass in his overthrow of Huang Silang in the final stages of the film's narrative. Although having many reasons to rebel against Huang Silang's brutal oppression, Goose Town's poor are portrayed as excruciatingly hesitant to be antagonistic. Indeed, the poor are only encouraged to be antagonistic in *Let the Bullets Fly* at the point at which Zhang Mazi returns to avenge Master Tang and Brother Two's deaths (and it is also suggested the deaths of the previous five Governors, who had also been caught out by the surprise attack of Huang's fake Pockey). At no point throughout the film's narrative does Zhang Mazi engage directly with Goose Town's poor, nor do the poor feature in any other way in the film except as background bodies when they are being terrorised by Huang Silang's henchmen, or at the film's conclusion, ransacking Huang Silang's citadel and pilfering his belongings.

Let the Bullets Fly takes painstaking efforts to emphasise the weakened ideological positions of Goose Town's unpropertied townsfolk. Zhang Mazi's decision to return to Goose Town to mobilise Goose Town's poor to storm Huang Silang's citadel takes up the better half of the film's climactic final half hour, which I will relay now in narrative detail, to reinforce the deep-set need for self-preservation Goose Town's poor are shown to have. Zhang Mazi first fills the streets of Goose Town with Huang Silang's silver, to appeal to the poor's support through the promise of a share in Huang Silang's wealth. The poor choose to wait until the dark of night to pilfer the offerings, and by morning the streets are empty. Outraged, Huang Silang releases his horses towing empty carriages through the streets of Goose Town and obediently the silver gathered during the night spews forth from windows into the carriages below and are towed back to Huang Silang's citadel. Zhang Mazi's gang are distraught at the willingness of the poor to return the silver with such obedience. Zhang Mazi, however, sees the situation differently. In his mind, what lies under fear of Huang Silang is in fact the poor's rage. Zhang Mazi discovers that this rage is not so dependable. Lining the streets with guns and ammunition, again in the dark of night, the poor collect the weapons and ammunition. When Huang Silang sends his horses once more to collect the weapons as he did the silver, the carriages remain empty. Encouraged by the poor's refusal to relinquish their weapons, Zhang Mazi and his gang take to the streets calling for the poor to join them in attacking the citadel. The poor do not follow. Realising that the poor need evidence of a weakened leadership, Flora, the prostitute who befriends Zhang Mazi's gang, arrives at the gates of the citadel with Huang Silang's decoy kidnapped earlier in the film. Acknowledging that arming the rage of the poor alone was not enough to convince them to rebel, Zhang Mazi's only option is to decapitate Huang Silang's decoy publicly to convince the poor that Huang Silang poses no threat to their storming the citadel. It is then, and only then, convinced of no chance of reprisal, that the poor finally take their weapons and, following Zhang Mazi's lead, storm Huang's citadel. In these triumphant scenes, however, the storming of the citadel is portrayed as a desperate exercise in scavenging rather than political mobilisation or emancipation; earlier reflections on audience rejection that the conclusion advocated an overthrow of capitalism or the introduction of democracy to Goose Town supports this reading.

To grasp the importance of these final scenes in *Let the Bullets Fly*, it is worth taking a moment to reflect on how the portrayal of Goose Town's poor's agency cinematically deviates from earlier portrayals of peasantry mobilisation from recent history. Take 《红色娘子军》 *Red Detachment of Women* (Xie: 1961), for example, a film that was first produced by director Xie Jin and reproduced as one of the eight model operas that dominated the screens and stage during the Cultural Revolution. The film's protagonist, Wu Qionghua, a maidservant, has finally captured the evil landlord, Nan Batian ("the tyrant of the south") and parades him among the local villagers. In this scene, Qionghua pulls Nan Batian cuffed in chains through the streets, while informing the village peasants of his crimes and promising the villagers a bright communist future. A shot/reverse-shot sequence captures not only Qionghua's political education of the village population as she spruiks the Communist party's ability to emancipate the peasantry classes, but also pointedly presents the willingness to listen and learn and to be actively engaged on the side of the peasantry (see Figures 3.2 and 3.3). There is a recognisable connection between mobiliser and the mobilised.

Figure 3.2 Overthrowing landlords in the *Red Detachment of Women*

Figure 3.3 The peasantry listen intently to Qionghua

42 *Let the Bullets Fly*

Figure 3.4 Zhang Mazi yells over his shoulder to mobilise the poor

In contrast, as the events described above in the final scenes of *Let the Bullets Fly* suggest, there was little narrative time given for the poor of Goose Town to be seen as benefactors of political education and emancipation by Zhang Mazi. Nor were they ever in charge of their mobilisation. In Figure 3.4 we see the moment that the "masses" join Zhang Mazi, who leads the crowd by yelling over his shoulder to the mob of poor villagers, to follow his lead and attack the citadel.

Featuring only in this final 20 minutes of the 132-minute-long narrative, the mob-like presentation of Goose Town's poor brings little depth to the role the underclasses play in the narrative. *Let the Bullets Fly* quintessentially defuses any assumption that the political education of Goose Town's poor is their motive for their storming the citadel. Moreover, the film's conclusion does not advocate the political education of Goose Town's underprivileged, of which a crude comparison can be made to, say, the illiterate audiences in Nanjing and less-privileged audiences in Taiyuan A and B, to alter their instinct for self-preservation (and thus passivity) that is borne out of political exclusion and socio-economic disadvantage.

Not one audience member believed that the poor had learned something from storming the citadel. When asked to explain the reasons behind the poor's hesitation to be antagonistic, a conversation between lower classed female audiences in Taiyuan B (although LBF28 came from a prestigious family, she herself claimed to have little privilege) was particularly insightful – especially because these females could be observed to draw associations between the poor's depiction in *Let the Bullets Fly* to explain their own personal preference to remain politically detached:

> Having previously received money freely offered and then abused for innocently accepting this money, the poor have been taught to wait and see which

group would win in the power struggle: Zhang's or Huang's.[4] The poor people only know that a struggle is taking place, but do not know the details of what is happening in the circle of power. Their instinct is to protect themselves. In these final scenes, they need to be sure that they are supporting the strongest, and ensuring their safety. People are not aware of matters high up in the political hierarchy, but they can tell from each subtle public event what might be going on. Then they follow who other people believe is the most likely to win.

(LBF28)

At which point LBF27 clarified:

Here [China] people will support whoever is in power. The most important thing for the common person is that their leaders will raise their living standards. People tend not to care about power for themselves. Powerful leaders can see the whole picture clearly from above, whereas ordinary people cannot. This problem is simplistically presented in these final scenes. I personally am a businessperson and focus on how to make money. But I cannot avoid the political authority! My business will not be successful without the authorities' approval. But that is the extent of my knowledge of their activities. Business only.

To which LBF29 explained:

I am too young to be aware of issues related to our government.

And LBF30 followed with:

People have different jobs and will mind their own business in general and avoid politics.

To which LBF28 concluded:

It is not worthwhile taking the risk to get involved. Whether it can be done through the media or another way, it is none of my business. I am nobody.

When rural migrant workers in Nanjing were asked whether they personally believed they understood the current leadership in China better than the poor townsfolk of Goose Town, the male of the group, LBF15, who showed the highest level of narrative comprehension, shook his head smirking and beckoned with his hand to move on to the next question. LBF15's response spoke on behalf of his focus group peers, who were happy for LBF15 to act as mediator on this topic. Without portraying the political education of Goose Town's poor, audiences appeared vindicated that remaining politically disengaged was the right and only option for them within an unpredictable and highly corrupt society as *Let the Bullets Fly* had portrayed.

44 *Let the Bullets Fly*

While rural migrant workers and low-level administrators in Taiyuan interpreted the lack of political education of the poor in the film's narrative as a reason to stay disengaged, the more privileged audiences in Lanzhou, Taiyuan C and Beijing interpreted the trepidation of the poor in Goose Town as a point of comparison for how much political information had improved. CCP membership and proximity to the political centre could be seen to influence the expression of a more positive interpretation of the poor's situation in *Let the Bullets Fly*. Audiences in Beijing (LBF1–LBF7) consisted of participants with and without CCP membership, but all were employed in professional occupations and educated. In contrast to the discussion relayed above, these audiences shared the impression that the Party-state's communication had improved significantly in comparison to *Let the Bullets Fly*'s depiction. Despite many weaknesses in state policy and their recognition of the state's neglect of public opinion in implementing policy, there was an overwhelming belief that the Chinese public were far better informed than the poor in Goose Town. LBF7 explained that the internet and media had improved accessibility to political information and the increase in education had closed the gap between the people and members of the ruling elite. LBF4 noted that in *Let the Bullets Fly* the poor "knew nothing", but now the average citizen "knows more, but is hard to objectively quantify". LBF2 specifically referred to the improvements in communicating public policy, and it should be noted that LBF2 was employed in a government department in public relations. Universally sweeping assumptions were made by Beijing audiences that the levels of access and awareness they had (despite their advantageous position to such information) were indicative of the levels of informed opinions of all Chinese, and political education was unnecessary as the internet had solved many information gaps.

In contrast to feedback gathered in Taiyuan B, Taiyuan C consisted of four female postgraduate students, who were adamant that the Chinese public were *much* better informed than the poor of Goose Town. Three of the four young women (LBF32–LBF35, ages 23–25) had full CCP membership. As for female audience members in Lanzhou (LBF8–LBF13), the furthest focus group from the political centre in terms of location, yet consisting of similarly aged young adults (22–25 years) in possession of CCP membership personally or in their family, they regarded as secondary the political implications of the narrative and diverted discussion towards the love story of the prostitute, Flora and Zhang Mazi's gang member, Brother Three. A number of the female students even named the minor character of the prostitute, Flora, as their favourite character, while in Taiyuan, Beijing and Nanjing the character of Flora was given no attention by audience members of either gender or class. The political centre appeared quite far from their realities and the issue of the poor in Goose Town less interesting. Instead, these female students believed the film was about "brotherhood, love, and being kind to the poor". Being kind, however, most certainly did not imply political education and mobilisation of the poor. Whereas in Beijing the internet was cited twice as the reason for believing political engagement was better for Chinese now than in comparison to the poor

Let the Bullets Fly 45

in Goose Town, LBF8 in Lanzhou believed the Chinese media was one forum within which information could be improved:

> At the time depicted in *Let the Bullets Fly*, the struggle between justice and evil was very clear to see. Since economic reforms, the struggle still exists, but we just cannot see it as clearly. The media only publicises positive information about [China's] economic development, so families are focused on their own economic development, not with the issues of who is in power.

Audiences that had already seen *Let the Bullets Fly* and had very much enjoyed the film were privileged young adult urbanites (Beijing, Lanzhou and Taiyuan C). They were also notably the groups that assumed political information between Party-state and Chinese society had improved and the information was as accessible for everyone in Chinese society as it was for them, stating, "Chinese are all the same." Their confidence was contradicted by the sentiments expressed by rural migrant workers in Nanjing and low-level administrators in Taiyuan. Inspiring cohesive class consciousness and mobilising Chinese audiences to overthrow capitalist corruption was a highly unlikely probability with the release of the blockbuster *Let the Bullets Fly*. Particularly if these audiences are indicative of the broader divergences in opinion between China's aspirational and lower classes about the political inclusion and education of China's broader population. While the abuses of power and the rule of law may be broadly assumed as endemic to the individuals that make up China's leadership, the inability to perceive an alternative system of governance, or a necessity for political education, ensured that *Let the Bullets Fly*'s narrative reaffirmed the need for the Party-state's leadership in contemporary China, in all its corrupt glory for the Chinese audiences who watched and discussed this film.

Criticism without political change

The power of *Let the Bullets Fly*'s narrative is that the film is in fact a thoroughly sophisticated and entertaining piece of cinema for those with film comprehension. A lack of media literacy or even a political voice ensured, however, that a portion of Chinese audiences found little enjoyment in the film, and thereby negated political mobilisation of those most likely antagonised by the film's themes. The dialogue is witty, the graphics captivating, the protagonist, played by director/actor Jiang Wen, is irresistibly charming. Audiences' inability to perceive possibilities of political change among those who did possess media literacy skills and could discuss *Let the Bullets Fly*, though, was not a sign of an audience ripe for class-based mobilisation. Rather, audiences seemed to assume that they were unable to challenge the status quo, or that the status quo was the only way forward. Audiences who were the benefactors of the current leadership's reforms supported their leadership's status quo after watching the film – albeit with some hesitation, while audiences who did not expressed assumptions that they would simply have to "make do" or "stay out of the way" to survive. Indeed, these audiences' preference

46 *Let the Bullets Fly*

to not become politically involved would not be so disconcerting if the attributes of Chinese leadership portrayed in *Let the Bullets Fly* were not so bothersome; to say nothing of the fact that audiences all drew lines between the fictional on screen and their perceptions of contemporary reality.

A leadership establishes the norms of what is right and wrong in broader society, the value and character of human relations and understandings of personal freedoms, and ultimately legitimises class and political access within these paradigms. If these audiences are indicative of how a broad section of Chinese society may draw assumptions about China's leadership from popular commercial film consumption, their comments would support the notion that it is highly unlikely a challenge to China's political status quo is waiting its metaphorical turn in the wings – most importantly, that China's popular cinema will not be the forum in which such a challenge will take its shape.

Notes

1 Box office figure as of 16 July 2016 (Entgroup Inc); approximate USD at historical exchange rate for 1 January, 2011 (XE Currency); URL: http://www.cbooo.cn/m/573439/
2 Douban rating: 8.7/10 from 542,624 reviews. URL: http://movie.douban.com/subject/3742360/ (last accessed: 16 July 2016).
3 Bruce Dickson (2008: 215) reports, "The price for an office was roughly commensurate with the amount of bribes a person could expect to receive in the course of a year," and Yan Sun (2004: 145) claims that the "office for sale" model which provides *shi quan* (实权, substantive power) for cadres had "special appeal in the market economy, as it means authority over tangible and cashable resources and projects. . . . These perks and benefits are particularly important for officials in the poor regions." The exploits of office holding have not been a one-way affair. Party-state officials have also been encouraged to plunge into the "commercial sea" (*xiahai*, 下海) and enter into private business to take advantage of their close political connections as a means of stimulating market economy activity. Jie Chen and Bruce Dickson (2010: 38–39) conclude that the CCP has become a resource for the most "well-connected" and "politically trustworthy capitalists" in economically reformed China.
4 LBF28 refers here to scenes in *Let the Bullets Fly* when Zhang Mazi and his men anonymously deploy parcels of Huang Silang's silver to Goose Town's townspeople during the dark of night without Huang Silang's approval. In retaliation, Huang orders his men the following night to return and retrieve his silver. In doing so, they gang-rape a woman in front of her husband as punishment. The details of the incident are spread around the townspeople and the couple visit the magistrate's court demanding justice be served by Zhang Mazi as Governor.

References

Chen, Jie, and Bruce J. Dickson. 2010. *Allies of the State: China's Private Entrepreneurs and Democratic Change*. Cambridge, MA: Harvard University Press.
Dickson, Bruce J. 2008. *Wealth in Power: The Communist Party's Embrace of China's Private Sector*. Cambridge: Cambridge University Press.
Guo, Yingjie. 2013. Political Power and Social Inequality: The Impact of the State. In *Unequal China: The Political Economy and Cultural Politics of Inequality*, edited by Wanning Sun and Yingjie Guo, 12–26. Oxon and New York: Routledge.

Hawes, Colin. 2013. (In)equality under the Law in China Today. In *Unequal China: The Political Economy and Cultural Politics of Inequality*, edited by Wanning Sun and Yingjie Guo, 125–138. Oxon and New York: Routledge.

Stockman, Norman. 2000. *Understanding Chinese Society*. London: Polity.

Sun, Yan. 2004. *Corruption and Market in Contemporary China*. Ithaca, NY: Cornell University Press.

Zhang, Yingjin. 2004. *Chinese National Cinema*. New York: Routledge.

4 *Lost on Journey*
Prejudice in class relations

Figure 4.1 Promotional film poster: *Lost on Journey*

50   *Lost on Journey*

《人在囧途》
(*ren zai jiong tu*)

Lost on Journey

Director: Raymond Yip
Starring: Baoqiang Wang (王宝强)
Box office: 37,635,000 RMB (USD 5,508,675)[1]
Exhibition period: June 2010 (4 weeks)[2]

Synopsis

Lost on Journey's (Yip: 2010) narrative gravitates around two central characters: Li Chenggong (李成功) and Niugeng (牛耿), both enroute from Beijing to Changsha during the Spring Festival season. Li Chenggong is undertaking his annual visit home from his Beijing base as a CEO of a toy manufacturing company for the Spring Festival holiday to see his daughter. He also plans to negotiate a divorce with his wife in order to marry his Beijing mistress. Niugeng on the other hand has undertaken the task of retrieving debts owed to the milk factory where he and his colleagues work to recoup wages outstanding to them. On the advice of his boss's handwritten "debt receipts" which Niugeng lacks the literacy skills to properly read, Niugeng sets off for Changsha. As fate would have it, Li Chenggong and Niugeng find themselves crossing paths more than once along their journeys, to the frustration of the high-flying business CEO, who finds his travelling companion a constant insult to his more civilised class sensibilities. While Li Chenggong is a seasoned traveller and accustomed to luxury travel and paying his way out of trouble, Niugeng is new to air travel, without money, and willing to "slum it" in rough travelling conditions.

The adventure these two men find themselves on occurs on different modes of transport. Challenged by weather and traffic conditions Li Chenggong is forced to reconcile his attachment to his country bumpkin travel partner, Niugeng. Over the course of the adventure they travel by plane (turned back after a thunderstorm), train (which becomes stuck by ice on the railroad tracks), bus (which has to be turned back due to bridge repairs), car (which they win through a raffle and then crash with Niugeng falling asleep behind the wheel), *nongminche* (农民车) (a rural tractor that transports them out of a village they find themselves in), a ferry (from which they disembark after spotting a beggar on the shore bank who has supposedly stolen Niugeng's money) and by foot (at desperation point). Each of the forms of transport provides an insight into China's development, the great divide between developed and underdeveloped China, and the classes that travel by each method.

As New Year's Eve falls upon the protagonists camping by the side of the road, they discuss the meaning of love and marriage, and whether Li Chenggong's love for both his wife and his mistress are equal and moral. At the end of the roadside heart-to-heart, Li Chenggong thanks Niugeng for making him see that his "life is more or less a sorry situation." Arriving home in Changsha, and after a surprise visit from his Beijing mistress, the audience is left understanding that Li

Chenggong plans to improve his attitude towards his role as father and husband by concluding his relationship with his mistress. Later, Li Chenggong realises that the debt receipts Niugeng has in his possession are useless and that Niugeng's employer has tricked him. Li Chenggong anonymously covers the payment of the debts, and to celebrate Niugeng's success, Li Chenggong offers to take him out to dinner. This is the last that the two see of each other for a year, until the following New Year and Li Chenggong waits seated once again on a delayed flight from Beijing to Changsha. Frustrated, Li Chenggong muses with the flight attendant what kind of nuisance passenger would hold a plane up like this. Suddenly, Niugeng boards the plane in a Western suit with his hair slicked back and polished black leather shoes – the poster image of a Chinese business and social mobility success story. What Nigueng's success actually entails, however, is left to the audience's speculation. "Hi!" he shrieks when he spots Li Chenggong, at which point the film ends with Li Chenggong's face freeze-framed in horror.

Introduction

> [O]ur views of how others relate to us in the world (and of what should be done about it) do not arise spontaneously. They are *mobilized*. And leaders do not mobilize prejudice by accident or by chance.
>
> Stephen Reicher (2012: 38)

Prejudice, as a preconceived opinion or feeling that lacks qualitative evidence, has very real consequences for social action, and *inaction*. Prejudice has real implications for how class relations take place and the assumption of the necessity for, or the natural condition of, class structures in any given society. In China, where the overwhelming majority are excluded from the political process of the economic initiatives that the Party-state instigates (which compounds their experiences of class), mobilising prejudices, as Stephen Reicher may agree, is crucial to legitimising this phenomenon. Not only does prejudice validate the continued labour exploitation of China's lower classes in general, but it also serves to negate the formation of class consciousness between urban and rural migrant workers who arguably share class interests but have been socialised to understand themselves as culturally different.

The rural migrant worker has become a feature of most developed cities in China that offer employment in factories, markets, construction sites and service work (Solinger 1999; Huang 2009; Sun 2009, 2014). For as many stories of entrepreneurial success told since China's economic reforms, there are multiple contradictory stories of discrimination, maltreatment and industrial exploitation of China's working classes, particularly its rural migrant workers who have swarmed to urban areas searching for work. As the immediate life realities of Chinese from polarised class spectrums grow further and further apart in experience and opportunity, the cognition of the class "other" grows starker and more robust in its application to everyday social interactions. As a result, the presence of the rural migrant worker character in China's popular cinema has evolved into a means of measurement by

52 *Lost on Journey*

which privileged filmgoers can gauge their own class status and position in China's modernity narrative of progress and development.

While the term "prejudice" typically has a connotation with hostility, fear and hatred, which renders the term negative, China's cinema of class socialises prejudice as an *affirmative* value system for film audiences to employ in their everyday activities and social encounters with the class "other". Affirmative prejudice in this case is knowing who the class other is and what the superficial indicators are of another person's value, so as to not only accurately distinguish one's own class position but, likewise, normalise social hierarchies, both industrially and socially.

Lost on Journey was filmed on location at bus stations, train stations, in villages and on suburban streets between Beijing and Changsha, which provides audiences of *Lost on Journey* an immediate capacity to project their conceptual understandings of "everyday China" onto the film's narrative. The visuals involve little post-production – urban areas are left grey and rural areas muddy and green. The adventure's *mise-en-scène* continuously exacerbates privileged protagonist Li Chenggong's out-of-place presence in each street-side location that is not the chandeliered restaurant where he typically conducts business. *Lost on Journey* is accompanied by what could only be described as "humorous" music – digitally constructed sounds that indicate when Niugeng is acting in a way that is either embarrassing, unacceptable or naïve, and suggest the audience should laugh *at* Niugeng. In contrast, the orchestral music that accompanies Li Chenggong's family scenes or moments of "moral clarity" indicates when Li Chenggong's character development is to be taken seriously.

Lost on Journey's box office takings were moderate considering the possibilities of the Chinese film market. Yet, *Lost on Journey* gained significant cultural traction since the film's exhibition in mainstream cinemas and subsequent broadcasting on Chinese state television, which is best captured by the overwhelming number of positive reviews the film has received on Douban, the highly popular social forum. *Lost on Journey* was the only film in this book that was mentioned by audiences as having been watched multiple times on state television specifically (as opposed to in a cinema or online streaming) prior to participating in this project. These audiences confirmed that the class stereotypes and the portrayal of class relations in the film were immediately recognisable to them. Perhaps encouraged by this, as well as the humorous script that centres on a hopeless rural migrant worker in an urban environment they could recognise, audiences were also noticeably confident in discussing the prejudices in the film as "truths" among their peers of a similar class position. With *Lost on Journey* promoted as a fun, all-ages family film too, the film ensured that the affirmative application of prejudice the film portrays was pitched not only at China's adult audiences, but affirmative prejudice was presented as a morality appropriate for all: young and old.

Audiences and discussion groups

The average age of an audience member for discussion groups about *Lost on Journey* was 35 years; 17 were male and 19 were female. Two discussion groups

Lost on Journey 53

were held in Lanzhou: one group with peasants (A), and a second group with undergraduate students from a variety of academic disciplines (B). Taiyuan consisted of three groups: the first with white collar professionals with higher levels of tertiary education (D), the second with a mix of administrators with low, moderate and high education levels and with career opportunities (E), the third with a mix of service workers with moderate-high levels of education or professional occupations, and one participant had a low level of education and employment status (F). University students in Lanzhou and the majority of urban residents in low to mid-level white collar occupations in Taiyuan had seen *Lost on Journey* prior to participating in the film screening. Audience members who had not seen *Lost on Journey* prior to the film screening were from polarised spectrums of privilege like those depicted in the film: peasants and mature aged established professionals. Of all five films considered in this book, *Lost on Journey* was the only film that was received positively by all audiences regardless of socio-economic background. Each audience member agreed that he or she would recommend *Lost on Journey* to friends and families. A number of privileged urbanites in Taiyuan and Lanzhou admitted they had watched the film multiple times when it was exhibited in the cinemas and then subsequently on television. Two of the audience members in Taiyuan confirmed on their subsequent viewings of *Lost on Journey* on state television that they had encouraged their children to watch the film with them.

The group that visibly enjoyed the experience of watching *Lost on Journey* the most were the peasants in Lanzhou. By the end of the film's screening, these men were smiling broadly and in very high spirits. The character of Niugeng provided them a hook on to which they could properly engage with the film's narrative, unlike other films in this book, which failed to resonate with rural migrant worker audiences. These men had never been to a cinema and it was a novelty for them to spend half a day to have a private screening in the government compounds of the village. Although they did confirm that sometimes in the village square a screen was erected for public movie screenings (usually state studio productions or tele-series), they confirmed people would watch only "in passing" on their way through the square.

In Taiyuan, LOJ26 agreed that he personally enjoyed the film but later as the discussion group progressed stated, "foreigners should not be watching these films." LOJ26's comment did not appear to display embarrassment at the film's narrative, but discomfort in the direction the group discussion had taken in prejudicially speaking about rural migrant workers. LOJ26's peers looked surprised at LOJ26's comment, assuring LOJ26 that they were simply clarifying that the rural migrant worker in *Lost on Journey* was not as genuine in reality, and performing a service for the foreigner who was the host of the discussion group. In all group discussions, albeit most vigorously so among those of privileged urbanites, prejudicial thinking and attitudes towards the class other appeared to flow freely, confidently and without embarrassment – yet noticeably more cautiously expressed by urbanites less-privileged and with rural ties. *Lost on Journey* appeared not necessarily to

54   *Lost on Journey*

be *the* precursor for prejudicial attitudes, but most certainly not a cultural product that encouraged prejudicial assumptions to dissipate.

Wanning Sun (2012: 6) asks her readers to contemplate the question "How are viewers positioned in the process of identification with the underclass?" in watching popular Chinese cinema. Audiences of *Lost on Journey* demonstrated that to identify with the underclass, an audience member had to share a class view with the underclass character. Without this reference, identification became merely a means of clarifying *who* and *what* audiences were not. Thus, this chapter proposes that audiences other than the underclass in fact do *not* identify or empathise with underprivileged characters on screen. Audiences rather learn in these theatrical occasions how to recognise and manage their prejudices towards the class "other" in an acceptable mainstream context. Group discussions indicated that audiences of *Lost on Journey* could only share a class view with characters and narratives that they recognised as members of their own "in-group" and were oftentimes oblivious to, or misinterpreted completely, the narrative trajectory of the class other in the film's script.

In-groups and out-groups: stereotyping the other

The narrative of *Lost on Journey* pivots around two protagonists: an urban professional "CEO", Li Chenggong (李成功), whose name translates as "Power and Success", and a migrant worker, Niugeng (牛耿), whose name translates as "Bright Ox". Encountering a series of transport mishaps, the protagonists mirror the two speeds of contemporary China: the high-flying owner of capital who exploits his workers, and the exploited labourer with only his labour to sell in China's reformed market. Li Chenggong and Niugeng are introduced to their audiences in relation to their social position within the means of production. Li Chenggong is introduced addressing his three employees in his capacity as CEO of a company that manufactures soft toys. He sits on one end of a banquet table, enjoying his meal, with a grand chandelier above, as his employees sit obediently across from him, acquiescing to Li Chenggong's abuse and, importantly, not eating. Niugeng in contrast, is introduced to audiences watching the news coverage of Chinese travellers returning home for the New Year celebrations, when Niugeng's boss confirms that he has no money to pay the workers their wages. Immediately, *Lost on Journey* establishes that the film's protagonists sit on polarised social positions of production. Li Chenggong is the owner of capital and controls the means of production and hence has the power to provide or deny a worker's employment and wage; and Niugeng, who only has his physical labour to sell in the market, is shown to be vulnerable to exploitation (Figure 4.2).

When audiences were asked to identify which protagonist was more privileged than the other, the responses were consistent across all discussion groups: Li Chenggong was privileged and wealthy and Niugeng was poor. LOJ12 even categorised Li Chenggong as from the "wealthy middle class". When asked for these

Figure 4.2 Industrial juxtapositions in *Lost on Journey*. (Left) Li Chenggong and his employees; (right) Niugeng and his colleagues at the milk factory

assumptions to be explained, the following points of distinction were provided; Li Chenggong was a *"laoban"* (老板, boss) because he:

- lived in a villa
- wore expensive clothes
- had a driver and surplus money
- was able to use his money to solve his problems
- did not have to carry his life possessions around with him
- retrieves Niugeng's bags when he drops them because his instinct is to look after his property, whereas Niugeng is not so materialistic
- had workers who performed administrative services on his behalf.

Peasants and students in Lanzhou also noted that Li Chenggong's wealth was indicated by his keeping a mistress. As LOJ11 explained, "only a man with money could afford to do that."

Niugeng, in contrast, was recognised as not having wealth or power and identified immediately as a "rural migrant worker" (*nongmingongren*, 农民工人) by privileged audience members, although peasants in Lanzhou referred to Niugeng as simply *"nongmin"* (农民), "villager" or a "rural man". From the outset this choice of language implied "in-grouping" and "out-grouping" indicative of the divisions that urban and rural Chinese believe they have. While peasants saw Niugeng as their own "in-group" from a rural context and referred to him as a "villager", urban audiences perceived Niugeng as a peasant from their urban context, and thus a "rural migrant worker". Privileged urbanites recognised Niugeng as a rural migrant worker because he:

- wore dirty clothes that were indicative of rural fashion, which indicated that he did not consume frivolously
- had limited literacy skills
- had a weak industrial position, as he had not been paid his wages and, importantly, "worked in a factory with animals"
- was ignorant of the etiquette of air travel

56 *Lost on Journey*

- consumed the entire contents of his 4-liter bottle of milk at the security gate at the airport, because he would rather drink the milk than waste it
- carried his life possessions around with him in large cloth bags (in contrast to Li Chenggong, who was able to store his belongings in two different homes and travel lightly)
- had to borrow money from Li Chenggong.

Dovidio et al. (2012: 250) explain that one of the traits of "in-group" and "out-group" behaviour is that

> Cognitively, when people or objects are categorized into different groups, extant differences between members of the same category tend to be perceptually minimized, and differences between members of different groups become exaggerated or over-generalized. Moreover, people retain more positive information about ingroup than about outgroup members, discounting negative information about the ingroup.

Accordingly, peasants in Lanzhou neglected to indicate Niugeng's clothing, his lack of literacy skills, or ignorance of air travel etiquette as their reasons for recognising him as a poor man from rural origins. Rather, they only nominated Niugeng's odd-job type of labour (known as *dagong*, 打工) in an urban context to clarify their assumptions. Similarly, middle-aged professionals in Taiyuan ignored the prominent element of the narrative that plays on stereotypes of wealthy businessmen in China having mistresses as a sign of their wealth, despite the glaringly obvious subplot the mistress plays in the film's narrative. Only undergraduate students and peasants nominated this stereotypical characteristic of Li Chenggong. Audiences interestingly ignored negative traits about the character with which they shared class views in *Lost on Journey*, while listing many more negative traits about the class "other". This was behaviour observed by audiences of both spectrums of the class division. The preferential selection of class traits became especially evident when students in Lanzhou, in the position of not exclusively identifying with *either* character's class at this stage in their lives, were evenly attentive to negative traits of both characters. After all, their comments did not reflect what they perceived to be representations of their current class positions, but identified privileged white collar professionals and underprivileged rural migrant workers, neither of which they were.

When audiences were asked whether they believed the depictions of the two classes were "realistic" and "accurate", all groups unanimously agreed with the statement but for different reasons. Peasants in Lanzhou confirmed that their clothes were similar to those worn by the character of Niugeng, yet interestingly had not nominated Niugeng's clothing as a sign of his poverty during the earlier discussion. The peasants also acknowledged that on occasion they received similar treatment to Niugeng from city-dwellers when working odd jobs in urban areas. Peasants were not disgruntled or offended by the representation of Niugeng, in fact these audiences believed Niugeng's honesty and optimism were accurate and that rural migrant workers were friendlier than the city dweller. In saying this, they emphasised that Niugeng was very fortunate, because the likelihood of a wealthy urbanite providing financial assistance as Li Chenggong does for Niugeng, was highly unlikely.

LOJ4 was quick to explain, however, that the economic capacities of the rural people were "closing in" on that of the city-dweller (*kaojin tamen*, 靠近他们) and therefore he believed that the relationship between Li Chenggong and Niugeng could potentially happen. LOJ4 was quite optimistic that in the future, rural and urban Chinese would be more closely aligned socially and economically. LOJ3 supported his peer's comments, explaining that the possibility to work two seasons – the harvest season and then odd jobs in urban areas during the off-season – meant that peasants could earn the same as, if not more than, some poorer city dwellers. These audiences acknowledged Li Chenggong's discrimination of Niugeng in the film but explained it as something they could also find humorous, as they were confident their life positions were improving. Peasants furthermore perceived themselves at the film's conclusion as advantaged, because they believed they lived in friendlier communities than that of the urban dweller. Indeed, these peasants did not critique or question Niugeng's portrayed moral superiority to Li Chenggong, taking it for granted that the filmmaker meant this as a true reflection of rural Chinese. Li Chenggong's discrimination was considered an issue of not liking Niugeng's dirty clothes, not an issue of Niugeng's rural origins or his class-based characteristics, as urban audiences subsequently indicated was the case.

Professionals in Taiyuan and students in Lanzhou believed the visual representation of Niugeng was accurate, but they were unconvinced by the purity of Niugeng's honesty. In group Taiyuan D, three females (LOJ14, LOJ16 and LOJ20) were particularly vocal, and in Taiyuan B, LOJ22 and LOJ24, who grew up in Taiyuan proper, were likewise critical of rural migrant workers' moral characters. In these cases, their group peers hesitated to agree openly with them, although no one vocally disagreed with their statements. This conscious act not to disagree implied, therefore, either agreement with the comments made by LOJ22 and LOJ24 or unwillingness to challenge the comments. Their silence also could have been taken as a contemplation of their own prejudices. When these same audience members were asked whether they would behave in the same way towards Niugeng if they were Li Chenggong, including the same LOJ26 who believed foreigners should not watch *Lost on Journey*, they confirmed that they would – even the quieter urbanites with rural backgrounds. Peasants in Lanzhou, in contrast, were not sure how to answer this question. After all, why would they ignore or avoid one of their own ingroup?

It is important at this juncture to note that when asked who audiences felt they most easily identified with in *Lost on Journey*, peasants without hesitation answered "Niugeng". Male and female middle-aged urban professionals in Taiyuan D, E and F responded "Li Chenggong". Five audience members in Taiyuan F with rural backgrounds and working in white collar jobs responded "in between Li Chenggong and Niugeng". Three of the eight students in Lanzhou had a similar reasoning to Taiyuan E audiences, with LOJ11 responding, "I am like Li

58 Lost on Journey

Chenggong, but in my heart I am like Niugeng," while LOJ8 clarified, "I hope to be like Li Chenggong." For the students and permanently settled low-level administrators in Taiyuan E and F, it could be conjectured that not only education, but also the type of labour they were employed in influenced their sense of distinction from Niugeng's character. While we cannot conclude whether these audiences who identified with both characters were influenced by the prejudices expressed by the more vocal city dwellers towards rural Chinese, or the representation of a superior morality in Niugeng's character, due to the negativity expressed towards rural Chinese within these group discussions, it would seem reasonable that these audience members did not choose to align themselves completely with Niugeng's character, even if they believed such identification was more appropriate. Furthermore, having depicted Niugeng without any flaws and Li Chenggong only with flaws, urbanites found more reason to denounce the validity of Niugeng's character as a false representation while consolidating in their minds the validity of their prejudices towards their class other. Most importantly though, there was no audience member who could not identify with either of the characters. And this ease in which familiarity was formed between audiences and characters is, of course, wherein the danger lies. For it is in this seemingly harmless and fictional connection that some of the most harmful prejudices establish their foundations for real and practical social action (and inaction) when audiences return from the imagined filmic world to their everyday lives.

The "buddy road movie" for Chinese audiences

The convenience of narratives interpreted by two different film industries, for different audiences, is that one has the benefit of comparison in hindsight. *Lost on Journey* was an unofficial adaptation of Hollywood's *Planes, Trains and Automobiles* (Hughes: 1987), starring John Candy and Steve Martin. Ina Rae Hark (2002: 205) categorises *Planes, Trains and Automobiles* as a "buddy-road movie"; a genre that she believes is American "popular culture's critique of the excesses of the neoliberal economics of the 1980s". Hark's comment is critical to understanding the adaptation by Chinese filmmakers for two reasons. Firstly, Hark implies that popular culture in America is self-determining in its freedom to critique, and secondly, that in American popular culture's self-determining capacities, popular culture may critique the economic conditions of the society it depicts and that the filmmakers' criticism is thus the framework within which to analyse *Planes, Trains and Automobiles*. In China, where culture only becomes popular with the approval of the Party-state and under the censors' watchful gaze, *Lost on Journey* is quite differently situated in its purpose for production and consumption. *Lost on Journey*'s portrayal of China's neoliberal economics can only exist as part of the broader economic reform agenda – *not* as an outlet for artistic criticism, as may have been the case for the producers of the Hollywood original. A comparison of the two narratives shows how *Lost on Journey* consciously exaggerates the class differences between the two protagonists compared with the Hollywood original, and how the script encouraged upholding social segregation between wealthy and

Lost on Journey 59

poor and rural and urban Chinese. From *Lost on Journey*'s outset, director Raymond Yip establishes how difficult it would be by the film's conclusion to close the class gap between the two protagonists.

A self-made entrepreneur, Li Chenggong is based in Beijing far from his family home in Changsha, and is planning on divorcing his wife to be with his mistress. The audience is introduced to Li Chenggong firing his workers with conceited abandon. In the opening scene he congratulates one of his employees for being promoted from "stupid" (*yuchun*, 愚蠢) to "retarded" (*ruozhi*, 弱智), then proceeds to bully another employee into resigning. Li Chenggong's arrogance is portrayed as a result of his wealth, and as an exploiter of workers. His wealth is not all negative though, as it also ensures his masculinity, symbolised by his ability to provide for two women, his wife and his mistress. Niugeng, on the other hand, is travelling to Changsha to recoup debts owed to the milk factory that he works at because the factory claims it is unable to pay his and his three factory colleagues' wages. Niugeng is travelling to Changsha rather than Chengdu (where debt receipts totalled 80,000 RMB) because he believes he and his colleagues must be "honest" and recoup the factory's debts for only the amount that they are officially owed in wages (20,000 RMB), and no more. Niugeng's family ties in comparison to Li Chenggong's are never disclosed and his lack of a wife or love interest serves to emasculate him. By the time Li Chenggong encounters Niugeng at the airport, an illiterate rural migrant worker, the audience can very well anticipate the superiority that Li Chenggong will assume over Niugeng.

In the Hollywood original, Li Chenggong's counterpart, Neil, and Niugeng's counterpart, Del, are not nearly as different as the two protagonists may appear in *Lost on Journey*. Neil Page is not a CEO, but rather a marketing executive answerable to a CEO. The reason he finds himself in economy class on a plane with Del is because he is delayed by his boss's indecision on an advertisement he was responsible for. Neil is a member of the aspirational middle classes, while Li Chenggong's great wealth situates him among China's elite. Neil's social distinction, therefore, is manifest simply in his distaste for anything culturally unsophisticated. His travel partner, Del, is a travelling salesman for shower curtain rings. Del is uncouth, chats incessantly, is overweight, wears garish and unfashionable clothes, and carries his life possessions around with him in his trunk, suggesting homelessness – in other words, unsophisticated. Despite Del's apparent lack of sophistication, though, he is a valuable negotiator with the average man and a clever problem solver with a high degree of self-awareness. Late in the movie, it is revealed that Del has *chosen* this lifestyle since the passing away of his much loved wife – he is by no means forced into his travels, like Niugeng has been because of unpaid wages. And while Li Chenggong and Niugeng find themselves to be strangers to each other on all fronts, Neil and Del have one thing in common: their family values. Before sleep each night, Del prepares a photo of his late wife by his bedside, which provides an equivalent to Neil's wife, who is often edited into scenes at night, sitting waiting by the phone for Neil to ring, yearning for her husband's return. With their masculinities confirmed for their audiences, the class division between Neil and Del does not appear nearly as stark as between Li

60   *Lost on Journey*

Chenggong and Niugeng. The immorality of the neoliberal lifestyle in America is depicted as the immorality of chasing capital gains at the expense of family values. *Lost on Journey*, in contrast, depicts neoliberal economics as simply a part of modern contemporary Chinese life, and chasing capital gains at the expense of family values (if any exist in the narrative at all) as far from immoral. As it is, Li Chenggong has a mistress, and Niugeng has no family at all.

Neil and Li Chenggong assume the quickest way to get from A to B is by plane. As Hark (2002: 205) says, "Flying embodies capitalistic success; the road is for economic losers." The greatest insult to both men is not being able to fly first class. Consequently, Li Chenggong is forced to the economy class ticket counter where he first encounters Niugeng. Both Neil and Li Chenggong display disgust with having to fly economy with commoners whom they must share their cramped seating spaces with. Del removes his shoes and socks and falls asleep on Neil's shoulder and in his banter the audience is made aware that he is familiar with air travel. In contrast, Niugeng is flying for his first time and is clueless to both the science and the etiquette of air travel. Rather than forfeit at security the four litres of milk in his luggage, Niugeng drinks the entire contents of the bottle to the amazement of those, including Li Chenggong, queuing for their luggage screening prior to boarding (accompanied by humorous soundtrack). To the horror of Li Chenggong seated next to him, upon the unfamiliar sensations of flight, Niugeng struggles to avoid vomiting, re-swallowing in desperation his valuable milk. Niugeng requests windows to be opened, wishes to stand up, calls out "waitress" to get the flight attendant's attention rather than using the call button and demands to be let off the plane mid-flight. Whereas Del is aware that his behaviour is perhaps a little undignified, he takes an antagonistic glee in offending Neil's pompous sense of superiority. In contrast to Del, Niugeng is clearly unaware of his ignorance and how others may perceive his ignorance. With the return of the airplane to Beijing due to bad weather, Li Chenggong's and Niugeng's next travel attempt is via train, a form of transport that Niugeng proves comfortable in, and Li Chenggong not.

When in *Planes, Trains and Automobiles* the characters require train travel it is in fact Del who arranges tickets through a personal contact, for himself and Neil. The two men sit in similarly classed carriages and when the train breaks down, despite having arranged for tickets far from Del, Neil empathises with his frustrating travel partner and assists Del to carry his trunk across the mud. After all, Neil is indebted to Del for arranging the tickets. In *Lost on Journey*, Li Chenggong calls on his employee to organise tickets for him for the High Speed Rail. His contact is only able to find him tickets for a hard seat on the slowest train. Surrounded by the masses of rural train travellers with their life possessions on their backs, frying-pan handles knocking him in the face, Li Chenggong is clearly out of place on the narrow hard chairs. The slow train network is the environment of the poorer traveller and is symbolic of the uncomfortable route that almost a quarter of a billion rural migrant workers have taken to participate in China's economic development. Although Niugeng appears right at home with his standing position in the cabin aisle, chatting freely with fellow travellers who are all, too, carrying their life possessions in their luggage, Li Chenggong is stony-faced and frustrated,

Lost on Journey 61

the juxtaposition to his familiarity with air travel establishing the protagonists' differing degrees of engagement with the luxuries that modern China provides.

A deviation in the Chinese narrative occurs when the ticket inspector arrives and discovers that Li Chenggong and Niugeng have tickets for the same seat. The ticket inspector jumps to the conclusion that Niugeng has a fake ticket. Li Chenggong secretly discovers that in fact *his* ticket is the fake one and that the inspector has wrongly accused Niugeng – but does not admit to his discovery. Rather he chooses to cover the cost of a new ticket condescendingly "for" Niugeng and immediately fires his employee who arranged the ticket for the embarrassment incurred by cell phone. Li Chenggong does not refuse Niugeng's deference that he continues enjoying the seat while Niugeng stands – Niugeng being highly apologetic for the inconvenience the ticket confusion caused (although clearly aware that Li Chenggong must have a fake ticket if his ticket was legitimately bought). Notably, at no point in *Planes, Trains and Automobiles* is Del's honesty questioned by a figure of authority (only by Neil), and this inclusion in *Lost on Journey* is an interesting twist that suggests figures of authority believe rural migrant workers have questionable characters too – not only China's wealthy classes.

As the original film would have it, the train becomes stuck due to ice on the railroad tracks and the passengers are forced to disembark, hobbling off to awaiting mini buses to drive them to the next town. Li Chenggong takes the opportunity to rid himself of Niugeng's company. Sitting up front of the minibus with the driver, to his dismay Niugeng boards the same bus at the last minute. Li Chenggong listens to his earphones in an effort to block out the sing-along that Niugeng initiates with his fellow passengers and hides his face in his jacket collar so as to avoid Niugeng's recognition. The bus encounters a heavy traffic jam on the highway and Li Chenggong insists that the driver to take a path through a village that has a "No Motorised Vehicles Allowed" sign. The bus passengers, including Niugeng, who try to object, are overruled by Li Chenggong's presumption of authority. Claiming he will take responsibility for ignoring the village's regulation, the minibus driver agrees to continue onto the virgin land. As fate would have it, the minibus crashes into an oncoming elderly peasant's hand-pulled cart upon which his wife sits eating a peach – the stone of the peach becomes lodged in the elderly woman's throat upon impact with the minibus. As the village peasants surround the minibus furious at the intrusion and violation of the village's no motorised vehicle rule, a riot starts to take shape. When the bus driver points to Li Chenggong and claims that "the man in the Western suit!" is responsible for the intrusion, the peasants turn their anger towards Li Chenggong. As the peasants surround the minibus, Niugeng performs a Heimlich manoeuvre on the choking elderly woman and saves the day. Niugeng becomes the village's hero and defuses the tension Li Chenggong has created. The intrusion of the minibus into the tranquillity of the village and its crash with the peasant's hand-pulled cart emphasises the void between the urbanite CEO, Li Chenggong, and the simplicity of rural China, which a Chinese audience immediately recognises as the natural environment for Niugeng. Thus, as minibus passengers and Niugeng enjoy a feast with the local peasants,

62 *Lost on Journey*

Li Chenggong remains alone on the bus smoking, disrespectfully putting out his cigarette on a rural migrant worker's frying pan.

These series of experiences on both the train and the minibus emphasise the personal characteristics of what those of privilege (Li Chenggong) believe they are entitled to, and the acts of deference that are given despite better judgement by those underprivileged (the bus driver and Niugeng), who are willing to comply in their sense of class inferiority. This is very different from that of the Hollywood version. *Planes, Trains and Automobiles* also has a bus ride that Neil and Del take. The two characters rather sit side by side, and when Neil tries to get involved in the bus sing-along at Del's insistence, the passengers stare blankly at Neil's poncy tune of a bygone era, only to return to singing with a vengeance when Del initiates the lowbrow theme song from the animation series the *Flintstone*s. Neil in fact never commands the type of authority or receives acts of deference from characters of lesser privilege that Li Chenggong does in *Lost on Journey*. Take the scene of Neil's miserable attempt to obtain a refund for a hire car that was not at the collection spot. Despite his aggressive tone and extensive use of the superlative "fuck", the sales lady refuses to let him have his way and points out that without his lost rental agreement, Neil himself is "fucked". A taxi rank conductor then punches Neil in the face for his loose tongue and conceit. Despite Neil's wealth and sense of superiority, those of lesser privilege in the Hollywood version never show him the deference that Li Chenggong receives from those around him. The only exception to Li Chenggong's assumed superiority and authority is in a village context. Yet, considering the backwardness that the village is depicted as having, for an urban Chinese audience, losing authority in a village where modernity never reached is a far lesser insult than in the Hollywood version when Neil cannot command authority over a lowly sales clerk. The village leader informs Li Chenggong as he leaves: "if it wasn't for this young chap, we would have had you," referring to Niugeng, but this divergence in the Chinese version does not nearly come close to the comeuppance Neil receives during his travels.

Taking the journey into a rural environment establishes a visual context for where Niugeng comes from. The "no motorised vehicle rule" encourages the impression that Chinese villagers in fact resist the intrusion of the modern world.[3] Leaving the village on a tractor bound for Fuzhou, Li Chenggong, Niugeng and the handsome youth (Shuaige) that Niugeng befriends on the train sit high on top of a haystack. The tractor splutters along painfully slow all the way to Fuzhou. The symbolism of the various forms of transport is clear: those who reside in rural areas are not fussed with the urgency and restrictions of time that yuppie business hotshots of the city are. The reason that rural Chinese may be backward, the film suggests, is that they actively resist modernising. By association, so do rural migrant workers who are found laboring in China's urban districts. Disadvantage is portrayed as the *choice* of lifestyle for rural Chinese, and Li Chenggong, as a man of modern China, is simply portrayed (and justly so, the narrative suggests) as relieved to finally be leaving such backward living.

The most telling deviation that *Lost on Journey* takes from *Planes, Trains and Automobiles* is in the narrative's resolution. Neil's mission is to return home for

Thanksgiving; his long absences away from his family are the price he pays for the salary he chases in New York. After his dismissive attitude towards Del throughout the film, Neil's personal integrity is restored when after parting ways after having reached their final destination of Chicago, and privately reflecting upon his journey, it occurs to Neil that in fact, Del does not have a family to go to for Thanksgiving. Rushing back to the train station to find Del sitting poignantly with his life's possessions, and learning that Del's wife in fact had passed away eight years prior, Neil invites Del to his home to share Thanksgiving with his family. After a tearful reunion, Neil pointedly introduces Del to his beloved wife as "my friend". Not only have the class divisions been overcome through the sharing of family values between the two men, but also Neil realises that he in fact enjoys Del's company enough to consider Del as part of his in-group.

In *Lost on Journey*, Li Chenggong never yearns for his wife whom he plans to divorce. In his wallet he carries a picture of his mistress. The audience is only visually introduced to Li Chenggong's wife upon his return to the family home. Even then, Li Chenggong's wife is an unusually stiff character and despite becoming aware of her husband's adultery, she obediently hands over an unread letter his mistress left Li Chenggong in the pot plant by the front door. After reading the letter, Li Chenggong's wife devotedly hugs him in a manner Harriet Evans (2002: 336) may describe as the "wife's self-sacrificing support of her husband . . . a gender-specific requirement of the ideal of happy conjugality". Li Chenggong's wife appears unemotional about his deception. At his attempt to explain and apologise, she interrupts him with a non-descript face and assures him, "as long as you have come home" and they embrace. Their embrace, however, seems far from the intimacy that Neil displays towards his wife upon returning home – and the embrace is certainly *not* given to his wife in front of his travel partner, Niugeng, like Neil does in front of Del. Li Chenggong's masculinity is accordingly never shown to be weak in front of his rural migrant worker travel partner – or the film's audience, it should be noted.

Li Chenggong's wife's self-sacrificing support of her husband lends to the thinking that Li Chenggong's behaviour only needs amendment within his domestic environment and not within broader society. Li Chenggong is forgiven by his wife, is appropriately rude to his mistress who has come to Changsha to visit him under the impression Li Chenggong is planning to divorce his wife and despite Li Chenggong telling Niugeng: "You've made me see that my life is in a sorry situation", his comment is far from being a statement of friendship. Moreover, his statement does not result in an invitation into his family home as Neil offers to Del for Thanksgiving. Li Chenggong simply arranges for Niugeng's debts to be covered (anonymously) and how Niugeng spends the New Year period is of no consequence either to Li Chenggong or the narrative, albeit he does offer to dine with Niugeng after Niugeng calls him excitedly to tell him he has recouped his debts. Li Chenggong may have corrected his attitude towards his role as figurehead of the family, but certainly *not* towards his lowly class other. After all, *Lost on Journey* reminds its audiences, Li Chenggong and Niugeng are fundamentally different characters with pre-determined life trajectories that are far too polarised

64   *Lost on Journey*

to traverse. Although Li Chenggong is willing to assist in funding the debts that Niugeng is chasing out of sympathy, there is no indication that Li Chenggong could ever see Niugeng as being of a similar in-group. Arguably, this has a lot to do with the narrative's refusal to allow Niugeng's character any self-assertion. While Del exudes self-determination when he defiantly declares to Neil at the turning point of their relationship:

> You want to hurt me? Go right ahead. I'm an easy target. I talk too much, I also listen too much, I can be a cold-hearted cynic like you, but I don't like to hurt people's feelings. You think what you want about me, I'm not changing. I like me. My wife likes me, my customers like me, because I'm the real article. What you see is what you get.

Niugeng's only social power is portrayed as that in the village scene when he saves the grandmother from choking. As Niugeng's social power is never portrayed outside of a village environment (in urban spaces he is repeatedly depicted as clueless or discriminated against), *Lost on Journey* functions quite unapologetically to diminish Niugeng's self-determination within an urban setting. Del's confidence in *Planes, Trains and Automobiles* is denied entirely to Niugeng's character in the Chinese adaptation.

As no audience member for *Lost on Journey* had seen *Planes, Trains and Automobiles* or was aware that the film they were watching was an adaptation of a Hollywood script, audiences did not contemplate that Li Chenggong and Niugeng's story could be resolved in any other way than in the two men's parting and agreeing to tolerate one another's existence in the urban environment they occupy. Audiences of *Lost on Journey*, therefore, were observed not to be critical of the film's exploitation of their prejudices to relay the narrative, but rather used the film's narrative to search for truths in the depictions of the stereotypes of the two classes that confirmed their own perceptions about who and what they were not. Criticism of the narrative's conclusion or portrayal of the two men's class divide was absent from the group discussions. Chinese filmmakers made sure to deviate from the Hollywood original enough to project an entirely different moral foundation for the adventures the two men have, and promote so effectively the illusion that the rural migrant worker is indisputably different from the urban man.

None of us are like "them": the beggar and the beggar's poverty

Mid-way through *Lost on Journey*, Li Chenggong and Niugeng encounter a female beggar at a long distance bus station. Kneeling down with her head humbly bowed, the beggar's plea for a loan to purchase medicine for her daughter is written in chalk on the asphalt in front of her. She cries as passengers at the bus station crowd around to read her plea and to watch her beg. Niugeng is instantly moved by the beggar's plea and urges Li Chenggong to help her, assuring Li Chenggong he can

Lost on Journey 65

Figure 4.3 All beggars are liars

tell the beggar is not a liar because of "her eyes". Li Chenggong automatically believes she is a fraud and refuses to join the group gathered around the beggar (Figure 4.3). Leaving Niugeng standing in the group, Li Chenggong boards the bus alone heading for Changsha.

When Li Chenggong's bus is forced back to the station due to road work, he finds Niugeng standing alone at the bus stop with no money to his name. Li Chenggong chides Niugeng for giving all his money away:

Li Chenggong: 你这样的傻瓜活该被人骗,知道吗?
  If you live your life like an idiot, you're going to be cheated by people, you know that?
Niugeng: 我愿意,骗了才好呢,骗了说明没人病。没人病更好
  I agreed to it, I'm sure the beggar is good. The beggar said no one would be sick. It's always best if there are no sick people.
Li Chenggong: 我怎么又落你手里了
  (Sighs) I really can't let you out of my sight again . . .

Audiences were asked at this point in the film what their impressions of the beggar had been, whether they had thought at the time of the above exchange that the beggar was a liar and had stolen Niugeng's money or not. Each audience member agreed at the first sighting of the beggar in the film that they believed she was a fraud. All males in urban Lanzhou, Taiyuan D, E and F believed at the point of Li Chenggong's return and discovery of Niugeng stranded that without doubt the beggar was a fraud. Two female students in Lanzhou expressed compassion, claiming they had thought the beggar had a legitimate need for the money, and that was why

66 *Lost on Journey*

she stole it (as the film eventually explains to its audiences), and this sentiment was expressed in the peasants group too. This cannot discount that at first she was understood to be a fraud.

Audiences were asked if they personally would gather around the beggar like Niugeng and the other bus passengers did, or whether they would be like Li Chenggong, try to avoid the beggar and the group milling around her. Audiences were also asked whether they gave money in reality to beggars. Peasants in Lanzhou all agreed that they would gather around the beggar. They explained they would do this out of curiosity, yet they confirmed they would not give money to the beggar, especially if the beggar were male. The group collectively explained that there was plenty of work available for able-bodied men and that begging was a false way to live unless the beggar was physically disabled and had a legitimate reason to beg. Each peasant also believed that the beggar in the film was a liar from the moment Li Chenggong and Niugeng meet her at the bus stop and showed no discomfort or embarrassment in their attitude to begging in China. To justify Niugeng's giving of his money, LOJ3 explained, "he has a good heart."

Privileged middle-aged workers and professionals in Taiyuan (D, E and F) all said that they would absolutely not stop to stand around and watch. They cited firstly, a lack of time, and secondly, the act of gathering to look at someone's misfortune as being an act of poor *suzhi*. Only a handful (Taiyuan E and F) said that they might give one or two RMB if the beggar were visibly disabled. The rest agreed, however, that they would not give the beggar any money. As LOJ20 clarified, "The majority of beggars are not honest like in the film." Although peasants believed Niugeng had given money because he had a kind heart, urbanites interpreted Niugeng's actions as that of the gullible rural migrant worker.

Regardless of whether an audience member had previously identified as most similar to Niugeng or Li Chenggong, it appeared that none was likely to believe that the beggar or the extreme poverty her character suggested was to be trusted. Privileged audiences agreed that they would have walked past and perhaps offered money if the beggar in *Lost on Journey* had had a severe disability, while peasants would be willing to gather and stare out of curiosity (unaware of the poor *suzhi* those of privilege associate with this behaviour) but not offer any money, again if the beggar were able-bodied. The presence of the beggar in *Lost on Journey*, therefore, reaffirmed for urban sophisticates and peasant audiences alike that their active engagement in China's economy meant that *they* were not like *them*, the non-working and lying beggars. While in *Planes, Trains and Automobiles* the protagonists may share a common ground over family values, in the Chinese version the common ground is an antagonism about, and a distrust of, those who claim poverty and destitution.

The only moment in *Lost on Journey* that Li Chenggong and Niugeng appear to share a common prejudice is their chasing down of the same beggar scenes later. Although it is short lived, the audience momentarily is led to believe that Niugeng and Li Chenggong will retrieve Niugeng's cash "together" as they chase after the beggar through the crowded streets. The audience hopes for Niugeng and Li Chenggong to triumph in their act of solidarity against economic deception. This enthusiasm is short-lived but because upon reaching the beggar's house, Niugeng discovers the beggar really does have not one, but ten, disabled children that she is caring for in her apartment. When Li Chenggong finally reaches the beggar's apartment, lugging Niugeng's belongings that he had dumped in his quest to catch the beggar, *Lost on Journey*'s musical score suddenly reaches a melodramatic crescendo. The camera pans laboriously over each disabled child and provides close-ups of the poignancy of their childish artworks. Although these production values are arguably used to emphasise Li Chenggong's and even Niugeng's (and indeed the audiences') incorrect assertions about the beggar's moral integrity, the scene's sudden overt sentimentality and excessive disproportion to what all audience members expected to be the case in reality meant that the scene failed to alter firmly held prejudices amongst audiences that beggars were all liars, as was the false poverty they represented. As LOJ16 stated:

> It was completely unrealistic that the beggar was housing ten disabled children and schooling them. There are services for disabled children and the authorities would never allow someone to do that.

Audiences who identified as Li Chenggong downplayed his comeuppance in this scene and audiences who identified as Niugeng took pleasure in Niugeng being proven to have a good heart. Yet, no one was able to acquit the beggar of her presumed guilt from their conclusions drawn already scenes earlier about her integrity. The beggar had originally lied to Niugeng and was, henceforth, always to be considered a liar.

Families and unexplained social mobility

Considering the ease with which audiences were able to interpret and understand the class-based stereotypes presented in *Lost on Journey* – that of the privileged Li Chenggong, rural migrant worker Niugeng, as well as the beggar – what became apparent was the difficulty that audiences had in understanding the plot's resolution and agreeing on the moral of the film. To prejudge is to have unqualified preconceived notions about a person or a narrative's rightful conclusion, and when the opposite occurs, an audience has to reconcile original prejudices with new possibilities, some of which may not be agreeable to one's class views.

Li Chenggong and Niugeng finally reach Changsha on the back of a truck hauling chickens. Covered in feathers, they enter a shop together wherein Li Chenggong purchases new clothes for him and Niugeng. Acknowledging that this is the point at which the two men will part ways, Li Chenggong tears in half a painting given to them by one of the children the female beggar cares for. The image of himself he gives to Niugeng, the image of Niugeng he puts inside his breast pocket. Saying their farewells, they walk off in different directions. Later, after Li Chenggong has returned home and reunited with his wife, the narrative cuts once more to Niugeng meeting a man in a black suit on a street corner. Niugeng is elated after looking inside the bag he has been given. The frame cuts

68 *Lost on Journey*

to Li Chenggong in the back of a chauffeured car speaking to Niugeng on his mobile, who excitedly tells Li Chenggong that he has successfully recouped the debt owed to him and his colleagues. The same man approaches the car window and asks Li Chenggong, "Who was that guy?" to which Li Chenggong replies, "My creditor" (*zhaizhu*, 债主) to imply the moral debt he is in to Niugeng for becoming a better man.

The screen then cuts to Li Chenggong sitting aboard an airplane, once more frustrated at his plane being delayed. The audience is told it is "one year later". Niugeng steps aboard the plane dressed in a Western suit, with polished black shoes, briefcase and slicked back hair, and shrieks "Boss!" when the two men recognise each other. The end frame freezes on Li Chenggong's look of horror. Gone is the image of Niugeng, the illiterate "peasant"; Niugeng is now the ideal image of the modern Chinese businessman.

In light of Niugeng's implied social mobility and Li Chenggong's personal development, audiences were asked whom they understood *Lost on Journey* to be principally about: Li Chenggong or Niugeng? Without hesitation, peasants responded in unison with "Niugeng". Similarly, professionals and students who had identified with Li Chenggong earlier answered "Li Chenggong". Only six audience members in the discussion groups conducted in Taiyuan and Lanzhou (students) answered "both" and four of these six audience members had previously identified as being a combination of the two protagonists. Only the peasants in Lanzhou had exclusively seen the film to be about Niugeng and the other overwhelming majority had understood *Lost on Journey* to be chiefly about Li Chenggong. Audiences were observed to keenly project their own self-identity onto the character that they believed most represented them, and therefore interpret the narrative's trajectory according to the character they most identified with. Not only could this be seen to influence audiences to overlook negative attributes of the character that they identified with (as previously discussed), but also by projecting their class views this further influenced their understanding of *Lost on Journey*'s narrative resolution and greater moral objective.

Audiences in Taiyuan, and the group consisting of students in Lanzhou, understood the moral objective of *Lost on Journey* as "upholding family values" and the desire to "return home to be with family during the New Year's celebrations". These first two interpretations were repeated multiple times. As LOJ33 explained, "no matter how poor you are, everyone deserves to be with family and loved." Although these interpretations arguably are true for Neil and Del in Hollywood's original version, this is not necessarily so in the case of the two men in *Lost on Journey*. By concentrating on the protagonist Li Chenggong with whom they personally identified with, the understanding these audiences drew from *Lost on Journey*'s narrative was observed to overshadow Niugeng's role within the film. Indeed, only Li Chenggong was returning home for the New Year's holiday. Niugeng was travelling to Changsha to recoup debts outstanding for *unpaid labour*. This was not only for himself but also for three work colleagues who had entrusted him with the task back in Beijing. For New Year's, Niugeng was clearly *not* with his family and neither were any of his work colleagues waiting for his

Lost on Journey 69

return at the milk factory. Their familial roots were completely ignored by the filmmakers and privileged audiences alike.

When these same audiences were asked what the Western suit that Niugeng wears when he boards the airplane in the last frame of *Lost on Journey* signified, they believed he had become a "boss" of some sorts with the money that Li Chenggong had given him a year earlier. Upon further discussion, though, they turned doubtful as to whether this could happen within the space of a year, as the scene suggested. Taiyuan white collar workers, professionals and students in Lanzhou were at a loss as to what kind of a boss he had become, or of what kind of business he had started. They confirmed that Niugeng's *suzhi* would not improve within a year even if he had been commercially successful. The ease of social mobility for rural migrants in urban China appeared to be a grey area for urban audiences, and it was concluded that the reason for Niugeng's implied social mobility in the film's conclusion was simply to "bring hope to audiences" (LOJ8).

In contrast, when peasants were asked what Niugeng wearing a Western suit and boarding the plane signified, they believed that Li Chenggong and Niugeng had established a good relationship and gone into business together. LOJ1 reminded his peers that Niugeng at the beginning had told Li Chenggong that he wanted to open his own cake business, to which his peers agreed in a chorus of, "ah, that's right!" The peasants had paid close attention to the expressed dreams of Niugeng and accepted that he had become a boss of this same cake business, and likewise, that Li Chenggong would think it reasonable to enter into business with Niugeng. When it was pointed out that Li Chenggong had looked horrified when Niugeng boarded the plane, the peasants agreed that they could not have a healthy relationship if Li Chenggong reacted that way and silently mulled over their understanding. LOJ4 then put forward the proposition to his peers that perhaps Niugeng had used his portion of the money to buy a new suit. LOJ4 explained, most likely for the benefit of the foreigner in the room, that when villagers migrate to urban areas to look for work they make sure to wear a suit to look like city dwellers. Having their fantasy of Niugeng's easy social mobility quashed by LOJ4's alternative interpretation of the scene, LOJ4's peers nodded in silent contemplation. Interestingly, when LOJ4's proposition was subsequently provided to audiences in Taiyuan F, however, they confirmed that they had never heard of this etiquette, suggesting that perhaps dressing rituals that are performed to indicate self-respect in urban areas by rural migrant workers may be missed entirely by more privileged Chinese in urban areas. Moreover, in contrast to the family values and the New Year celebration themes nominated by privileged audiences as the moral of *Lost on Journey*'s narrative, peasants believed *Lost on Journey*'s message was to "work hard" and "respect others"; family themes were nowhere to be heard.

The presence of family values and Niugeng's suggested social mobility in *Lost on Journey*, therefore, appeared to serve two purposes and both appeared to pander to privileged audiences. On the one hand with only Li Chenggong's family introduced to audiences, the rural migrant worker's familial life became unimportant and superfluous to the concerns of privileged Chinese society. On the other hand, Niugeng's social mobility confirmed that the aim of rural migrant workers was to

70 *Lost on Journey*

become privileged urbanites. Yet, in the perceived inability to do so within a year, *Lost on Journey* confirmed the pre-determined and eternal low *suzhi* of the rural migrant. Not only were privileged audiences' senses of purpose therefore inflated beyond their lower classed audiences', but the film's ability to be interpreted differently by peasant audiences easily sidestepped possible accusations of the narrative not being all-inclusive or derogatory to Chinese from the lower classes.

Lost on Journey is a story where everyone is happy: the boss rediscovers his moral backbone and the exploited labourer wins his wages and unexplainably becomes overnight a business success story. If *Planes, Trains and Automobiles* was Hollywood's critique of America's neoliberal economics, *Lost on Journey* is the celebration of them in China. By encouraging in-groups to remain in-groups and privileged in-groups to see value in the ongoing devaluation of their rural "out-group", not only is China's class society culturally legitimised, but also such social distinctions become normalised as reasonable and natural ways of everyday social organisation. Affirmative prejudice, popular cinema such as *Lost on Journey* suggests, is the crux to achieving and maintaining social harmony during a time of intense social transformation.

Class-based tolerance

Without doubt, *Lost on Journey* is a very funny film. In upbeat spirits, audiences unanimously believed the film was an "optimistic" film. Director Raymond Yip's ability to humorously portray the complications that arise within class relations is, on the one hand, a sign of his skill in storytelling and, on the other, a sign of how in order for his storytelling to have applicability to his audience, he could call on already existing prejudices that underpin class relations in China today for his success. While the box office figures suggest that the commercial appeal of the film was not realised during its exhibition period, the subsequent multiple broadcasts on public television ensured that *Lost on Journey*'s narrative has become a household favourite.

Class relations can be good or bad; effective or ineffective; exploitative or fairly negotiated. These standards are established by a country's leadership through policies, legal frameworks and economic design – and conceptualised into lived realities by those in positions of cultural authority, such as filmmakers through their storytelling. In this position of authority, cultural producers provide tangible frameworks for their audiences to make sense of the world, and the "unknowns" around them. Affirmative prejudice encourages a society to be confident that their doubts, scepticism and lack of trust in strangers are reliable convictions. De-personifying the class other, as say Niugeng is in *Lost on Journey* by having his family roots undisclosed and personal development somewhat lacking in comparison to his wealthy counterpart Li Chenggong, whose family we come to intimately know, legitimises the subordination of an entire social group. While Li Chenggong is an individual, Niugeng represents a class, farcically ignorant and lacking intellectual depth. *Lost on Journey* did not *weaken* or *shame* privileged Chinese men and women by the narrative's conclusion, despite its attempts to portray Li Chenggong's morals as questionable. If these audiences of *Lost on Journey* are anything

Lost on Journey 71

to go by, the potential for reducing the gap between China's privileged and lower classes in the near future appears much gloomier than the hopeful peasants in Lanzhou may have perceived their chances to be. As such, the framework of China's social harmony appears to be a harmony that relies on class-based tolerance, as well as ignorance and desensitisation to inequality – fictional or otherwise. As audiences of *Lost on Journey* can reveal, Chinese audiences are responding to this framework with as much vigour as could be anticipated.

Notes

1 Box office figure as of 16 July 2016 (Entgroup); approximate USD as at historical exchange rate for 1 June 2010 (XE Currency); URL: http://www.cbooo.cn/m/588601/
2 Douban rating: 7.4/10 stars from 266,313 reviews. URL: http://movie.douban.com/subject/4237879/ (last accessed: 16 July 2016).
3 A male discussant in Taiyuan explained that the type of tractor that Li Chenggong and Niugeng leave the village on is now prohibited from coming closer than a set distance to the city centre of Taiyuan, as they present traffic hazards. Villagers who may rely on agricultural machinery between rural and urban areas to transport produce for sale or for general travel where public transport is not available therefore are now excluded by regulation from the city space. In the newly paved eastern section of Taiyuan city, for example, the few tractors I saw looked particularly out of place.

References

Dovidio, John F., Tamar Saguy, Samuel L. Gaertner, and Erin L. Thomas. 2012. From Attitudes to (In)Action: The Darker Side of 'We'. In *Beyond Prejudice: Extending the Social Psychology of Conflict, Inequality and Social Change*, edited by John Dixon and Mark Levine, 248–268. Cambridge: Cambridge University Press.

Evans, Harriet. 2002. Past, Perfect or Imperfect: Changing Images of the Ideal Wife. In *Chinese Femininities, Chinese Masculinities: A Reader*, edited by Susan Brownell and Jeffrey N. Wasserstrom, 335–360. Berkeley, Los Angeles and London: University of California Press.

Hark, Ina Rae. 2002. Fear of Flying: Yuppie Critique and the Buddy-road Movie in the 1980s. In *The Road Movie Book*, edited by Steven Cohan and Ina Rae Hark, 204–229. London and New York: Routledge.

Huang, Phillip C. C. 2009. China's Neglected Informal Economy: Reality and Theory. *Modern China* 35 (4): 405–438.

Reicher, Stephen. 2012. From Perception to Mobilization: The Shifting Paradigm of Prejudice. In *Beyond Prejudice: Extending the Social Psychology of Conflict, Inequality and Social Change*, edited by John Dixon and Mark Levine, 27–47. Cambridge: Cambridge University Press.

Solinger, Dorothy J. 1999. *Contesting Citizenship in Urban China: Peasant Migrants, the State, and the Logic of the Market*. Berkeley, Los Angeles and London: University of California Press.

Sun, Wanning. 2009. *Maid in China: Media, Morality, and the Cultural Politics of Boundaries*. London: Routledge.

——. 2012. Screening Inequality: Injustices, Class Identities, and Rural Migrants in Chinese Cinema. *Berliner China-Hefte: Chinese History and Society* 40: 6–20.

——. 2014. *Subaltern China: Rural Migrants, Media, and Cultural Practices*. Lanham, MD: Rowman & Littlefield.

5 *Go Lala Go!*
Secretaries, shopping and spinsterhood

Figure 5.1 Promotional film poster: *Go Lala Go!*

74 *Go Lala Go!*

《杜拉拉升职记》
(*du lala sheng zhiji*)

Go Lala Go!

Director: Xu Jinglei (徐静蕾)
Starring: Stanley Huang, Karen Mok, Xu Jinglei
Box office: 124,412,000 RMB (USD 18,230,198)[1]
Exhibition period: April–May 2010 (6 weeks)[2]

Synopsis

Go Lala Go! (Xu: 2010) follows the professional trajectory of a 27-year-old female, Lala, who enters an American Fortune 500 company based in Beijing, "DB", as a newcomer secretary at an annual salary of 36,000 RMB, which by the age of 33 years increases to 300,000 RMB, as the result of four promotions. Lala lives with her brother and his girlfriend in Beijing and is determined to succeed. Her colleague, Helen, takes her under her wing on her first day and provides her counsel about the office policies, including hierarchies, what the salaries of the various personnel are and thereby what their class positions are. Helen also relays DB's strict "No Romance" rule – which Lala tries her hardest to abide by. Succumbing to temptation, however, on a DB holiday bonus trip to Thailand, Lala has a one-night fling with the irresistible regional sales manager, David. After turning down David's subsequent requests for a dinner date upon the office's return to Beijing, as fate would have it Lala is promoted to become David's senior secretary.

Despite trying to deny their desires, Lala and David find themselves back in each other's arms. At this point Lala discovers David's former partner is none other than her immediate superior, Rose, DB's cold, hard Human Resources (HR) manager. Misreading the intentions of a farewell embrace between David and Rose at the end-of-year office party (Rose has decided to quit her job and leave China to reconnect with herself after the pressures of the white collar world), Lala ends her relationship with David. As a result, David, like Rose, and unbeknownst to Lala, relocates to Thailand and establishes a tourism business. Unable to contact David, Lala commits herself to the lonesome grind of her office work and is finally promoted to HR manager for her efforts. Her personality, once happy and carefree, becomes that of her former superior, Rose. Two years on, despite professional success and wealth accumulation, Lala still pines after her lost love. For nostalgia's sake, she returns to Thailand. As luck would have it, she and David are reunited under a prayer tree. David has established a successful tourism company in Thailand. The final montage consists of David and Lala canoodling as the sun sets in the far distance . What happens to the young lovers' careers is left open to audience speculation.

Introduction

Go Lala Go! is a story of social mobility that overwhelmingly appealed to the sensibilities of female audiences with aspirations and opportunities to mobilise into

China's expanding white collar workforce. The narrative is not to be confused with that of a rags-to-riches story that would imply the protagonist Lala triumphs over poverty, hardship and injustice. Rather, *Go Lala Go!*'s premise is the plight of the post-reform generation of young female urbanites born into, and with access to, the advantages that come with being a member of China's expanding aspirational middle classes. The prominence of the female white collar worker in a successful homegrown blockbuster pinpoints the social importance of the new worker category in China's labour force for reasons both optimistic and negative. On the one hand, the female white collar worker is an exemplary example of China's modernity narrative of development and the middle class ideal, both as a white collar labourer in a foreign corporation and for her economic capacity to be an avid participant in China's consumer market. She too reflects man's ability to manage a healthy economy. On the other hand, the female white collar worker's presence is symbolic of the efforts currently invested into negating the growing trend for these same white collar women to remain unmarried (Fincher 2014). The unflattering term "剩女" (*shengnü*) given to this social group of women translates as "leftover women", and refers to women who are in their 30s and 40s who, for whatever reason, have not married or produced children.

Shengnü are categorised as women earning high incomes that are well educated, and either stuck in her single status and hoping for love; unmarried as a result of her sense of uncharacteristic individuality and bogged down by a demanding work schedule; or self-determining, career-focused and disinterested in wedlock and rearing children. The character "剩" (*sheng*) in its literal translation as "leftover", though, cannot but carry negative connotations. As it is, the term does not refer to a woman's professional or economic achievements that confirm her socio-economic status, but to her metaphorical expiration date on the marriage market. In September 2007, the State Education Bureau officially ranked "剩女" (*shengnü*) first of 171 new phrases to the Chinese lexicon, officially earmarking the Party-state's awareness of the so-called threat to social harmony these educated and single women pose. Yang Yantao (2011) even warns that the emergence of the *shengnü* in first-tier cities may soon have cultural implications for women in second- and third-tier Chinese cities, and can only result in the suffering of lonely women, the women's parents who expect grandchildren and the countless Chinese men hoping to marry. To retreat from the labour force and adhere to the ideals of domestic bliss should not be confused as an ideal for *all* Chinese women but – this ideal really only refers to women of privilege. *Go Lala Go!* does not advocate a retreat from the labour force by women of the lower classes. Crudely explained, the labour, and easily exploitable labour at that, of lower classed women in China, continues not only to be important for the perpetuation of China's economic growth, but likewise, the socialisation of middle class feminine sensibilities that are recognised as middle class by *not* being working class.

Women as agents of public and professional life on China's big screens are not a contemporary phenomenon.[3] As Chris Berry and Mary Farquhar (2006: 110–112) note, typically cast as "martial arts fighters, businesswomen, labor heroines in

76   *Go Lala Go!*

the factories and fields, and as guerrilla fighters and Communist Party cadres", Chinese women have not typically been portrayed onscreen "as objects of the gaze, nor excluded from agency in public space". Importantly for the chapter at hand, Berry and Farquhar also note that in earlier socialist cinema, "instead of the mother, it was the unmarried daughter figure that provided a "traditional" role model fit for Chinese modernity". While Lala, the protagonist of *Go Lala Go!* is unmarried, *Go Lala Go!* clarifies that unmarried modern Chinese women most certainly are no longer expected to be married to the state, the revolution or the party, but rather the economy, herself and hopefully a wealthy man. And while China's leaders in recent history were seemingly confident that regardless of the public agency or the unmarried status Chinese women had onscreen, daughters off-screen would continue to wed and rear children as a matter of due course and social planning prerogatives. Presently these assumptions are no longer so confidently taken for granted. With the retreat of the state from the institutional control over marriage in reformed China, and a gender imbalance borne out of the single child policy, privileged women's marital and professional preferences can no longer be assumed; and popular cinema is responding accordingly.

The production values of *Go Lala Go!* are highly sophisticated, like those of *Let the Bullets Fly*, and similarly were designed to appeal to a sophisticated audience. CFGC's role as key producer of the film ensured the high quality of the production and the Party-state's stamp of approval. Beijing is depicted with piercingly blue skies and a skyline of high-rises with sparkling glass windows. Inside these high-rise office spaces, luscious green plants and perfectly groomed women and men prowl the corridors busying themselves on Chinese manufactured Lenovo computers with their perfectly manicured fingernails. Interiors are minimalist and office partitions are glass to allow for Beijing's sunlight to fill the open-space office plan. Living quarters are high-end apartment blocks with modern appliances. Beijing's notorious traffic is notably absent on the highways that the white collar characters' luxury cars drive on between offices, apartments and meeting locations. White collar China is, simply put, much *cleaner* than that of the environments the lower classes occupy. Product integration and placement throughout the film is far from subtle, providing convenient links between products and privileged personalities and urban lifestyles. Despite the film's impressive box office takings, review feedback on Douban was disproportionately negative from website users due to the overt product integration.[4] Hence, *Go Lala Go!* should be understood to be a film that very easily divided its audiences, not only for the gendered bias of the film's narrative, but for its highly opportunistic commercial overtones.

Audiences and discussion groups

The average age of an audience member for discussion groups about *Go Lala Go!* was 29 years of age; 15 were male and 18 were female. The discussion group in Beijing was conducted with educated professionals, while in Hangzhou and Nanjing the discussion groups were conducted with rural migrant workers. Two discussion groups were conducted in Lanzhou: the first took place with middle-aged factory supervisors and one of their younger female staff (C) and the second took place with postgraduate students studying humanities (D). In Taiyuan, the discussion group was held with undergraduate business students. Female white collar workers and students had all seen *Go Lala Go!* prior to the film screening. An overwhelming number of this same cohort confirmed they had watched *Go Lala Go!* multiple times. The lone male audience member in Beijing who had not seen the film (a company CEO), stressed that his reason for not having already seen *Go Lala Go!* was his busy schedule that did not allow him time to visit the cinema, not out of a disinterest in the film. Only one female migrant worker in Hangzhou had previously seen "parts" of *Go Lala Go!*, but for all other rural migrant workers and factory workers, their first viewing of the film was by participating in this project.

The clear gender bias in *Go Lala Go!*'s narrative approval from privileged female audiences was the most pronounced of all films in this project. Male white collar workers and university students all clarified that *Go Lala Go!* was a film for women, not men. Young female students sat on the edges of their seats swept up in Lala's narrative and full of energy at the conclusion to discuss the film's content. Their male classmates in contrast treated their contribution to the group discussion as a display of their analytical skills. Privileged male audiences consistently prefaced their comments about *Go Lala Go!* with "this is not the type of film I would normally watch" or "although this is a woman's film . . .", in case their well-thought-out answers were mistaken for enthusiasm (Taiyuan, Lanzhou and Beijing).

Middle-aged coal factory supervisors in Lanzhou became visibly frustrated and fidgety in their seats during their screening of the film. GLG9 fell asleep and GLG12 searched his mobile phone and answered two phone calls during the screening of the film. Rural migrant workers in Nanjing and Hangzhou sat quietly throughout the film's screening, but appeared baffled by Lala's tale as the end credits started to roll. In contrast to their enthusiastic female university student counterparts, audiences in Nanjing offered a lukewarm response to the question of whether they had enjoyed the film, judging *Go Lala Go!* to be just "ok". By the conclusion of the group discussion, these same rural migrant workers were notably more confident in expressing their opinions and admitted that they would not recommend the film to other friends to watch, and were not sure who would like the film within their extended social network. For rural migrant workers in Hangzhou and Nanjing, the distinction of being a "woman's film" was furthermore not apparent. Rather both male and female audiences alike were alienated by *Go Lala Go!*'s depiction of white collar labour, Lala's femininity, conspicuous consumption and even Lala's moralities.

Audiences were asked what social status Lala had. In contrast to the responses provided for *Lost on Journey*, whereby "boss/CEO" (*laoban*) and "rural migrant worker" (*nongmingong*) were easily recognised by privileged and lower classed audiences, the term "white collar" (*bailing*, 白领) was only offered by audiences in Lanzhou, Beijing and Taiyuan. In Nanjing, only GLG20 was familiar with the term "white collar worker" after being prompted.[5] GLG20's rural migrant peers

78   *Go Lala Go!*

had never heard the term before and did not understand the symbolism of what being white collar entailed. Professionals and university students in Lanzhou, Beijing and Taiyuan were well aware not only of the labour association with the term, but also the lifestyle implications of the white collar worker. As such, much of the white collar innuendo in *Go Lala Go!* proved irrelevant to rural migrant worker audiences.

Responses to the question "What was your favourite scene?" emphasise this point. Rural migrant workers in Hangzhou and Nanjing, and male factory supervisors in Lanzhou unanimously responded with the scenes set on beaches in Thailand during Lala's company's staff holiday. Each of these audience members confirmed they had not travelled outside of the province they lived in (except for GLG20, who had worked in Beijing) and the images of Thailand's shoreline proved to be very appealing. No one in this group had ever seen the ocean. Importantly, the appeal of the images of the ocean had nothing to do with the flirtatious interaction between Lala and David that was taking place in these scenes set on the beach, as it did for a female student in Lanzhou who nominated "Lala's and David's flirtation" at the beach as her favourite scene. The fact that the beach's landscape was repeated by similarly classed rural migrant workers (male and female) unprompted in Hangzhou, Nanjing and among male factory supervisors, who were alienated by the gendered bias of the film's narrative, supports the thinking that the applicability the film's narrative had to these audiences was very minimal.

In contrast, female university students of a comparable age group in Lanzhou and Taiyuan focused their attentions on two scenes that were related to the romantic agenda of the film's narrative. The first was the scene where Lala and David playfully chase each other under a fountain found in the middle of Sanlitun on a late night date (Beijing's commercial shopping hub). The second was the film's closing scene, when Lala and David are reunited by chance after a long separation under a prayer tree in Thailand. The scene is shot in slow motion and has an overpoweringly melodramatic soundtrack, so great that GLG9 in Lanzhou was notably startled from his slumber, and in Nanjing, the young male GLG23 looked around to see if his peers were as surprised by the music as he was.

When these same groups were asked what they did not like about the film, the female university students in Lanzhou and Taiyuan said "nothing" because they had enjoyed it immensely. Despite the criticisms of Beijing audiences about the misleading facts related to Lala's professional salary and consumer capacities, similarly nothing seemed to inspire dislike among them. This was not the case for a young male in Nanjing, GLG23, who nominated the way the "removalists were treated" by Lala in a scene that features an office renovation Lala coordinates in her position as HR administrator for DB (and is one of her first administrative breakthroughs that wins her professional recognition). GLG23 explained that Lala had acted rudely to the removalists (she also speaks up to her male boss in public as well in this scene) and it frustrated him that the employees in the offices were not organised enough to make the task of the removalists easier. Indeed, in this scene Lala herself was frustrated with her colleagues for not assisting *her*. Yet, GLG23's focus had been on the removalist that he could project his understandings of his own type of labour onto, and as a result, he overlooked Lala's, the protagonist's, similar complaints of frustration. He did not empathise with Lala, but with the removalist. It should be noted that the removalists feature in *Go Lala Go!* in only two scenes as extras and are the only non-white-collar workers in the entire film. One removalist has one speaking line, but they are by no means key characters in the narrative. Faced by a narrative that was beyond GLG23's reality, GLG23's attention to the removalist echoed the manner in which the favourite scenes were nominated as the landscapes of Thailand's beaches, and provides an insight into the alienation that rural migrant workers may have felt throughout their two hour viewing of *Go Lala Go!*.

When discussion groups were asked what type of audience would enjoy watching *Go Lala Go!*, responses from young professionals (Beijing) and university students (Lanzhou and Taiyuan) were very specific about a person's motive. They included, "someone looking for a job" (the most common), "graduates wondering what to do after graduating from university", and "someone looking for inspiration". Audiences believed *Go Lala Go!* conveyed true professional realities and provided recommendations for success. Professional and life pedagogy, therefore, is a reliable framework within which to understand the audience engagement with *Go Lala Go!*, especially for female audiences receptive to the film's narrative.[6]

Lala: an idol for a vanguard generation

The absence of protagonist Lala's parents or broader extended family other than her brother, with whom she shares an apartment, is in stark contrast to the majority of mainstream films produced for Chinese audiences. Filial piety, so often referred to as the backbone of Chinese culture, is conspicuously missing in Lala's narrative of professional and economic success. The rupture from the family lineage is clear: Lala's narrative relates to a *new* generation of young women, unmoored from historical experience and customs of either her mother's or her grandmother's generation. The concept of the protagonist, Lala, originates from the 2007 best-selling novel of the same name, by author Li Ke (李可). The appeal of the fictional ambitious Lala was so great that the narrative was subsequently adapted for the stage and performed at the Polygon Theatre in Beijing (2009). Lala's story was then adapted into a 30-part TV series (2010) for CCTV and subsequently produced as the feature film that is the focus of this chapter.

The white collar woman, most often characterised as a secretary, has long been romanticised in mainstream American popular culture. American readers' imaginations were titillated by white collar literature in the late 1800s to early 1900s (Mills 1953: 198–209); filmgoers then learned about the white collar secretaries through early Hollywood films (Haigh 2012); and more recently, women's magazines from the 1960s to the present have provided an abundance of information and guidance on white collar "do's and don'ts" (Berebitsky 2012). Over the course of America's industrial history – and by extension other Western societies that have consumed American popular culture – generations of white collar women have contributed to popular culture's evolution of the Western white collar woman's class identity. If

80 Go Lala Go!

Chinese scholar Dai Jinhua's (2002: 112) claim is true that during the Mao era, the "vigorous call to assimilate into society alienated the gender identity of women by requiring them in the same capacity as men to undertake public responsibilities and duties and to accept all male behavioural standards", *Go Lala Go!*'s professional and life pedagogy for young female audiences that lack accessible historical references through their mothers' generation, should be understood as being very real. There are not many other fictional narratives available in Chinese popular culture for the emerging social group of white collar women from which to draw inspiration. In 2012 when these film screenings and group discussions were conducted, *Go Lala Go!* was the Chinese white collar woman's instruction manual.

Director and lead actress Xu Jinglei was herself marketed as a white collar icon as part of the film's promotion: professionally established as a film director and film actress and, at the time of *Go Lala Go!*'s release, editor of the now-defunct celebrity e-zine "开啦" (*Kaila*).[7] In her late 30s at the time of the film's release and single, Xu's promotional campaign included her appearance as guest editor of the Chinese *Harper's Bazaar* for a special edition about white collar women. Xu was marketed as an authority on white collar identities. *Go Lala Go!* not only rode on the success of its well-established reputation, but also on Xu's.[8] The quaint reality of Xu Jinglei, herself a *shengnü*, finding love in her co-star, Stanley Huang, further advocated the film's morality with its leading lady, director and real-life *shengnü* finding love in Lala's story and Lala's love interest. Lala and Xu Jinglei alike filled a vacuum of historical reference for educated privileged Chinese female audiences, and as the following sections will show, it was this demographic that responded most enthusiastically to Lala's story.

Performances of "cuteness" and navigating hierarchies

Lala's "cute" behaviour, a phenomenon that Tzu-i Chuang (2005) describes as "female infantilization", is established early on in her employment with DB. While performing her administrative errands, Lala discovers DB's marketing archival materials in the library. Due to an unexplained inspiration, Lala makes a scrapbook collage (Figure 5.2) of the advertisements and articles about DB that she finds in the archival materials. The American CEO of DB upon discovering it (how he finds

Figure 5.2 Cuteness has its rewards. (Left) Lala's collage; (right) DB's CEO applauds Lala for her collage

Go Lala Go! 81

it is unexplained), requests Helen (another secretary) as a matter of urgency to find out who pasted the scrapbook together, because it is "very, very cute". So highly impressed by the collaging in the scrapbook is the CEO that he singles Lala out for recognition at the next staff gathering, claiming the scrapbook is a "reminder of what we [DB] stand for". Lala is called on to make a speech about her inspiration for the scrapbook. With her hands clenched behind her back, she skips to the stage excitedly, her animated speech accompanied by projected pages from her collage on a screen behind her. The audience can only wonder how a company that praises an activity like this on the company's clock (not to mention a staff member who assumes liberties to cut up archived marketing records) would have ever made it to the Global Fortune 500 list. Yet, director Xu demands her audience suspend belief as DB's upper management applaud Lala for her efforts. Being cute clearly has economic value in the personality market, especially when it is followed by a promotion and salary increase, which is the case for Lala shortly after her collage is publicly acknowledged.

Lala's performance of cuteness appeals to the majority male managerial force. During an office refurbishment that Lala coordinates, the heartthrob Regional Sales Director (who becomes Lala's love interest), David, takes Lala out for respite – and an excessive amount of Dove chocolate. In her cute eating manner Lala smears chocolate all around her mouth. Not easily fooled, David wonders how intelligent Lala is. Through conversation with her he has started to realise that her childish behaviour does not seem to correlate with the level of conversation she provides. As Lala jumps out of David's sports car, he asks her, "How high is your IQ?," "My IQ is very high," she replies nasally and accompanied with a pout, as she declares "I'm probably the smartest person in the office." Despite revealing crafty scissor skills up until this point in the film (little else of her professional work is in fact revealed to the audience) there is very little evidence to support Lala's claims of intellectual prowess. This is until we learn that Lala's cuteness and the childish innocence it suggests were simply a performance by which to manage the hier-archies and competitive secretarial atmosphere that she faces within DB's office environment. Not only does cuteness win her male superiors over, but her female colleagues as well.

When Lala does indeed become HR manager by the film's conclusion her demeanour is far from cute. In the final frames of the film, we see Lala walking haughtily through the corridors of DB with a stern face and authoritative coun-tenance. Lala's cuteness has eroded under the pressures of a life in upper man-agement. Indeed, at this point, Lala begins to resemble Rose, Lala's assertive supervisor and DB's HR manager – and as fate would have it, David's former partner. Rose and Lala represent two different femininities that undergo a transi-tion throughout the course of the film's narrative. Lala's personality develops into that of Rose's as she becomes more ambitious and loses her cuteness, while Rose's personality becomes more like wide-eyed Lala when she decides to leave the cut-throat white collar world to "rediscover herself" by travelling abroad at the end of the film. Cuteness, *Go Lala Go!* makes its audiences understand, is easier to project when navigating the lower-middle echelons of the white collar world, but

82 *Go Lala Go!*

in a high-pressured managerial position, is difficult to maintain. If taken too far, like Rose, a woman could lose her childish innocence so much so that she will be obliged to rediscover herself by leaving her job; even *leave the country* to have to do so; and unmarried at that.

Rose has been introduced to audiences already in this professionally pressured state. Audiences suggested that, indeed, neither male nor female audiences approved of Rose's assertive attitude. Audiences described Lala as "naïve", "conscientious", "hard working" and "pure"; a male rural migrant worker in Nanjing simply described her as "beautiful", even when she becomes pressured and cold like Rose towards the film's conclusion. In contrast, audiences described Rose as "ambitious" and "strict", "not able to care for her partner's feelings or understand David", "self-orientated", but likewise "hardworking" and "industrious" for having reached her senior position. A male student in Lanzhou, GLG14, explained that his impression of Rose was like this because unlike David, whom the audience sees smoking cigarettes on a break with colleagues, the audience never saw Rose with others in the office, implying that she was not a team player. A female rural migrant worker in Nanjing believed that Rose's repeated pleas of desperation for her long-awaited promotion made her "calculating". These adjectives in fact describe the characters in the first instances that they are introduced to the audience in the film, and ultimately excused, or excused ignoring, changes in both Lala's and Rose's personalities by the end of the film. Indeed, no audience member understood Lala to be similarly calculating in her hiding the news of David's impending redundancy from him when she is HR supervisor, or in her hiding of her forbidden affair with David. Convinced by Lala's implied vulnerability and innocence through her cute performance at the beginning of the film, and juxtaposed against Rose's stern demeanour, audiences were convinced that the two women were inherently different personalities with different moral agendas. And in doing so, were inclined to prefer the cuter female protagonist. Rose was not acknowledged for her decision to pursue other dreams by audiences. Nor were her frustrations for promotion ever raised as indicative of how Rose may have been the victim of discriminatory industrial relations, even though Albert, the senior recruitment manager, confirms Rose is long overdue one. There was furthermore no audience member that suggested David's advice to Rose, "Perhaps there was something more that you could do?" to secure her promotion was playing into common beliefs that women have to perform up and beyond in order to equal their male counterparts as potentially chauvinistic and condescending. Rose's stern personality simply turned off her audiences and her onscreen colleagues alike. David, on the other hand, was positively described as "hard-working", "stern", "handsome", "good-hearted", even "wise" – not "cruel" for his initial harsh treatment of Helen, his secretary prior to Lala, or "opportunistic" for dating his secretary, despite his position of power and knowing DB's "No Office Romance" rule. Lala's cute demeanour functioned to engender agreeability from audiences for her morality, and by extension, other characters associated with her. Although *Go Lala Go!* indicated that cuteness has its rewards of easing the navigation of the white collar world's hierarchies, the negative aspect of such a professional trajectory is depicted as a woman losing her cute feminine charm and becoming a woman that, simply put, men and office colleagues (and audiences) alike, will no longer find enjoyable. *Go Lala Go!* warns its female audience, that while cuteness may have its rewards, a woman should know when the rewards have "dried up".

Cuteness and social mobility

As a 27-year-old newcomer, Lala's entry-level secretarial wage is 3000 RMB per month and she is wide-eyed, bubbly and friendly. By 29 years old, Lala is secretary to the Regional Sales Director and her wage is 6000 RMB per month. Lala has snared a successful lover (David, her boss) and is excited by love's possibilities. By 30 years old she has been promoted to HR Supervisor at 12,000 RMB per month and in her new position of seniority has had to execute the retrenching of her best friend, Helen, for her office romance, and cracks appear in her relationship with David. Finally at 33 years old, Lala has reached DB's lower management on 25,000 RMB per month, but her relationship with David ended two years earlier, and she has lost her wide-eyed enthusiasm for life that made her so attractive at the beginning of the film. At 33, despite her success, Lala is still seen outside of office hours to be making futile efforts to call her ex-partner David's former cell phone, which has ceased to be connected. Lala's cuteness has been diminished to eating Dove chocolate alone and disgruntled in her sports car. While her personal traits have been exchanged for a higher salary than she started on, an earlier conversation between Helen and Lala on her first day at DB indicates that she could have used her cuteness to benefit herself in a much more lucrative manner than seeking professional promotion.

Helen: 在公司里人与人的区别是很大的，经理以下级别叫"小资"，其实也就是穷人的意思，月薪不超过4000
This company really has different personnel levels. People below managers are small potatoes *[cuts to a screen share of their female colleague desperately trying to hail a taxi in busy Beijing]*. That means they are poor, making less than 4000 RMB per month.
经理级别算是中产阶级，有自己的私家车。年薪超过20万。
The managers are middle class, they have their own cars *[cuts to screen share of a BMW driving through streets of Beijing]* and an annual salary of over 200,000 RMB.
总监级别是高产阶级。年薪超过50万。保守派喜欢出国度假，少壮派为了跟他们区别开来，往往在体力上折磨自己。
Directors are upper class *[cuts to screen share of HR director, Lester and his wife (westerners) reading a book together on a couch]* their annual salaries are over 500,000 RMB. The older ones take their vacations abroad. The younger ones, trying to be different [cuts to image of David, Lala's soon to be love interest and regional sales director with a backpack on climbing a mountain], torture themselves physically.

84 *Go Lala Go!*

总裁呢，年薪超过百万，是标准的富人。什么是富人？

The CEO makes more than a million a year, typical upper crust *[cuts to image of a westerner walking through a villa's garden admiring his flowers]* Helen sighs. What does it mean to be rich?

By Helen's categorisation Lala has reached the middle class by the time she has reached the role of HR manager at 33 years old after seven years of service to DB. Her wage of 25,000 RMB per month would put her in the category of middle class on an annual salary of 300,000 RMB. Lala would still have a long way to go before being promoted to a director's level, which would have mobilised her into the upper class by earning over 500,000 RMB annually. As the screen cuts to David in this sequence, Helen has conveniently revealed to the audience that David is, by Helen's rationale, upper class. Lala's own professional efforts, and exchange of her adorable cuteness, only mobilised her to the middle class by the end of the film's conclusion. Yet, Lala's love affair, a result of her cuteness, could have propelled Lala to the upper class if she had chosen David over her own professional ambitions. Losing her cuteness for a managerial role (which audiences agreed was a personality trait in Rose that nobody approved of), as well as her chance to become upper class through marriage, is portrayed as the fate of the woman who follows the path of Lala: the *shengnü*. Cuteness in *Go Lala Go!* presents an interesting proposition for young female audiences to think strategically about how cuteness can aid their social mobility in ways other than through their labour. Young women should weigh up their earning power and that of her male counterpart's, and pay heed to when the optimal time may be to retreat from the labour force and prioritise *his* career.

To gauge whether audiences had vigilantly paid attention to the details of Lala's professional progress, audiences were asked whether they could recall the salaries and job titles for each of Lala's promotions. This was to see who may most likely be influenced by *Go Lala Go!*'s subtle clues about social mobility and earning power. GLG22 in Nanjing and GLG5 in Hangzhou (Helen's "small potatoes") recalled Lala's job titles only on behalf of the group. While GLG22's peers in Nanjing could not help her with the salary figures, GLG5's peers could offer ballpark figures of 3000 RMB and 6000 RMB only. Migrant worker salaries in Nanjing were just higher than 1000 RMB per month and participants in Hangzhou were approximately 1700 RMB per month. None of these wages came even close to reaching Helen's "small potatoes" category of 4000 RMB per month. Coupled with their disinterest in white collar lifestyles, their attentions bypassed Lala's salaries that appeared to be figures beyond their realities.

When audiences in Hangzhou and Nanjing were asked whether they believed their salaries would reach those of Lala's in their lifetime, they were unsure how to answer the question and looked to each other for guidance. After some tentative discussion, in both cities audiences came to the conclusion that their wages would most likely not accelerate as quickly as Lala's did in the film (although they would not rule out completely the possibility), but believed their children's generation may have a better chance for earning salaries like Lala. These audiences showed optimism that "hard work" would lead to rewards, albeit Lala's salaries were not retained as crucial details to take away from the watching of *Go Lala Go!*.

In stark contrast, professionals in Beijing (GLG2–GLG4) could recall exact figures and titles with confidence and familiarity. GLG3 even claimed the salaries were "laughable", because in his employment with a leading State-owned research institute he had encountered employee wages in foreign corporations, or in positions of senior management such as Lala and her colleagues are portrayed to have, that were much higher than the salaries presented in the film. GLG4 agreed with GLG3's claim. Middle-aged factory supervisors in Lanzhou could only recall ballpark figures of Lala's promotions like the audiences in Hangzhou, but could recall the *speed* in which her salary increased, noting her age at each promotion. These factory employees laughed off their chances of reaching salaries like Lala's and so quickly, but like the audiences in Nanjing, believed their children's generation would be the beneficiaries of any such opportunities. In contrast, university students in Lanzhou and Taiyuan could recall Lala's salaries as well as her administrative titles with astute precision; in both cities the students raced each other to recall the details in their enthusiasm to answer. University students believed that it was very likely they would reach Lala's salaries if they sought out a white collar career after completing their studies. Without critique of the value of the salaries (and well aware that they were not entering into manual labour), Lala's professional trajectory confirmed to student audiences their future white collar labour expectations and earning potential.

If GLG3's claim that Lala's wages are undervalued in *Go Lala Go!* is correct, the decision on the part of the filmmakers to undervalue Lala's wages would suggest that they foresaw their target audience as less informed about white collar labour within foreign corporations – such as the university students who paid close attention to the salary details in Lanzhou and Taiyuan. It could therefore be argued that the salaries displayed in *Go Lala Go!* were consciously pitched at more conceptually accessible amounts for this younger aspirational demographic. Another explanation could be that salaries were undervalued so as to appear *less* appealing for this same demographic to encourage a retreat from the labour market. Either way, university student attentions to Lala's salaries, career projection and behaviour attached to her social mobilisation suggested that these details were highly important to their consumption of *Go Lala Go!*, even taking on pedagogical qualities. This however, is not to detract from the more pressing issue of *Go Lala Go!*'s narrative: that being Lala's career trajectory at the expense of love.

Professional sacrifice for white collar romances

Although *Go Lala Go!* tries to capture the work environment of the white collar world as a step forward for women's labour, the fundamental concern for the successful *shengnü* is her marital status. Lala is often encouraged by her brother "at her age" to be thinking about focusing on her relationship with David, rather than her career. When David vanishes from Beijing after he and Lala end their

86   *Go Lala Go!*

relationship, Lala devotes her focus to climbing the professional ladder without joy. Despite Lala's economic capacities, the threat of spinsterhood suggestively underlies her depression. *Go Lala Go!*'s moral to the narrative is clear: women who prioritise their career will end up spinsters, because social mobility via a career results in hardened female personalities that no longer make the woman desirable to upper class male suitors. David ends his relationship with Rose because of her assertive and argumentative personality, and likewise ends his relationship with Lala, making sure to let her know her career was the reason for their relationship problems:

David: 不知道你有没有认真对待过我们的感情. 你更在意你的工作跟公司
　　　　 对你的看法
　　　　 I can't believe that you ever took our relationship seriously. You only care
　　　　 about your job and what the company thinks of you.

Go Lala Go! confirms that upper class men will reject career-minded women. And not any upper class man at that – *Go Lala Go!* assures that these upper class men are, above all else, as sexy as American-Taiwanese pop star heartthrob Stanley Huang, who is cast as David. After Lala and David's melodramatic reunion under the prayer tree in Thailand after their two years apart, the final frames of the film capture Lala and David embracing on a boat out to sea. Their joyous reunion would strongly support the assumption that their commitment to the relationship has been reaffirmed. This leaves the audience to speculate how this will impact on Lala's employment with DB, if audiences speculated at all unprompted. Yet, with Lala's notably uplifted spirits upon reunification with David and the final cut of their silhouettes in each other's arms with the sun setting behind them, *Go Lala Go!* hints that following David would make Lala *happier* and it would be a sound decision for Lala to forgo her career. Indeed, audiences interpreted *Go Lala Go!*'s plot resolution in this way.

Audiences were asked at the conclusion of *Go Lala Go!*: which did they believe was more important for Lala's character – love or career? Additionally, in light of Lala's experience, which did they think was more important for their own futures? Female university students and all rural migrant workers responded with "love" for both Lala and themselves personally. Two female university students in Lanzhou and GLG1 in Beijing even claimed that they would not want Lala's high-powered white collar life, as it was clearly, "too stressful for a woman". If the ambitions of *Go Lala Go!*'s narrative was to inspire an attitude among its female audiences of the intensity of white collar work and a preference for marital bliss, the film proved to have had success in encouraging these sentiments in a portion of this audience sample.

Male audiences overwhelmingly claimed that "love" was important for Lala, but "career" or "both" were important to them personally, an attitude that echoes Jieyu Liu's (2013: 79) claim that "[t]raditionally, the proper place of women was closely linked with the inner domain of the family while the proper place of men was associated with the outer public world." Professional men in Beijing (GLG3 and GLG4) and male students in Taiyuan and Lanzhou explained that a "career was more important in order to *afford* to have love", with GLG32 in Taiyuan following his answer shyly at the playful behest of his female classmates with, "of course love". Male responses reflected not only the sentiments in the plot resolution of *Go Lala Go!* but indicated that conventional norms in Chinese culture still prevail: woman's role is to love man unconditionally and prioritise this emotion, while man's is to work and earn in order to be able to afford the love women offer. This chapter does not argue that *Go Lala Go!* inspired these sentiments alone, but the overwhelming responses by young female audiences to the reunion of David and Lala under the prayer tree, and the distinctions made about love and career, indicated that the subplot of Lala's romance (as opposed to her career trajectory) certainly featured strongly in their understanding of Lala's narrative. This was even though these same female audiences had keenly paid attention to Lala's professional salaries and promotions. This being the case, *Go Lala Go!* provides a solution to its female audiences as to where to find a man: her workplace. The film portrays the white collar workplace as an environment where similarly classed men are concentrated and the capacity to use her sexuality or cuteness to catch a superior's attention is at its strategic prime – as an early altercation between Eva and Helen (fellow secretaries) suggests:

Helen: 看什么看我走了也轮不到你
What are you looking at?
[Slams down her papers on her desk]
If I leave you will not get my position.
Eva: 海伦这么大气呢,别忘了千万别得罪女同事,说不定有一天她就会成为你的老板娘啦
Oooh, Helen's got quite a temper ***[chiding voice]***. Be careful not to displease your female colleagues, she might be your boss's wife one day.
Helen: 我倒是要看看谁是我老板娘
[Spinning around to face Eva]
Ha, I would like to see that!

Sex and romance as the unspoken (but often real) promise at the point of exchange in DB's office environment is important to understanding the tensions between the white collar workers in the DB office. Despite a "No Office Romance" rule, the female secretaries appear to have romantic agendas in their dealings with their male bosses. Rose was a long-term secret partner to David; Eva flirts desperately with David in Thailand as Helen and Lala watch their flirtations jealously; Lala is called on to fire Helen for a romantic fling she has with Albert the HR manager after accidentally emailing to the entire DB mailing list a picture of the two of them snuggling in each other's arms; and Lala first has a one night stand in Thailand with David, then subsequently becomes his love interest when promoted to be his direct secretary.

88   *Go Lala Go!*

Zhu Yan (2013) claims that the production of *Go Lala Go!* heralded the arrival of a new feminist ideology fresh from the West to Chinese screens. Zhu understands *Go Lala Go!*'s production as assisting the reconfiguring of emotions in male and female relations in contemporary China, and goes so far as to claim that this new women's feminism has gone hand in hand with the male characters (presumably David) in DB shown to treat their female white collar colleagues with respect. Yet, Lala and her secretarial colleagues' sexualities in *Go Lala Go!* are far from portrayed as an expression of progressive independence – albeit the attempt has been to package it in this manner – but rather appear to be means to an end. The sex appeal of the female secretarial staff of DB is portrayed as assisting these women in hopefully finding a long-term partner or husband. Furthermore, each of the secretaries must gamble with her employment to do so. If it was not this way, the fear of the scandal and threat of dismissal that the airing of Lala's relationship with David may bring would not loom over her conscience as deeply as it so unfairly does for her throughout the film. Instead, Lala is constantly faced with managing the fine balance between a secret romance with David and her professional ambitions to climb the administrative hierarchy of DB.

After joining the ranks of DB's lower management, Lala is required to carry out Helen's retrenchment from DB. No clarification is provided (or is necessary, the film suggests) about what might have occurred to Albert's employment with the firm. From a discussion Lala has with David about Helen's dismissal, Lala notes that if Lala and David were to publicise their relationship, either she or David would "have to go". As such, the audience can assume that Albert maintained his position within the firm if Helen was made redundant; after all, Albert's value to the firm is greater than that of a secretary. Lala is happy to maintain her and David's secret, because she too understands that her value to the firm is less than that of David. Sex is for DB's secretaries one way of avoiding spinsterhood, if the sex results in commitment. Accordingly, the warning needs to be heeded in gambling with one's sexuality to get ahead: a female secretary's labour is valued less than that of her male superior, who may simply be taking advantage of his secretary's availability, like Albert does of Helen.

Audiences were asked whether the retrenchment of Helen was fair because of her relationship with Albert and whether they believed Lala should have confessed her own relationship with David to DB in light of being given the task to fire Helen. Rural migrant workers were in steadfast agreement in Hangzhou and Nanjing that it was unfair that Helen was retrenched for her affair. GLG22 claimed Helen's relationship with Albert had no relationship to the company. Migrant worker audiences likewise all agreed that Lala should have admitted her relationship with David to the company if Helen was her friend. The disappointment towards Lala's lack of solidarity with her friend and colleague among rural migrant worker audiences was clearly visible. Students, middle management factory workers and young professionals rather believed that although it was unfair that Helen lost her job, Helen should have worked harder like Lala did to *hide* the affair in order to protect her job. They also believed that Lala was not obliged to tell DB about

Go Lala Go! 89

their relationship, because "she would lose her job" (GLG17). For female student GLG15 in Lanzhou, when Lala gave Helen a business card of a contact that could help her find a new job, she believed Lala was absolved from accusations of double standards for not disclosing her own relationship. Upon hearing GLG15's reading of the scene, the other students nodded their heads in agreement.

The difference in moral readings of the Helen and Albert affair was quite striking but explainable. The groups with migrant workers had married couples working together for the same employer. Although undergraduate student GLG25 in Taiyuan commented that he thought businesses worked together better when families were involved (and the profits could be kept within the family), his fellow students were quick to point out that in a global corporation, conflicts of interest may arise financially and organisationally if colleagues were romantically involved. The professionals in Beijing and managers in Lanzhou were acutely aware of this too, reading their own workplace experiences into the narrative. Male professionals understood and even morally justified Lala's self-preservation and condoned her secrecy. GLG3 rationalised, "if you get caught, there are rules, but if you don't get caught, then continue."

The advocacy of using sexuality to gain advantage within the white collar workforce as portrayed in *Go Lala Go!* and seemingly encouraged by privileged audiences is in stark contrast to the "limitations of sexual enticement" (Otis 2011: 42) that the regulation of women's wearing of the standardised blue Mao suit, for example, was meant to negate during the Mao era. In contemporary popular cinema, women's sexual enticement is promoted as an opportunity that she should grasp and utilise, and while lower classed audiences could not entirely grasp what that meant in terms of securing benefits, female university students and white collar workers alike were well aware of how Lala's sexuality could work to her social mobility prospects.

Using one's sexuality, however, comes with a catch: successful men like David and Albert will not be willing to work for, or commit to, just any woman's love. A man's opinions will count when choosing a suitable female for serious commitment and women should pay heed to both Helen's and Lala's predicaments. David is both content and willing to walk away from his relationships with Rose and Lala when they start to prioritise their career over him and their personalities are no longer "cute". The film also suggests that Albert has no qualms about Helen losing her job for their affair. *Shengnü* like Lala, therefore, have new rules to adhere to in order to catch and keep a successful suitor like David. The fact is, David's and Albert's range of choice as upper class men is much greater than Lala's and Helen's as lower-middle class women. In order to be successful in the marriage market, not only will *shengnü* have to maintain their appealing personalities, but they will also have to recognise the timing to address their call to marry and make professional sacrifices, and moreover, make sure they are targeting the right man or her profession will be sacrificed on her behalf. As *Go Lala Go!* depicts in the plot resolution, though, the ideal conclusion is that of the narrative of Lala and David, who once reunited, drift romantically into the sunset.

90   *Go Lala Go!*

Consumption as female behaviour

Although criticism about the product integration in *Go Lala Go!* was ripe at the time of the film's release, university students in Taiyuan and Lanzhou did not perceive that the product integration was a negative attribute of the film. Rather the students perceived the presence of brand logos throughout the film to be positive reinforcement of China's modernity. Their sentiments echoed survey results collated in the early 1990s by Pollay, Tse and Wang (1990: 88–89) that concluded that Chinese approved of advertising for numerous reasons, including: "driving them to work harder . . . and making them proud of the country's economy". As the white collar worker carries broader Chinese society's expectations of being able to afford luxury items to distinguish their social status (Li 2011: 139–141), the product integration in *Go Lala Go!* confirmed not only Lala's status, but the film's status as appropriate for more privileged audiences who saw themselves as actively involved in the nation's economic growth and the status of the audience member who could recognise the products placed throughout the film.

Forty-three (43) brands placed 246 times throughout *Go Lala Go!* were counted in the course of the film. Eleven (11) were Chinese and 32 non-Chinese. Lenovo (Chinese) and Lipton Tea (American) received the most amount of exposure at 44 and 41 placements, respectively (Table 5.1). The greatest concentration of product integration in *Go Lala Go!* strategically occurred in the first thirty minutes of the film, when audiences are arguably most attentive and alert. To put this into perspective, Galician and Bourdeau's (2004: 21) study of product placement in the fifteen top-grossing Hollywood films in 1977, 1987, and 1999 found that the mean number of *total placements in all fifteen films* combined was 182. In one film alone, *Go Lala Go!* surpassed Galacian and Bourdeau's count, and the scale of the film's product integration can only be indicative of the aggressive expectation *Go Lala Go!* makes that young female audiences should become active consumers.

Through Lala's fashion, the audience also learns how Lala distinguishes herself as a white collar worker. The engagement of Patricia Field (*Sex and the City*: HBO 1998) as wardrobe stylist for *Go Lala Go!* had a very clear goal. As Jacqueline Elfick (2008) discovered, the TV show *Sex and the City* was hugely popular among *shengnü* in Shenzhen, with her informants perceiving a strong connection between their own lived experience and the show's narrative. Patricia Field's association with *Go Lala Go!*'s production brought certification to the fashion and consumer behaviour for young female audiences already familiar with Field's previous work on *Sex and the City*, and most likely inclined to seek out the film to watch. Take the simple gesture of the importance of Lala's footwear that Field stylises with each of Lala's promotions (Figure 5.3).

As a newcomer to DB, Lala wears sneakers to work that she swaps outside of the office building for fashionable flat-soled shoes. Lala's preference for comfortable sneakers is an indication of her commuting to and from work via public transport, as the audience is shown Lala commuting by subway to work. At Lala's first promotion, she changes these fashionable flats to mid-low heeled pumps of a playful green colour, with open toe and a style commonly seen available at shoe stalls in

Table 5.1 Product placement count for *Go Lala Go!*

Brand	Product	Placements
Lenovo	Technology (computers)	44
Lipton	Black Tea	41
Lotto	Sportswear	25
Kartell	Home design and furniture	18
Wrigley's Extra gum	Confectionary	18
Mazda	Auto	17
Dove	Confectionary	13
Nokia	Telecommunications	12
COGI	Cosmetics	5
Industrial Bank Co. Ltd.	Banking	5
Zhaopin	HR website	4
IKEA	Home design and furniture	4
Harper's Bazaar	Magazine	3
Giorgio Armani	Fashion	3
Bobby Brown	Cosmetics	2
CBN Weekly	Chinese Business and News magazine	2
Miffy	Soft children's toys	2
OZZO	Fashion	2
PICC	Insurance	2
SOHO building	Commercial/construction	2
Agnona	Fashion	1
Beijing Yintai Center	Commercial/construction	1
Canon	Photography	1
Cartier	Fashion	1
China Mobile	Telecommunications	1
China World Hotel	Hotel	1
D&G	Fashion	1
Fuji Film	Photography	1
GUCCI	Fashion	1
Hermes	Fashion	1
Lee	Fashion	1
LG	Television	1
Marlboro	Cigarettes	1
MaxMara	Fashion	1
Nikon	Photography	1
Prada	Fashion	1
Sony	Photography	1
Toga	Fashion	1
VW	Auto	1
Watson	Pharmaceuticals	1
Yamaha	Jet Ski	1
Union Pay/Mastercard	Credit Card	1
	TOTAL	246

Figure 5.3 Shoes as power in *Go Lala Go!*

Chinese markets. These green pumps indicate in fashion terms a woman not quite aware of what style-as-power is, but who is trying to imitate it nonetheless. Once reaching a managerial level, Lala wears streamlined black stilettos that would be considered highly impractical on public transport. Lala's stilettos are the only shoes she does not change into outside her workplace, thus confirming that Lala is now travelling by car to work and that she wore her stilettos from the front door of her house to the office. The intensity of Lala's footwear, the colour and even the functionality of the shoes all become indicators of Lala's consumption that complements her social mobility.

Shopping, and knowing what to shop for, is paramount for respectable women of the aspirational classes to distinguish themselves. Whereas manual labourers may wear uniforms, the white collar world relies on fashion to be an extension of the individual's personality. Active engagement with China's beauty economy is hence positioned as an extension of the unique female self and is rewarded by a man's desire for her in the sexually charged environment of the white collar workplace. When successfully enjoyed by a man, for reasons relating to female objectives of procuring a husband, a woman's fashioning of her femininity is shown to be a worthwhile investment. Moreover, fashion is an investment that will ultimately distinguish her from her manual labouring sisters, less informed by the in-built codes of fashion that allude to social distinction (as Lala's footwear indicates).

To investigate product awareness along class lines, audiences were requested to list the products that they recognised in *Go Lala Go!* on a piece of paper while they were watching the film's screening. Product placement in *Go Lala Go!* spoke almost exclusively to a younger educated urban audience – and those who lived in the proximity of shopping districts with international brand outlets, or who had travelled overseas. Interestingly, although male university students in Taiyuan and professional men in Beijing proved much better at brand recognition in the film than females, they were adamant that shopping was an activity undertaken primarily by females. This also could have been a sign of their disinterest in Lala's love story, and hence their attentions were focused on the task of spotting products as they appeared in the film. Privileged audiences in Taiyuan, Lanzhou and Beijing listed anywhere between 11 to 24 brands and company names in their viewing (GLG27, male, recognised the most, with 24 brands). The labels easiest for audiences to recognise proved to be Chinese. Foreign brands proved recognisable only to professionals in Beijing (although they clarified that this was not indicative of their consumption patterns). As such, many of the 43 brands eluded audiences' attentions. This is not to say that for these companies their placement was in vain. Young female urbanites were agreeable to watching *Go Lala Go!* multiple times and were enthusiastic about recommending the film to their friends to watch. Many even indicated that their awareness of happenings in the film and their brand spotting improved upon each viewing.

Only Mazda and Lenovo caught the attention of male rural migrant workers and coal factory supervisors. Female rural migrant workers followed their male peers' answers by nodding their heads in agreement to suggest that they too had recognised the Mazda brand. It was clear, even when pre-warned of the task to list the products they might see watching the film, that rural migrant workers and middle-aged men were far less aware of brands in *Go Lala Go!* than their urban counterparts. In the case of the middle-aged factory supervisors, their lack of brand recognition had a lot to do with their overall disinterest in the film. For migrant workers, it appeared to be a mixture of limited literacy skills, an unfamiliarity with a great deal of the brands and logos integrated into the film, and interestingly, a task that they quickly abandoned once they started watching, whether consciously or not. Regardless of which option was correct, those who eagerly consumed and attended to the task of counting product placements were young urban university students and white collar professionals in Beijing.

Binge consumption

Lala's temperament is often vulnerable to emotional outbursts, the remedy for which is retail therapy. When Lala discovers David's ex-partner is Rose, her

94 *Go Lala Go!*

heartbreak sends her into an extravagant display of what can only be described as binge consumption. In this scene, high-fashion retail labels flash across the screen accompanied by loud music and hands passing credit cards, and a Mazda convertible sports car zips noisily through the streets of Beijing. Lala looks thoroughly pleased at the conclusion of her retail therapy and *Go Lala Go!*'s director, Xu, advocates through Lala's behaviour that audiences likewise should not feel guilty about superfluous and conspicuous retail therapy. Not to feel post-retail therapy guilt is portrayed both as a symbol of a young woman's economic capacities and a young Chinese female's rightful response to emotional outpouring. The montage affirms that shopping, if anything, is therapeutic if one can afford it, good fun with friends and cute if undertaken by a woman scorned.

Audiences generally indicated that retail therapy was a female attribute, albeit an attribute of privileged females only. Rural migrant workers confirmed that they would not binge consume if they were unhappy and had never done so. Audiences in Nanjing seemed particularly uninformed of the protocols of retail therapy, appearing bewildered at why unhappiness required Lala to shop. Nor did female rural migrant workers in Nanjing realise how much the clothes modelled onscreen by Lala and her colleagues were sold at retail price for, or approximately how much Lala may have spent during her shopping spree. When provided with approximate values of the dresses worn by Lala and her colleagues, these female audiences did not believe that clothes should cost the amount that the fashion brands featured in the films do. As GLG24 generously deferred to her more privileged female counterpart, though, "If people want to buy these clothes, then what can you do?"

Female students in Lanzhou and Taiyuan and professionals in Beijing confirmed that they did often rely on retail therapy and all of them admitted to feeling some degree of post-consumption regret. When asked if they believed that Lala regretted her retail therapy, young females in Lanzhou noted that Lala could not have felt guilty for her consumption because when Lala gets out of her newly purchased Mazda car and proclaims to David that all her savings have gone into buying it, she says it excitedly (and notably with a particularly cute voice). The fact that these young women recognised Lala's lack of guilt is not without relevance. Their recognition indeed indicated that they gave a high degree of attention to Lala's countenance throughout her spending spree. In saying this, the notion of consumption as an act performed by a successful and desirable young woman without guilt was seen to be both symbolic of her economic capacities and a filmic confirmation that conspicuous consumption was a privileged female's natural inclination. Arguably, the film also confirmed for male audiences that retail therapy and conspicuous consumption was a woman's calling, and therefore they (the men) were expected to earn in order to support their female counterparts' unavoidable compulsions to shop. Perhaps this is why they claimed a career was more important in order to "afford" love earlier in the group discussions. Lala's economic capacity to consume as a result of being career-minded, therefore, is effectively diminished to unavoidable behaviour due to her being female; not an economic capacity she has achieved through her professional success. Most importantly however, Lala's consumption is an indicator in broader society of who she is *not*, and that is indeed understood by audiences as *not* being of the subordinate classes.

Mixed messages

For all the allure and excitement that *Go Lala Go!* provides its young female audiences, the film's narrative offers conflicting messages. On the one hand, *Go Lala Go!* promotes active employment in the white collar labour market and encourages young women to aspire to educate themselves in order to obtain this well-paid professional work. The benefits of doing so, the film suggests, is a lifestyle of extravagance, conspicuous consumption and romance. On the other hand, the film's narrative advocates that successful women should avoid finding themselves alone with only money to spend to show for their efforts – particularly because their choice impacts on the emotional stability of China's unmarried and unsatisfied men as Lala's behaviour is seen to impact on her beau, David, whose heartbreak drives him to migrate to Thailand. The conflicting messages, though, are not necessarily surprising, for the expectations of these young professional women are exactly that: conflicted. While some room is required to allow China's female professionals to lead the vanguard of the consumer revolution as curious trendsetters, they are also expected to conserve the moral status quo of middle and mainstream Chinese society and to bear children.

As female and male rural migrant worker audiences of *Go Lala Go!* alike proved unfamiliar with the retail therapy and brand recognition required by the film, it became apparent that lower classed women are unfairly placed in their ignorance of the social cues that privileged women are privy to. In lacking the "know-how" to project their sense of worth to broader society or utilise their sexuality for personal gain, the codes of respectable femininity remain inaccessible to their social group and understood only by women of the aspirational classes. Understandably, this comes at the lower classed woman's expense by decreasing her value in the labour market and her chance to socially mobilise – or marry "up".

What was perhaps most intriguing about audiences of *Go Lala Go!*, though, is the distinction that emerged between audiences of the lower and privileged classes in their understanding of Lala's narrative as deeply gendered. While male audiences from urban areas and with some degree of privilege repeatedly recognised *Go Lala Go!* as being a "women's film" or a "film that only women would watch", rural migrant workers, both male and female, said nothing of the film's gendered bias. Male migrant workers, moreover, did not appear burdened by discussing *Go Lala Go!*'s themes and narratives – it was simply a film that featured a woman working and in love. Similarly, love and relationships did not appear embarrassing or emasculating topics to discuss in front of their peers. This is not to say that within China's lower classes women do not face gender politics that disadvantage them – but that gender politics for China's women differ from class to class. In the case of privileged Chinese women, the gender politics presented themselves as a deep polarisation between them and their similarly classed male counterparts, who in reality could be potential suitors. Men did not want to know

96 *Go Lala Go!*

about "films for women", yet young female university students seemed thoroughly captivated by them. One can only muse how this socialised polarisation (keeping in mind that this distinction was not observable among lower classed audiences) may in fact contribute to China's more independent *shengnü*'s decisions to abstain from marrying. This being said, China's "Lala's" are the nation's opportunity to rear the next generation of aspirational middle class daughters and sons. Mothers play an important role in the cycle of privilege that a class society requires for its sustainability. Finding a harmony in the socialisation of respectable female class distinction and improved privileged female–male relationships, therefore, will be China's next hurdle. For if China's *shengnü* do not marry and pass on these codes of class distinction to the next generation, then who will?

Notes

1 Box office figure as of 16 July 2016 (Entgroup); approximate USD at historical exchange rate for 1 May 2010 (XE Currency); URL: http://www.cbooo.cn/m/572815/
2 Douban rating: 5.7/10 from 165,672 reviews. URL: http://movie.douban.com/subject/3820191/ (last accessed: 16 July 2016).
3 For further reading, see Shuiqin Cui's (2003) historical overview of women in Chinese cinema.
4 Consider "Gentle Dominatrix's" [温柔的母夜叉] review posted on 19 April 2010: "看《建国大业》数明星，看《杜拉拉升职记》数广告。", translated as "Watch *Founding of a Republic* and count the celebrity appearances, watch *Go Lala Go!* and count the advertisements." Accessed: 15 August 2014. URL: http://movie.douban.com/people/logorrhea/collect?start=1740&sort=time&rating=all&filter=all&mode=list
5 GLG20 had worked in construction in Beijing in the late 1990s. In the discussion group for *Lost on Journey* peasants commented that those who worked in first-tier cities such as Beijing returned with "open eyes" to their villages.
6 At the conclusion of a group discussion for *Lost on Journey* in Taiyuan, a young female privately recommended that I should screen and discuss *Go Lala Go!* to understand contemporary Chinese society. She was unaware that *Go Lala Go! was* part of the broader project, so she explained how her female manager had organised the female staff in her office to go on a work excursion to the cinema to watch the film. She explained the work excursion was not only an opportunity for the female employees to learn about office culture, but also how to dress and behave.
7 Ecns.cn claims that at the peak of Kaila's popularity, the celebrity e-zine "enjoyed annual advertising revenue of 20 million yuan ($3 million), with the click through rate for a single issue once exceeding 100 million".
8 See Jingyuang Zhang's chapter (2011) on Xu Jinglei's previous work prior to *Go Lala Go!*

References

Berebitsky, Julie. 2012. *Sex and the Office: A History of Gender, Power, and Desire*. New Haven, CT: Yale University Press.
Berry, Chris, and Mary A. Farquhar. 2006. *China on Screen: Cinema and Nation*. New York: Columbia University Press.
Chuang, Tzu-i. 2005. The Power of Cuteness: Female Infantilization in Urban Taiwan. *Stanford Journal of East Asian Affairs* 5 (2): 21–28.
Cui, Shuqin. 2003. *Women through the Lens: Gender and Nation in a Century of Chinese Cinema*. Honolulu: University of Hawai'i Press.

Dai, Jinhua. 2002. *Cinema and Desire: Feminist Marxism and Cultural Politics in the Work of Dai Jinhua.* Edited by J. Wang and T. E. Barlow. London: Verso.

Elfick, Jacqueline. 2008. Sex, Television and the Middle Class in China. In *Patterns of Middle Class Consumption in India and China,* edited by Christophe Jaffrelot and Peter van der Veer, 207–229. Los Angeles: SAGE.

Fincher, Leta Hong. 2014. *Leftover Women: The Resurgence of Gender Inequality in China.* London: Zed Books.

Galician, Mary-Lou, and Peter G. Bourdeau. 2004. The Evolution of Product Placements in Hollywood Cinema. *Journal of Promotion Management* 10 (1–2): 15–36.

Haigh, Gideon. 2012. *The Office: A Hardworking History.* Melbourne: Melbourne University Publishing.

Li, Chunling. 2011. Characterizing China's Middle Class: Heterogeneous Composition and Multiple Identities. In *China's Emerging Middle Class: Beyond Economic Transformation,* edited by Cheng Li, 135–156. Washington, DC: Brookings Institute Press.

Mills, C. W. 1953. *White Collar.* New York: Oxford University Press.

Otis, Eileen M. 2011. *Markets and Bodies: Women, Service Work, and the Making of Inequality in China.* Stanford, CA: Stanford University Press.

Pollay, Richard W., David K. Tse, and Zhen-Yuan Wang. 1990. Advertising, Propaganda, and Value Change in Economic Development: The New Cultural Revolution in China and Attitudes toward Advertising. *Journal of Business Research* 20: 83–95.

Yang, Yantao [杨艳涛]. 2011. Reflections On Our Country's "Leftover" Women [对我国社会"剩女"现状的思考]. *Canzhou shifan kejiao xueban* [沧州师范专科学校学报] 27 (3): 69–71.

Zhu Yan (朱艳). 2013. Films of New Women's Ideology: Researching *Go Lala Go* [新女性主义视阈下的电影《杜拉拉升职记》研究]. Zuopin toushi/dianying wenxue [作品透视/电影文学]: MOVIELITERATURE May: 93–94.

6 *House Mania*

Homeownership, marriageability and masculinity

Figure 6.1 Promotional film poster: *House Mania*

100 *House Mania*

《房不剩防》

(*fang bu sheng fang*)

House Mania

Director: Sun Da (孙达)
Starring: Zhou Yi (赵毅), Li Nian (李念), Li Qing (李菁)
Box office: 3,785,000 RMB (USD 577, 968)[1]
Exhibition period: March–April 2011 (2 weeks)[2]

Synopsis

House Mania (Sun: 2011) is set in contemporary Beijing where a young real estate agent, Xiao Ke, is struggling to lift her dismal sales figures that her manager reminds her of on a frequent basis. Her boyfriend, Yingming, is employed as a lifeguard at the local pool but has convinced Xiao Ke that he is in fact a surgeon. Yingming is desperate to make a good impression on Xiao Ke and her mother in order to marry Xiao Ke. But, Xiao Ke's mother has made clear that "good" means owning "a house, a car and having potential". When Yingming's employer discovers he cannot swim, he is fired. Concurrently Xiao Ke is also fired for her poor record as a real estate agent, and matters become even more desperate for Yingming to keep up the impression that he has a steady income and is able to become head of a family.

To start, Yingming borrows a basement apartment belonging to his friend, Xiao Hei, to show Xiao Ke's mother proof of his financial security. Unbeknownst to him, Xiao Hei's apartment is in very poor condition and neighbours a brothel. Xiao Ke's mother is horrified when he takes her to see his apartment. On the spot, Yingming claims that his intentions are to engage Xiao Ke to sell the property for him so he can upgrade to a larger apartment. Xiao Ke receives a timely phone call from a wealthy customer who is indifferent to what apartment he is buying (it is alluded it will be for his mistress). Xiao Ke sells Xiao Hei's apartment (believing it to be Yingming's) for an impressive sum on the spot. The sum surprises Xiao Hei, who did not realise the potential value of his underwhelming property. This initial sale sets the wheels in motion for what becomes Yingming's adventure into property speculation of unsellable properties across Beijing.

With the impression that the properties being bought and sold belong to Yingming, Xiao Ke agrees to steal customer files from the real estate agency she was earlier employed by to assist Yingming in finding potential buyers. Together they employ a variety of tactics of deception tailored to the buyers' egos, superstitions and needs, to assist the property sales. As Yingming's reputation expands, his earning power increases. Accordingly, the commissions he earns for each sale increase too. Ever more inventive, after a series of successes and profits, a guilty conscience drives Xiao Ke to question whether deceiving their buyers is morally correct. Returning to their earlier sales, they find that the new homeowners are each delighted with their living arrangements. Encouraged by their satisfaction,

Xiao Ke agrees to continue assisting Yingming's property speculation. Until the day she unwittingly introduces Yingming's parents to Yingming as their next prospective customers.

Yingming's parents reveal to Xiao Ke that he is not a surgeon, has never been a homeowner, never completed high school, has had many girlfriends just for "fun", and has twice been to jail for public disorder. In shock at these revelations, Xiao Ke ends the relationship with Yingming for deceiving her. Yingming does not take the breakup well, but with the news that a buyer is interested in Yingming's parent's rundown *siheyuan* (四合院 a traditional Chinese house in Beijing), located in the historical alleyways in Beijing known as a *hutong* (胡同), for an impressive one million RMB price, he is reinvigorated with hope of making another quick buck.

For the first time, though, Yingming is swindled and the sale falls through. In fear of disappointing his parents, Yingming buys their *siheyuan* with all his savings and is left penniless. All is improved, however, when Yingming is reunited with Xiao Ke. Spurred on by feelings of security, Yingming seeks creditors from far and wide to invest in a plan hatched to buy an island from a bankrupt Russian billionaire. When things do naturally go awry (the bank seizes the island in order to cover the Russian's debts) Yingming is admitted to a psychiatric hospital suffering from stress. Plagued by guilt, Yingming considers leaping to his death from the hospital roof. Xiao Ke begs him not to jump and insists that even though he does not own a house or have money, she will marry him, regardless of her mother's wishes. Xiao Hei arrives on the scene to tell them that due to the time difference between China and Russia, the money transfer was not successful: Yingming's creditors' funds were still in his bank account. *House Mania* concludes with Yingming and Xiao Ke working together, although in a capacity not entirely clear, either high-end real estate, or hotel service work. Whichever the occupation, it is clear that they do not own property but are satisfied because they have each other. In the closing scene, fireworks explode over Beijing at night as, arms around each other, they muse how it can be that in such a big city they are not able to find a home of their own.

Introduction

The housing reforms introduced by the Party-state throughout the 1980s and into the late 1990s have played a significant role in shaping China's class society. Transforming the provision of urban welfare housing into a real estate market and constructing new urban environments on a scale and pace never seen before, China has systematically replaced historically negative connotations of being a "landlord" (*dizhu*, 地主), with the contemporary prestige of being a "homeowner" (*fangzhu*, 房主 or *fangdong*, 房东). Indeed, so negative was the landlord character in Chinese socialist cinema, that Xiaoning Lu (2015: 235) reports that Chen Qiang, who built his theatrical reputation on playing villainous landlords in classics such as *The White-Haired Girl* (1950) and *Red Detachment of Women* (1961), was drawn to publishing a reflective essay in the popular film periodical *Masses Cinema* in 1962 discussing his theory of "negative pedagogy". The theory of negative pedagogy, Lu claims, gave Chen a necessary chance to create "a critical distance

102 *House Mania*

between him and his roles", so careful was Chen to manage his theatrical obligations to the communist narrative onscreen, and how Chinese audiences may perceive his actual ideological positioning off-screen.

Fast-forward half a century, and the prestige of homeownership has played a central part in propagating ideals of China's aspirational middle class narrative. Although the middle class narrative does not specify that this obligation to be a homeowner lies with men, audiences of *House Mania* confirmed that man's role in the propagation of the homeownership ideal is very much at the forefront of China's homeownership narrative. A man's investment is not simply the act of buying with the aspiration to become middle class, but by indicating he fits the middle class homeowner narrative, he confirms his marriageability, and by extension, his masculinity. By portraying corruption and deception in property speculation as a means for the male protagonist to "resolve" his masculinity crisis and therefore humanise deception and corruption as an individual, not a structural issue of the housing market, *House Mania* engenders a pragmatic acceptance among audiences that the corruption in the property market is a secondary matter to the much greater issue: the capacity for males to be "men" and invest. The inequalities borne out of housing reforms are reflections of man's economic capacities – not Party-state designed housing reform policies.

As property prices rise, and legal and financial responsibilities of property investment and mortgage repayments follow in severity, commercial cinema's propagation and reaffirmation of the cultural expectations that men should provide housing in order to be worthy of marriage, places young men (chiefly urban) and their families as financially and legally accountable within an already unequal property market demarcated by class and regional lines. Furthermore, they must bargain in a competitive marriage market with a depleted number of females due to the impact of the single-child policy (and apparently the growing numbers of *shengnü*; see previous chapter). This should not detract from the rise in women's homeownership in Chinese society or overlook the hidden rates of women and their families as co-financiers of mortgages due to cultural practices that place the man's name on deeds of property ownership. Indeed, researchers have sought to emphasise how homeownership as a man's domain unfairly discriminates against women in circumstances of divorce and economic power (Davis 2010; Sargeson 2013; Fincher 2014). Yet the reality is that man's obligation to provide a home in order to be considered an eligible suitor for marriage is still very much alive in Chinese mainstream popular discourse, amongst all classes and without regional disparities. While the popular discourse does in fact advantage Chinese men over Chinese women for the greater part, this cannot ignore how the discourse also challenges feelings of self-worth, privilege and masculinity of young urban males in weaker economic positions, and critically, between rural and urban men.

House Mania was the lowest earner commercially of the films surveyed in this book and represents an alternate perspective of the Chinese film market from the highly successful blockbusters and films that circulate at international film festivals. *House Mania* is an example of the numerous Chinese films that disappear with little fanfare into the pirate DVD market, file-sharing websites and public

House Mania 103

television broadcasts (if fortunate enough to have the rights to broadcast bought) and are typically consumed in online streaming platforms. The modest box office revenue should not detract from the fact that the box office for the two-week period the film exhibited was in fact quite strong, and extended exhibition may have revealed a different box office figure. Although *House Mania* could be described as somewhat lowbrow in its comedy and production values, the film's very real applicability to all group discussants meant that sense making of *House Mania*'s narrative was the most consistent across focus groups of any of the films discussed. The film is light-hearted, the characters could easily be your best friend in reality, and the imagination does not need to stretch to grasp the scenarios presented. On-location shooting within Beijing's residential areas provides an insight into modest Beijing, the opposite spectrum to Lala and her white collar colleagues discussed in the previous chapter. The young couple are appropriately modest in their physical contact as young lovers. There is minimal product integration in the film, but the products that are visible in Yingming and Xiao Ke's shopping sprees, including numerous fashion labels, Chinese banks and a fairly indiscrete Audi car, suggest *House Mania*'s commercial exhibition for two weeks may have been advocated because of the products associated with the film. Overall, class did *not* affect the comprehension of the narrative's trajectory that follows a young man desperate to secure homeownership in order to win the approval of his girlfriend's mother so the young couple may marry.

Audiences and group discussions

The average age of an audience member for group discussions about *House Mania* was 32 years of age; 22 members were male, and 16 were female. The discussion group in Beijing consisted of young urbanites earning modest incomes, but who were educated, regularly consumed foreign media and associated with Beijing's expat community. Discussions in Hangzhou and Nanjing were conducted with rural urban migrant workers; and in Taiyuan, the group consisted of both mid-level white collar workers and established professionals. Two discussion groups were conducted in Lanzhou, one with university professors from the social sciences and the second with bachelor students from the humanities. Only one male in Taiyuan had seen *House Mania* prior to attending a film screening and discussion group, although a number of students and young adults had heard of the film's title. These audience members reported seeing the film advertised, but none of them had pursued the film, either in the cinema or online. Only one rural migrant worker in Hangzhou had heard of the film's title prior to the screening.

All audiences enjoyed *House Mania*, albeit groups with young adult urbanites were full of criticisms about the film's "low budget" and "old era" production values (Beijing and Lanzhou). As such, only migrant worker audiences in Nanjing and Hangzhou agreed they would recommend the film to their broader social network. The elder who recruited participants in Nanjing even nominated *House Mania* as his favourite film of the five screenings for which he recruited participants (all except for *Lost on Journey* were screened in Nanjing). Young

104 *House Mania*

urban Beijing residents who were educated but in the same financial situation as Yingming and Xiao Ke believed that they would not recommend the film to their friends. They explained that *House Mania* reminded them of Chinese comedies they had watched when they were younger, when the commercial film industry was still in its early days of reform. HM5 and HM6, who work in media production, also believed the film's production values were outdated. HM5 commented that the director "must be in his 50s or 60s" to produce a film like *House Mania* to stress the outdated aesthetics of the film. In fact, the director Sun Da was 29 years old when he directed the film, yet Sun Da's career and training had been through the state film studio system, which arguably influenced his directorial style described by HM5 and HM6 as "old-fashioned". In the case of *House Mania*, therefore, it appeared that having "old-fashioned" production values could also have meant "having state studio qualities". HM4 in Beijing firmly disapproved of the performance of "cuteness" of the female protagonist, Xiao Ke. Although this particular act of cuteness is similarly performed in *Go Lala Go!*, Lala's privileged white collar cuteness did not seem to annoy educated young female urbanite audiences, whereas Xiao Ke's lower classed "cuteness" was deemed to be borderline whinging. Students in Lanzhou would not consider visiting the cinema to see *House Mania* but had enjoyed the film and would agree to watch it online for free. Academics in Lanzhou and middle-aged professionals in Taiyuan were also negative about watching the film at the cinema. As these audiences believed the houses featured in the film (low-end properties in Beijing) would be of "little interest to their social and professional networks", they agreed they would not recommend the film to friends and colleagues. Academics in Lanzhou understood the film to have been pitched at audiences below their social stratum.

Audiences were asked what class they understood Yingming and Xiao Ke to be from and they unanimously responded that the young couple were from the "lower class", albeit rural migrant workers used their hands to indicate lower class as they lacked the class terminology to categorise the characters in this manner. This being the case, it is possible that young male urbanites in Beijing who were inadvertently categorised by their peers as the lower end of the class spectrum may have perceived this to be a judgement on their own class predicaments. This, as well as the production values, may have also explained their particularly lukewarm responses to *House Mania*.

Lanzhou, Taiyuan and Beijing discussion groups consisted of audiences who owned property and audiences who did not. A dynamic among audiences similar to the behaviour in discussion groups for *Let the Bullets Fly* could be observed when audiences who were homeowners (or anticipated one day owning a home) spoke with confidence about China's housing market and the market's representation in *House Mania*, while audiences who did not own property withdrew from the discussion. This was not age specific, as the change in body language among non-homeowners was observed both among mature audiences in Taiyuan and young adults in Beijing. It should be noted, though, that non-homeowners still believed that *House Mania* was positive about homeownership, so pervasive is the homeownership discourse to everyday life in China. Furthermore, the defensive behaviour observed within urban discussion groups was *not* observed in groups consisting of rural migrant worker audiences in Nanjing or Hangzhou – neither towards others who owned land in their hometown, nor towards urbanite homeowners. As homeownership was considered an achievement of "hard work", migrant worker audiences treated homeowners with respect. Accordingly, homeownership in *House Mania*'s narrative took on different meanings for differently classed audiences. For audiences in urban areas, homeownership was perceived as an advantage of the fortunate; for audiences of rural origins, homeownership was a sign of personal and deserved achievement.

"没车没房没戏" "No car, no house, no potential"

Luigi Tomba (2011: 193) begins his chapter about the relationship between China's middle classes and homeownership by quoting a demand often prominently featured in personal classifieds: "Must have car and house". Yet Tomba does not mention that typically it is women who stipulate these requirements of men – not men of women, as a Chinese study of personal classifieds has reported is the case (Dong and Yao 2011). Indeed, the conclusion that Dong and Yao reach is that middle class men in particular will be the hardest pressed to find a suitable partner because of this homeownership obligation. When Xiao Ke's mother shoots the above comment "No house, no car, no potential" in Yingming's direction with a look of maternal disdain, no audience member can be confused about her sentiments towards Xiao Ke's choice of future life partner. Although Xiao Ke's mother delivers this prediction to the fictional character of Yingming, if the audiences in this chapter are indicative of broader Chinese thinking, she spoke the minds of the greater majority of Chinese parents with an interest in their daughter's future. Simultaneously, Xiao Ke's mother also confirmed for every young man and his family, who do not own a car or a house, that his future likewise holds little potential. Despite being humorously portrayed, *House Mania* from the outset establishes that a man's ability to provide housing determines his class position and, by extension, marriageability.

Whether it be as "castrated sexuality ... repressed by tradition and history" (Cui 2012: 502), brotherhood and filial piety to the patriarchal line and the nation-state (Berry and Farquhar 2006), or symbolism of colonial resistance in the martial arts films of Bruce Lee, Jackie Chan and Jet Li (Szeto 2011; Yu 2012), analysis of masculinity in Chinese cinema has typically complemented Kam Louie's (2002: 83) dyad of traditional Chinese masculinity: *wen-wu* (文-武), i.e. intellectual (civil, *wen*) and physical (military, *wu*) prowess. Yet, what is rarely mentioned is the relationship Louie in fact draws between the *wen-wu* dyad and man's claim to class positioning. As Louie explains, *wen-wu* is

a continuum along which masculinity can be correlated with class. . . . Those with more *wen* belong to a higher class, but having minimum *wu* is better than no masculinity at all. And to be a really powerful man, it is essential to have both *wen* and *wu*.

106 *House Mania*

Yet, does the *wen-wu* dyad effectively reflect Chinese masculinity's relationship to class in films set in contemporary Chinese society? *House Mania* and audience reception to the film suggests that a man's masculinity is now judged by a triad of factors: 文–武–产 (*wen-wu-chan*). No longer is man's class judged by merely civility (professional employment) and physical prowess (attractiveness), but also ownership of and access to property (homeownership). For this is how Yingming's weaknesses (unemployment, *wen* and physical inferiority, *wu*) are used to explain his lack of homeownership (*chan*) and thus his marriageability and masculinity crisis in present-day urban Beijing.

The film opens with Yingming working as a lifeguard at a swimming pool. Panic-stricken women squeal in alarm for Yingming to rescue a child struggling to stay afloat. Yingming frantically throws floating devices to the drowning child as he simultaneously resists the force of five distressed women trying to push him into the water to save the child. He is eventually overpowered by the bikini-clad women, upon which the camera cuts to Yingming being made redundant at the revelation that he, in fact, cannot swim. The scenario is set: Yingming is a man who is physically unable to save woman or child, and hence lacking physical might, or *wu* (武). Subsequently, the audience is made aware that Yingming has been hiding his employment as a lifeguard from his girlfriend, Xiao Ke, and has been pretending that he is a surgeon. Now unemployed, Yingming turns to driving an illegal taxi, or "black taxi", to make ends meet. The audiences see Yingming sneakily donning his white lab jacket in order to meet Xiao Ke at the hospital "after work" to keep up appearances. The reason for his inability to secure more prestigious employment is that Yingming never completed high school, never attended university and has two police arrest records for social disturbance. As such, Yingming is proven to also lack civility and intellectual credibility. Yingming's lack of *wen* and *wu* is proposed as to why Yingming has no property, or *chan*.

In introducing Yingming this way, Yingming's subsequent housing speculation that is the feature of the film's narrative functions to depict him as useful and entrepreneurial. This is a message to male audiences who lack the *wen-wu* advantage of their privileged counterparts that they, like Yingming, should take responsibility for their masculinity crisis. As migrant worker HM22 confirmed,

> You don't look for a man whose parents bought him his house and car. He may not be intelligent enough to be able to support you in the future. You want an intelligent man who can work things out, like Yingming.

In reality, audience responses to *House Mania* suggested that young Chinese males in a similar position to Yingming, who do not have such opportunities to improve themselves in a society riddled with inequalities, would not be as warmly received. Only 4 of the 38 group discussants voiced their agreeability to the idealistic morality of love conquering all challenges, which *House Mania* loosely suggests in its plot resolution of the young couple who are content to marry without homeownership. The remaining audience members pragmatically reasoned that in reality it would not be the case that a young couple (more so the young female) would agree to being homeowner-"less" at the time of marriage.

When asked if Xiao Ke's mother's comments were particularly exaggerated, audiences in Lanzhou, Taiyuan and all rural migrant workers supported Xiao Ke's mother's position. The following comments are provided at length to reflect the momentum of support for her that audiences had:

> A marriage cannot be realised without a residence, no matter how much the couple love each other. Although the film has a comic and idealistic conclusion, I think it is far from reality. Young people will only consider marriage after having bought property.
>
> (HM20)

> If the man has the means to provide a house, then he should.
>
> (HM28)

> Ninety-nine percent of the time, the responsibility of buying is the man's. I have a daughter who is not married yet, and if she does get married, I will encourage her to choose a man that has an ability to buy a house. We assisted my son to organise a house, but will not our daughter.
>
> (HM35)

> We have a daughter and we covered most of the payment for the property. But ours is a special case. He purchased their property in the US, so we purchased the property in Taiyuan.
>
> (HM34)

> Absolutely, all men require a house to marry.
>
> (HM27)

> There is no choice but to buy a house [in order to get married].
>
> (HM12)

> I will try to buy a house when I have a stable income as I can appreciate my girlfriend's thoughts on this. I have not seen any case, though, even people older than me that have purchased a house without support from their family.
>
> (HM5)

And among migrant workers in Hangzhou and Nanjing:

> Nowadays, if a young couple gets married, there must be a house. That is the case for most marriages, and if you do not have a house, there is a possibility that you will face divorce in the future.
>
> (HM23)

108   *House Mania*

> Even if the girl is willing to get married without a house and car, her parents will not agree. If we do not buy a house now, it is unrealistic to leave the task to our son.
>
> (HM24)

> As for our local customs, the house is a necessity before marriage, because the man must provide a better standard of living for the girl. As for owning a car . . . that is not as important. We all ride motorbikes.
>
> (HM7)

> If I had a girlfriend, I would be quite agreeable with the requirements her family raise. We might not think it is important, but the girl's parents will think it is important. Chinese people are all pretty much the same.
>
> (HM9)

> For our generation we do not think it is so important, but for older generations, they believe it is more secure to have a house. And if you have a house and a better income you will not live with so much difficulty.
>
> (HM10)

> This is the most important factor for a young couple's marriage.
>
> (HM26)

> It depends on the couple. When we got married we did not have a house but at the very least you need a place to live. If you work hard, you will have these things later on.
>
> (HM22)

Opinions towards the mother's comments only differed among the young urbanites in Beijing. Female audiences here displayed a slightly more understanding attitude to Yingming's plight, although it should be noted that this could have been out of sensitivity towards their male counterparts in the discussion who were part of their friendship circle. As their male peers had declared their weakened economic positions, they were careful to answer diplomatically. Although making assuring comments that the quality of their relationship with their boyfriend was the most important factor for them, these young female audiences employed the language of "what their parents would want" or spoke in the third person to conclude with comments that nonetheless hinted at approval of cultural obligations for males to provide:

> For me it is not that important, but it is important for my parents. If my boyfriend does not have a house, *my parents* will feel that it would be unreliable for me to marry him . . . but it would not be a big problem for me to marry him. All parents' attitudes towards their children and their safety are the same.

The question of a male's homeownership is largely based on concern about a stable life for their daughter in the future.

(HM3)

As long as I am happy and can get along with my boyfriend, it should not matter so much because I am the one who is marrying him. The way of life, though, whether you have or do not have a house, will definitely be different.

(HM4)

HM2 had property purchased by her parents under her name, but her opinion still rested on the understanding that the male should be able to provide for the household in the form of rent "at the bare minimum". HM6 in Beijing (a lower earner of the group), expressed a fairly disheartening outlook to his romantic prospects and lowered self-worth as a result:

The girl may want to have a house and whatever other needs, but I have to rent. I just simply will not have her as a girlfriend.

(HM6)

Yingming is not the only male character whose masculinity is in a state of crisis in *House Mania* due to homeownership. Homeownership in fact affects the majority of male characters in the film. Third Uncle, who is unable to sell his property, claims the dragon tattoos on his chest have been turned to "mere shrimps" after his decade-long struggle to sell his apartment. Another young male has employed Yingming's services at the insistence of his girlfriend, who feels it is inconvenient to have his parents living with them. She talks over the boyfriend in the meeting with Xiao Ke and he is seen to comply with her expectations of comfort. A single mother, whose son is completing the entrance exams, claims to have left her husband, who gambles on Mahjong all day long. Despite the less than ideal location and the intrusive noise of trains that pass the apartment's window, the noise's ability to keep her son awake and focused on his studies is better than "any gambling father". All of these characters are juxtaposed to the suggested virility of Xiao Ke's wealthy customer, who at the very beginning of the film buys Xiao Hei's (Yingming's best friend) apartment to house a mistress for his pleasure without even needing to see the apartment.

As class has been linked to the marital prospects of Chinese men as far back as the Tang and Ming dynasties (Telford 1992), *House Mania*'s confirmation that class and marriage are still very much deeply intertwined in China is no revelation. Yet the film suggests that if a man does not have homeownership it must be that he cannot afford it, as homeownership is simply what "everyone does" now, rather than being a conscious choice not to invest. A failure to invest is an issue of the man's capacities as an individual, not indicative of the broader economic structure that from the outset places him at a disadvantage to his fellow wealthier male.

110   *House Mania*

"Know the enemy, yourself, the law and the rumours": the property market in *House Mania*

You-Tien Hsing (2010: 213) cites figures that indicate: "Between 2000 and 2007, about 14,000 cadres were issued warnings by the Communist Party or under criminal investigation for land-related charges." Endemic corruption is not surprising considering owners of real estate development companies, construction firms and real estate companies have been revealed to be children of high-ranking officials who have "relied on illegal or improper connections with officials for their business success" (Zang 2008: 65). This reality did not escape two audience members, HM17 and HM20, who believed that *House Mania* was a negative reflection of China's housing market:

> I am relatively negative about China's real estate market, for I do not have my own property to live in, and do not plan to buy one. Since I cannot buy, I rent. From a macro-market point of view, this is not a market. Ordinary people cannot participate like speculators do, as they have neither capital nor internal information. As for regulating the house prices, the government has the last word, and there is a difference in attitude of central and provincial governments. Housing price is irrelevant to "The People", because the property owners are all the powerful and the rich. But at the end of the day, the government owns the land. The government initially claimed all people owned the land, but in reality it was nationalised. Of course we are not supposed to say so, but that is the case.
>
> (HM17)

HM20, a more senior professor and homeowner continued:

> This film reflects two patterns of the real estate market: 1. Overheated, 2. Unregulated. Why? Firstly, throughout Chinese history the majority of Chinese people lived in the countryside. Urban centres developed along with social progress. More and more people want to live in the city, leading to an expansion and overheating of the urban housing market. In addition, most people use real estate as a means of capital speculation, which further promotes an overheated real estate market. Secondly, real estate as capital is most likely to be possessed by political elites. Officials or dignitaries may own several houses, whereas other people may find it impossible to own a property due to their lack of resources. The ability to own multiple properties increases with the rise of the socio-economic level of the owner. This phenomenon forces up house prices to the detriment of the many and exacerbates market chaos. This is why this film I believe actually has a negative message.

Yet these responses were from senior social scientists and their concern for the motives behind *House Mania*'s narrative starkly contrasted with the optimism shown by the rest of the film's audiences from the other less privileged classes.

House Mania 111

Other audiences were in fact assured by the film's conclusion that homeownership was important, because they (or their children) did not want to end up homeowner-less like Yingming and Xiao Ke. Privileged audiences even saw the theme of inequality and corruption in the housing market in *House Mania* as a positive warning to viewers to be cautious; not a reason to be deterred from investing or demanding greater protections and transparency for investors within the housing market. As HM35 in Taiyuan shared his experience of being cheated of 20,000 RMB when buying his property explained:

> I feel it is good for a director to present a film like *House Mania*. The title suggests it is about the housing market and all the tricks in it. In particular, corrupt public officials, either in their collaboration with agents, or their encouragement of this type of devious behaviour by agents. *House Mania* is a warning that house buyers must be cautious in every aspect of society. We must be cautious about doing anything in this corrupt society, do not be cheated!

Although HM35's comments refer to the corruption in China's housing market, *House Mania* in fact never suggests public officials are behind Yingming's deception. Indeed, deception is perceived as something that Yingming, an individual, engages in to "resolve" his masculinity crisis, and is by extension forgivable. Although audiences agreed that corruption and deception were endemic to the housing market in China, they understood that *House Mania* encouraged investors simply to be wary of individual traders within the market – only HM17 and HM20 believed the film was indicative of the broader structure of the market. Even though audiences agreed that swindlers are a feature of the Chinese urban housing market and were disapproving of this fact, the humour employed in Yingming's deception resulted in audiences (including HM17 and HM20) applauding Yingming's approach to deceiving his potential buyers.

There was no audience member who claimed that he or she did not find humour in Yingming's deception. Rather, audiences expressed empathy for Yingming's plight to impress Xiao Ke's mother, and no audience member believed that his actions were explicitly wrong. Love was the reason Yingming deceived his investors. *House Mania* quite clearly sought vindication for Yingming's deception when the narrative takes a reflective detour that sees Yingming and Xiao Ke return to the investors they have deceived in a moment of moral uncertainty about their actions. In doing so, the protagonists find that the new homeowner have each found themselves overwhelmingly satisfied (despite the odds) with their new homes that they were swindled into buying. The old parents have found a sense of community with the hordes of urban stragglers who live next door; and the single mother is very pleased how the train keeps her son awake to study for his university entrance exams. *House Mania* explicitly excuses deception and corruption as a pragmatic means to an end, and a small price to pay for an improvement to the lifestyles everyone has enjoyed through homeownership.

Yingming's dedication to provide for Xiao Ke was thus considered admirable by all audiences. Partly this may have been because Yingming and Xiao Ke's investors are not the only victims in *House Mania*, in fact everyone is. The protagonists are victims of cultural discourses that discriminate against economically weakened men and their families; the poor who crowd into a single room are unable to afford better living conditions; homeowners are desperate to be rid of underperforming or uncomfortable properties that they acquired during the reform period; and lastly, Yingming's parents fall victim to local government plans to build a subway through their *hutong*, which renders the land their *siheyuan* is built on worthless. No character has a particularly good experience in the housing market, and as such, no one is specifically to blame for the difficulties that characterise the market. Deception therefore, is simply an obstacle that investors need to pragmatically avoid.

Audiences were asked which of Yingming's deceptions they believed was the smartest or the funniest. Female students in Lanzhou enjoyed the clip where a young female and her mother in an apartment block's elevator pass Yingming's friends masquerading as famous directors to appeal to the young woman's desire for social distinction and fame (Figure 6.2). HM17 in Lanzhou enjoyed Xiao Hei being "cured" of his paraplegia (Figure 6.3), and HM4 thought the businessman committing suicide from the opposite office block was funny (Figure 6.4). Young males (university students and rural migrant workers) thought funniest the scene where Yingming dons a biohazard suit and announces traces of the H1N1 virus in an apartment block so as to empty a studio apartment of its migrant workers and urban poor who had crammed together for cheap rent (Figure 6.5). After the tenants flee, the apartment Yingming is trying to sell next door is sufficiently peaceful during the home inspection by his potential buyers, making the apartment appear to be located in a respectable neighbourhood. Lastly, academics in Lanzhou judged Yingming masquerading as an elderly scholar living in a downbeat area to trick a mother seeking housing for her son to prepare for the competitive university entrance exam as the cleverest deception Yingming concocted (Figure 6.6).

Frames of deception

Figure 6.2 "Many film directors live in this building"

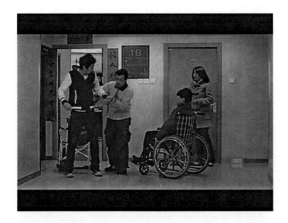

Figure 6.3 Xiao Hei is "cured"

Figure 6.4 "All companies that have rented this space have made it to the Fortune 500 list"

Figure 6.5 Yingming announces an evacuation due to the H1N1 virus

Figure 6.6 Yingming as an aging university entrance examiner

This said, *House Mania* engendered a mixture of both idealistic and exasperated opinions from less-privileged audiences in Beijing. HM5, a self-employed videographer who was hoping to expand his business and work towards owning property, stated, "I think the film is positive about real estate, it gives people hope. People may not have thought about selling their house, but once they've seen the film, they might realise by selling one of their properties they can make money," to which HM4 retorted in frustration, "Anyone who wants to buy a house or apartment in China is crazy. The prices increase every day. No matter how much you earn you cannot afford to buy a house in order to sell it like they do in the film." This discussion came to a halt when the only audience member in Beijing whose parents had purchased an apartment under her name, HM2, stated, "The people who can afford to speculate in the property market in China are simply not people employed in common jobs." HM2's reference to "common" jobs left the group in a pregnant silence. "Common" in this context implied not only a lower status, but also lower wages. HM2's comment also implied that the middle class narrative of homeownership equated with an *uncommon* advantage – not with the common nature of the broad "middle of society" to which the middle class narrative typically refers.

For young adult audiences, homeownership was something they could observe taking place around them on a daily basis but which excluded them unless their parents assisted. In this way, homeownership was a somewhat abstract notion. Knowing the "enemy, themselves, the law or the rumours" of the property market was very far from their immediate realities, although they understood homeownership inevitably to be important to their quality of life in the future. Their sense making of the film's narrative, though, did seem to be influenced by where they lived. For students in Lanzhou who lived within a housing market more favourably priced, the antagonism present in Beijing towards the ideals the film espouses, and to a lesser degree in Taiyuan (as audiences were of mixed generations and therefore peer comparison was not a defining feature of the discussion), was far less noticeable. Arguably, where an audience member lived and her or his experience of that particular property market compounded that member's feelings of agreeability or cynicism towards the film. When the young adults in Beijing were asked if they would consider investing (or living in order to invest) in Lanzhou to take advantage of cheaper options than that which Beijing presented them, the room burst into laughter and HM4 responded in English: "Hell no!" The audiences in Beijing confirmed that despite the enormity of the challenge they faced ahead of them to achieve homeownership as portrayed in *House Mania*, leaving Beijing to do so was not an option. Beijing urbanites were frustrated by their predicaments but would not trade their cosmopolitan lives for the economic advantages of homeownership their counterparts had in other cities across China. They would prefer to be a Yingming, and hope for an understanding Xiao Ke to appear.

Where and how to live?

On a map, Beijing is contained within six concentric ring roads. Within the third ring road alone (established as early as the mid-1990s), the architectural sprawl is a visually interesting mix of buildings both very modern and reminiscent of a bygone era. This includes the historical dwellings, *siheyuan* located in Beijing's *hutongs* and apartments deemed liveable for subsidised sales to former work unit employees. There are the properties redeveloped (expedient high-rise apartment buildings) and built during the 1990s when work unit welfare housing deemed too dilapidated to transfer to private ownership was torn down and residents relocated if they could not afford the newer dwellings. Wealthier residents could then purchase and move into the city centre. Lastly, throughout the 2000s the addition of luxury apartment blocks and commercial office spaces with all the living comforts expected by China's new rich have come to characterise Beijing's inner city district. Visually, this makes for an architectural mix of old and new urban spaces and, as such, has been and still is the inspiration for numerous cultural producers such as artists, theatre and film producers, who have sought to document and make sense of the city's physical changes and accompanying social transformation, as Yomi Braester's book *Painting the City Red* (2010) relays in detail. For residents in Beijing, the real estate market and homeownership "has a social function: to mark status and support new modern, urban identities" (Fleischer 2007: 289), and *House Mania*'s fictional protagonist, Yingming, is just one male trying to outsmart the odds stacked against him to achieve this new ideal.

Audiences were asked which property in *House Mania* they would be willing to live in. This was to gauge their sense of self-distinction, keeping in mind that early in each group discussion, audiences had judged Yingming and Xiao Ke to be of a lower class – and hence, living in lower class areas in Beijing. Responses revealed that class mattered to the taste and the willingness to live in the properties presented in the film. Bachelor students and academics in Lanzhou and homeowners in Taiyuan responded that they would live in *none* of the homes presented in the film. Two audience members in Taiyuan mentioned the renovated *siheyuan* of the esteemed gentleman who plans to purchase Yingming's parents' rundown

116 *House Mania*

siheyuan, because they appreciated the "historical value of the property" (his house is adorned with calligraphy and pottery to indicate his degree of *suzhi*). Aside from these two preferences, there was a clear rejection of all other living quarters (including all references to Yingming's parents' *siheyuan* considered to be outmoded living) by audiences in Lanzhou (students and academics) and homeowners in Taiyuan. The esteemed scholar's *siheyuan* was again nominated as fashionable living by HM1 and HM3 in Beijing, who currently lived in a renovated *siheyuan* together. HM6, HM4 and HM5 noted that they lived in apartments similar to those being sold in the film and, as such, thought that the majority of the apartments one could "easily live in", although this was far from declaring a preference for the homes depicted. Rather the homes were seen as a means to an end.

Audiences in Hangzhou and Nanjing were the exception to the rule. Rural migrant workers in Nanjing indicated that they preferred none of the apartments that Yingming was selling, but not because they believed the properties to be beneath them. Rather, these audiences looked for different qualities in the homes presented. In contrast, rural migrant workers chose the open plan room with the hordes of misfits who Yingming tricks into evacuating with the threat of the H1N1 virus. "The room is like our dormitories now" explained HM22 about her colleagues' choice. These workers lived in on-campus dormitory accommodation provided to them as employees of Nanjing University. Rural migrant workers in Hangzhou showed a similar preference for living quarters that promoted a sense of community. This group chose Yingming's parents' rundown *siheyuan*, because they believed that the quadrangle-style living meant that neighbours could "get to know each other" and "not feel lonely" and that for many neighbours it would be "easier to have dinner together". Similarly, rural migrant workers in Hangzhou were co-sharing their bedrooms in groups of two or three in privately rented apartments in urban Hangzhou.

Current living standards could be seen to directly inform preferences for living quarters amongst audiences who watched *House Mania*. Privileged audiences defined themselves by not liking any of the properties; less-privileged urbanites approached the properties with pragmatic reasoning; and rural migrant workers chose properties that placed importance on the communal and social opportunities of the living quarters' environment – properties that were presented as the least desirable by the film – regardless of how living in such a home may socially distinguish them. Rural migrant workers did not express a desire or need to "live upwards" from the properties present in *House Mania* like their privileged counterparts. Moreover, they did not seem concerned by the suggestion that they were choosing properties associated with lower class Chinese, or perceive this to be a negative issue in the case that they *did* understand the connotations the properties had for such a class distinction. As the next section discusses, this appeared to be due to rural migrant workers engaging with *House Mania*'s narrative from a different reference point to their urban peers. Rural migrant workers understood their interest in homeownership lay in rural or fringe areas of urban centres. While urbanites may perceive this to be a disadvantage, for the rural migrant worker audience member, *House Mania*'s narrative confirmed that access to rural land was in fact to their advantage. As such, a rethinking of how privilege was interpreted by migrant worker audiences of *House Mania* is worthwhile.

Rethinking "privilege"

Rural migrant workers understood that the morality of *House Mania* was to "work hard to achieve one's goals" – in this case, homeownership. Audiences in Nanjing and Hangzhou discussed homeowners with a notable degree of respect in contrast to their similarly aged urbanite peers in Beijing. Rather than voicing complaints against an unfair system (either governmental or vocational) that restricted their and their friends' attachment to land in rural areas due to the household registration system, these audiences placed emphasis on a good work ethic as a means of changing their current situations, and were far from pessimistic about their homeownership outlooks. As explained by HM10 in Hangzhou, "The film is quite motivating for people to work harder to buy houses for their loved ones." And in Nanjing:

> The film is a motivation that everyone should work hard for what they are entitled to later on in life. They should not wait for things to happen. You cannot cheat, but you should work hard, do not be selfish, but consider other people.
>
> (HM22)

For a middle-aged married couple in Nanjing, working hard to purchase property within the fringes of urban areas was considered worthwhile only to gain access through residence to better schooling opportunities for their children:

> Even if we did consider buying a house [in an urban area], we are buying for our children, otherwise we would just go back to our hometown where we have land.
>
> (HM23)

His wife concluding,

> The next generation may not be able to endure the hardships as easily as us. If you do not study well you cannot do well in society. So we must work for them.
>
> (HM24)

David Goodman (2014: 123) notes that the "family farm is the security blanket for the migrant worker[s] and represents both their fall back in case of unemployment and their plan of retirement." What he does not mention is that access to a family farm may also increase a young rural man's confidence in his marital prospects. In the case of the young males in Hangzhou, there was a sense of pride about the

118 *House Mania*

personal effort expended in the building and renovating of their family properties, which they retreated to when they required respite from urban working life. The option of returning to one's property in their rural hometown for marriage did not concern these younger males in Hangzhou. In fact, having left school at very early stages of their teenage years, their identities as homeowners and experiences with real estate came much earlier than to their urban counterparts:

> Cheating in housing sales is very common. Sometimes you pass a house in the city with "shabby house" or "the agents profited from our hard-earned money" written on them in protest, but the writing is removed after the matter is resolved. For myself, my family built a home on my family's land for me in 2003. It was very cheap [to build], about 80,000–100,000 RMB. Nowadays, with 120,000 RMB you can build a two-story house because materials are still cheap. There are many people building new houses in my village.
>
> (HM8)

And as his work colleague confirmed,

> If you want to have a house in your own village you normally build it yourself, but in another area you have to buy it. If you have money and you are planning to live in another city, you normally buy a house.
>
> (HM9)

In light of the couple's plight in *House Mania*, migrant worker audiences in Hangzhou and Nanjing expressed sympathy towards the younger generation of urbanites without access to land like they had. While HM7 in Hangzhou explained it was "not a joke, we like to return to our village when we have had enough of the city", in Nanjing, HM23 explained, "The pressure is greatest for university graduates. They have just started working and do not earn much. We can return to our hometown, it is a different concern for university graduates." In one of the rare instances in this project, rural migrant workers could be observed to perceive their life situations as *advantaged* in comparison to their urban counterparts through watching popular Chinese cinema.

Although *House Mania* was arguably aimed at soothing the frustrations of young urban males who lacked homeownership, the narrative's resolution confirmed rather for rural migrant workers that their positions were better than those of young men in urban areas because they had access to rural land, and because the opportunities for building were so much cheaper than in urban areas. These young men's confidence in their ability to provide a home in order to marry was also evidently greater than that of male audiences who arguably had the privilege of an urban household registration and maybe even tertiary qualifications. If a crisis of masculinity was the impetus behind *House Mania*'s production, audience discussions about the film indicated that this was a perceived crisis of *urban*, not rural, males – the presence of peasants with grossly exaggerated wealth at their disposal serving to compound this reality of a suggested urban-only male crisis.

Peasants (apparently) in the urban housing market

The respect shown by migrant worker audiences for urban homeownership was interestingly not mirrored by urban audiences towards the peasants who approach Yingming to assist their village in speculating on the Beijing property market. At the peak of Yingming and Xiao Ke's speculating successes, a village head from northeast China seeks Yingming out to engage him on behalf of its residents who have collectively pooled together funds in order to speculate on Beijing's property market. Offering gifts of ginseng and a chicken to Yingming, the village leader flatters Yingming by telling him that peasants deep in the villages of northeast China have heard about his success and hope that his speculating can acquire the village wealthy returns. Yingming asks in surprise, "Are they that rich in the villages that they can invest in Beijing?" to which the village leader with a serious expression responds, "Their fates are in your hands," implying that the response to this is in fact, "yes".

When the peasants arrive in Beijing by minibus, they are characterised in a familiar manner to the milk factory migrant worker, Niugeng, in *Lost on Journey*. Eating corn, the peasants wear rural fashions and project a wide-eyed fascination and ignorance towards the urban space that they are seeing for the first time (again, stereotypical devices employed to identify that these characters are from rural areas – and confirmed by audiences as symbolic of the peasant character). Yingming's role is to coordinate their group purchase of apartments in a complex currently under construction on the very outskirts of Beijing, or "almost Hebei province", as he describes the location on his first inspection. Xiao Ke expresses her concern about the absence of construction workers on site but is assured by the construction manager that the workers are on their lunch break. Despite these uncertainties, Yingming persists to encourage the off-the-plan purchase to the peasants who place complete trust in Yingming. It is only at the point of signing contracts that Xiao Ke discovers from documents unearthed at the last minute that in fact, a year earlier, the construction site had encountered financial difficulties and construction had stalled. Yingming cancels the purchase at the very last moment, and is declared by the village leader a benefactor of the villagers for showing "an act of conscience" because "honesty has no price". Only one audience member, HM20 in Lanzhou, hesitated in his approval of this subplot in *House Mania*'s narrative. HM20 cautioned, "Most peasants cannot afford to buy a property in urban areas. Only a minority can. There is a disparity in economic development between different rural regions too." Despite this, younger urban audiences (Lanzhou students and Beijing) and even professionals in Taiyuan expressed strong convictions about the economic capacities of peasants to invest in the urban real estate market.

Data are difficult to access in order to verify the claims of strong economic capacities that peasants have to speculate on urban property markets to which *House Mania* alludes. Yet, some indication of this phenomenon is provided by the 2007 China Household Income Project (CHIP) data. The data account for only a small degree of homeownership in urban areas by rural Chinese. The percentage in 2002 was 7.2 per cent and in 2007 decreased to 3.9 per cent (Sato et al. 2013: 92).

120 *House Mania*

The 2007 CHIP data also indicate an increase in private rentals by rural migrant workers and accordingly a reduction in collective housing rental arrangements (such as dormitories and living arrangements similar to where Yingming declares potential H1N1 contamination). These statistics, though, do not indicate a manic surge of wealthy peasants with armloads of cash in the manner depicted in *House Mania*, or explain why audiences (particularly younger urbanites) were so defiant in their convictions of a surplus of wealthy peasants investing in urban areas when the data do not support this thinking. Arguably, the subplot of the wealthy peasants served to exaggerate the crisis of masculinity among young men in urban areas, playing on prejudices that if the lowly classed peasant can afford property, so should the urban male. The male audience member who believes he shares class-based attributes with Yingming's character is henceforth informed that his social status is below that of an uncouth and uncivilised peasant if he is unable to invest.

Although this subplot of the film could be interpreted as an effort on the part of the filmmakers to depict the peasant's willingness to trust Yingming as a vulnerability that should not be taken advantage of by those in the urban areas, comments made about these characters in *House Mania*'s narrative indicated that this was not how they were received. This may be due to the portrayal of the peasants as eager to invest, money hungry and ill-informed in their naïve business manner. One peasant, Baldy, is particularly comical in his initial wish to buy the Bird's Nest (the landmark stadium of Beijing's 2008 Olympic Game grounds) when he arrives in Beijing. His enthusiasm is emphasised when he rushes his series of inquiries about his investment, gushing, "Once I have bought this apartment, when can I sell it?" followed closely by, "When I resell it, how much will the apartment be worth?" In *House Mania*'s credits, Baldy features once more, returning to Beijing with bundles of 100 RMB notes piled high in his arms (Figure 6.7). The camera pans to show Baldy's 360-degree view of the high rise apartment blocks around him, as he claims "I will buy this building!" in a manner that Augusta Palmer

Figure 6.7 "Baldy" arrives with his cash to buy property

House Mania 121

(2007: 181) describes as a cinematic device to indicate the "country bumpkin" who has plans to be literally "upwardly mobile". The portrayal of the peasant eager for easy profits in *House Mania*, and the visibility of the country bumpkin with cash piled high in his arms, appeared to pander to urban audience's prejudices towards rural Chinese's economic capacities, which they were quick to confirm exceeded those of urban Chinese. As HM4 in Beijing commented,

> They are the new rich of the village. They are like that in real life. It does not parody them. It actually makes them look *better* than they really are. The rich peasants are much richer than us. Their economic status is much higher than ours.

When urban audiences were asked whether they understood peasants to be as wealthy as they were depicted in *House Mania*, audiences unanimously agreed, and not one audience member believed that the characterisations satirised Chinese peasants in a derogatory manner. Similarly, audiences in Hangzhou and Nanjing were proud that rural Chinese were depicted as economically capable. HM25 in Nanjing stated in surprise at the question whether the portrayal was derogatory with, "So many peasants came to buy homes. It made peasants look really good!"

Migrant workers in Nanjing and Hangzhou had witnessed the economic improvement of fellow villagers and agreed that there were some very wealthy peasants. HM10 in Hangzhou, though, mused whether she and her peers were inferior to the wealthy peasants depicted in *House Mania* (this is despite having properties in their hometowns) because she did not have the cash that Baldy did. Rural migrant workers did not question the wealthy peasant character, because in their mind anything was possible with hard work. HM26 noted that she knew of two outskirt towns close to Nanjing that were full of peasant-purchased properties (similar to the new constructions alluded to by Yingming when he claims they are "almost in Hebei"). She elaborated:

> They are not renting these houses. They certainly own these houses. They want to earn money by buying and selling houses. If they are buying property, it is in the outskirts, though. The city centre cannot accommodate so many sales.

As *House Mania* films Baldy next to the iconic Bird's Nest, the film could easily confuse an audience unfamiliar with Beijing that in fact *House Mania*'s peasants are able to invest in Beijing proper. Audiences in Hangzhou and Nanjing did not consider that this portrayal of rural wealth might fuel prejudices among urban audiences towards rural Chinese. Urban audiences in contrast conjured up a variety of explanations for how peasants could have accrued so much surplus wealth in order to invest in urban property:

> A village where villagers live communally could be worth a few million RMB, so there is enough money to invest, and there may be resources in the village to gather for reinvestment.
>
> (HM28)

122   *House Mania*

> Even if bosses exploit the resources of a village, the villagers may also have a chance to benefit from the profits. The peasants cannot be ignored. There are many rich peasants now. China's peasants are earning lots these days.
>
> (HM34)

> They may have had large plots of land and the government purchased the land at a high price, and they do not know how to spend their money, so they come to the city to invest.
>
> (HM5)

A couple of audience members in Taiyuan did muse that the average peasant as characterised in *House Mania* may not be able to invest in property in Beijing. They believed that rural investors would more likely be owners of coalmines or other large ventures that earned them capital to invest. By depicting the peasants as "average" peasants, however, not village officials in positions of capital power, *House Mania* encouraged the understanding that the average peasant was comparatively privileged to the average urbanite. Urban audiences did not receive this suggestion favourably.

The impression created by the filmmakers of *House Mania* of the surge from rural to urban investment in China is undoubtedly exaggerated. Despite this poetic license on the part of the filmmakers, the exaggeration of regular peasants' wealth reinforced its conceptual possibility for audiences of every class. Most strongly this was the case for audience members who believed that they were disadvantaged in the property market as it currently stands. Rather than encouraging discussion about the need to protect rural investors in urban areas (particularly the exploitation of their willingness to invest in outskirt towns that hold lesser market value), *House Mania* appeared to clarify for privileged urban audiences the advantages regarding homeownership that rural Chinese have over their urban counterparts, exacerbating prejudices that already appear to exist among mainstream urban Chinese people. This time, though, the tension was not only between urban and rural Chinese, but between younger urban and rural men interested in homeownership to secure their marriageability in a competitive marriage market.

Normative social behaviour

House Mania cannot boast impressive commercial success or rest on a hope that word of mouth would ever assist the film becoming a cult classic in its post-exhibition stage as *Lost on Journey* did – especially if we consider the nature of audience feedback from the key consumers of China's popular cinema who stem from the privileged classes. With only migrant worker audiences agreeing to recommend the film to their social networks, which have already proven not to attend the cinema, *House Mania* is left destined for sporadic (if any) state television broadcasts and copies on the pirate DVD market. Despite this, *House Mania* is in fact an engaging film. Audiences were seen to be positive in their consumption of the film, and the film's contribution to the investigation into China's cinema of class is not without value.

Homeownership is central to understanding class, both for its relationship to capital growth and as a means of social distinction. The introduction of homeownership in China has disproportionately benefited some Chinese and not others. As was the case of the protagonist Yingming's parents' experience, whereby their *siheyuan* was assumed by the government in order for a subway line to be built, making their land suddenly worthless, homeownership in China is not entirely predictable. Chinese private property laws have still yet to relinquish the state's overriding claim to the land that individuals are buying and leasing. The property market takes place on the land at the behest of the Party-state's will and under its management. To date, millions of Chinese have been resettled from land that the Party-state has deemed desirable for infrastructure objectives, and continue to be as China develops. This process has taken place without clear laws related to the individuals' claims to their homes and resulted in instances of corruption and deception, as this film so quaintly captures. Homeownership in China can bring one great wealth, or conversely, deliver one to financial distress. *House Mania*'s title is thus quite aptly applied to the Chinese housing market that the film tries to depict.

What is most disconcerting is that *House Mania* was clearly targeted at China's lower classes, both male and female. This belief is supported by the production values the film employs and reiterated by audiences in their assessment of who the target audience was for the film. With the implication that a man is only worthy of marriage if he owns a home, *House Mania* exploits supposed "traditional" norms and the emotional responses of underprivileged men in an already competitive marriage market with depleted numbers of available women to encourage their investment. The film also ensures that young female audiences understand that these demands of men are acceptable. Lower classed men and their families however, are arguably China's least likely to have stable employment or the potential for professional mobility in their futures. With an unpredictable and "manic" housing market, as the title suggests, the question of why China's lower classed men would be an acceptable target for a film like *House Mania* can bring one to two conclusions: either (1) popular cinema is employed to conceptualise homeownership and investment by underprivileged urban males to provide them the opportunity to grow their wealth by making investment seem appealing as a "public duty" – after all, many Chinese have indeed profited greatly through the housing boom; or (2) popular cinema is involved in the propagation of a social narrative around homeownership for the benefit of those who build and sell these properties; to say nothing of the banks (chiefly state-owned) that provide the mortgages.

The argument exists that China's market economy requires a property market, as property ownership is central to any capitalist economy. The question must be asked, though, whether underprivileged males are the ideal targets for stimulating this investment – the sums of money this entails are significant and the labour economy is not so generous in terms of the ease in social mobility for these potential investors. If the attitudes expressed towards wealthy rural investors in

124 *House Mania*

these focus groups are anything to go by, tensions clearly have the potential to accelerate, as economically disadvantaged audiences were willing to turn their blame and prejudices on others who appeared to be "outside" competitors. While employing prejudices towards China's rural investors is one way in which commercially exhibited cinema can assist in diverting attentions from the inequalities of the housing policies the Party-state has implemented, how long this diversion can be maintained is yet to be seen. If the audience engagement with *House Mania* is anything to go by, as long as men believe that homeownership is their individual and gender-prescribed duty in order to marry, antagonism towards the powers that be appear safely negated. The pressures of homeownership lie for now safely with the individual Chinese male, his family and his extended social networks – and last of all, she who will accept his proposal for marriage, if at all.

Notes

1 Box office figure as of 16 July 2016 (Entgroup); approximate USD at historical exchange rate for 1 April 2011 (XE Currency); URL: http://www.cbooo.cn/m/587986/
2 Douban rating: 5.9/10 stars for 4,382 reviews. URL: http://movie.douban.com/subject/4960204/ (last accessed: 16 July 2016)

References

Berry, Chris, and Mary A. Farquhar. 2006. *China on Screen: Cinema and Nation*. New York: Columbia University Press.

Braester, Yomi. 2010. *Painting the City Red: Chinese Cinema and the Urban Contract*. Durham: Duke University Press.

Cui, Shuqin. 2012. The Returned of the Repressed: Masculinity and Sexuality Reconsidered. In *A Companion to Chinese Cinema*, edited by Yingjin Zhang, 499–517. West Sussex: Wiley-Blackwell.

Davis, Deborah. 2010. Guess Who Gets the House? Renegotiating Property Rights in Post-Socialist Urban China. *Modern China* XX (X): 1–30.

Dong, Jinyou (董金权), and Yao Cheng (姚成). 2011. *Ze'ou biaozhun: Ershiwunian de shanbian (1986–2010)* (Choice of Mate: Changes in 25 years, 1986–2010) [择偶标准: 二十五年的嬗变]. *Zhongguo qingnian yanjiu* [中国青年研究] 2: 73–78.

Fincher, Leta Hong. 2014. *Leftover Women: The Resurgence of Gender Inequality in China*. London: Zed Books.

Fleischer, Fredericke. 2007. "To Choose a House Means to Choose a Lifestyle." The Consumption of Housing and Class-Structuration in Urban China. *City & Society* 19 (2): 287–311.

Goodman, David. 2014. *Class in Contemporary China*. Cambridge: Polity.

Hsing, You-Tien. 2010. *The Great Urban Transformation: Politics of Land and Property in China*. Oxford and New York: Oxford University Press.

Louie, Kam. 2002. *Theorising Chinese Masculinity: Society and Gender in China*. Cambridge: Cambridge University Press.

Lu, Xiaoning. 2015. Villain Stardom in Socialist China: Chen Qiang and the Cultural Politics of Affect. *Journal of Chinese Cinemas* 9 (3): 223–238.

Palmer, Augusta. 2007. Scaling the Skyscraper: Images of Cosmopolitan Consumption in *Street Angel* (1937) and *Beautiful New World* (1998). In *The Urban Generation: Chinese Cinema and Society at the Turn of the Twenty-First Century*, edited by Zhen Zhang, 181–204. Durham and London: Duke University Press.

Sargeson, Sally. 2013. Gender as a Categorical Source of Property. In *Unequal China: The Political Economy and Cultural Politics of Inequality*, edited by Wanning Sun and Yingjie Guo, 168–183. Oxon and New York: Routledge.

Sato, Hiroshi, Terry Sicular, and Ximing Yue. 2013. Housing Ownership, Income, and Inequality in China, 2002–2007. In *Rising Inequality in China*, edited by Li Shi, Hiroshi Sato and Terry Sicular, 85–131. Cambridge: Cambridge University Press.

Szeto, Kin-Yan. 2011. *The Martial Arts Cinema of the Chinese Diaspora: Ang Lee, John Woo, and Jackie Chan in Hollywood*. Carbondale and Edwardsville: Southern Illinois University Press.

Telford, Ted A. 1992. Covariates of Men's Age at First Marriage: The Historical Demography of Chinese Lineages. *Population Studies* 46 (1): 19–35.

Tomba, Luigi. 2011. The Housing Effect: The Making of China's Social Distinctions. In *China's Emerging Middle Class: Beyond Economic Transformation*, edited by Cheng Li, 193–216. Washington, DC: Brookings Institute Press.

Yu, Sabrina Qiong. 2012. *Jet Li: Chinese Masculinity and Transnational Film Stardom*. Edinburgh: University of Edinburgh Press.

Zang, Xiaowei. 2008. Market Transition, Wealth and Status Claims. In *The New Rich in China: Future Rulers, Present Lives*, edited by David S. G. Goodman, 53–70. Oxon and New York: Routledge.

7 *The Piano in a Factory*
Suzhi, industrial heroes and the spectacle of poverty

Figure 7.1 Promotional film poster: *The Piano in a Factory*

128　*The Piano in a Factory*

《钢的琴》
(*gang de qin*)

The Piano in a Factory

Director: Zhang Meng (张猛)
Starring: Qianyuan Wang (王千源), Amanda Qin (秦海璐)
Box office: 6,526,000 RMB (USD 1,013,590)[1]
Exhibition: July–August 2011 (5 weeks)[2]

Synopsis

Set in Liaoning, northeast China, *The Piano in a Factory* (Zhang: 2011) follows the plight of a retrenched steel-factory worker, Chen Guilin, to build a piano in order to win custody of his daughter. With the absence of the universal welfare that the work unit system formerly provided to workers after the restructure of the SOEs which employed them, Guilin now makes ends meet performing at weddings and funerals in a brass band that is fronted by his sometimes-girlfriend, single mother Shu Xian. His wife, Xiao Ju, after migrating alone to an urban area in order to find work, has met a new man that has made his wealth from (allegedly) selling fake medicine, and has announced her desire for a divorce. Their young daughter, Xiao Yuan, claims that whoever is able to acquire a piano for her first, she will choose to live with. Chen Guilin, desperate for custody and control of Xiao Yuan's music education, tries to find a solution.

Unable to afford to buy a piano, Chen Guilin initially convinces his friends to help him steal a piano from the local school. When this fails, Chen Guilin recruits a group of colleagues from the former steelworks to assist him in building a piano for Xiao Yuan. There is history among the men; history that often comes to the surface. Each man has his own economic and family battles that he is privately trying to overcome in order to survive in the post-economically reformed environment, where the "system" is no longer there to fall back on. Reunited, the men find solace in returning to their labouring roots, nostalgic for the collective atmosphere of the bygone era, all the while painfully aware that it cannot be a permanent return and that China is not as it used to be. The men successfully engineer a piano made entirely from steel. Despite this, Chen Guilin concedes his custody of Xiao Yuan to Xiao Ju. Meanwhile, the smoke stacks that once proudly symbolised the industrial hub where Chen Guilin lives are imploded to make room for developments in line with the new priorities of the nation and the region. The forgotten industrial heroes of Mao's China watch on and contemplate the predicament they now find themselves in.

Introduction

The Piano in a Factory would not usually be included in a discussion about commercial popular cinema – or at least not in the "classical narrative" (Bordwell

1979) or the Hollywood formula sense of the films discussed in previous chapters. *The Piano in a Factory* was produced with little expectation of mainstream release across Mainland China but was a welcome outcome when the permission was granted (interview with Kam 2013). The film's presence on the international film circuit prior to being released within China, and the premise of the narrative being the sensitive topic of poverty and class disadvantage of China's "retrenched workers" (*xiagang gongren*, 下岗工人) – not usually the fodder of commercial big screen narratives – supports this thinking. Nevertheless, *The Piano in a Factory* received approval from the ideologically attentive and commercially attuned SARFT (now SAPPRFT) for an impressive five weeks of mainstream theatre exhibition – longer periods of exposure than the two family-friendly audience pleasers *Lost on Journey* (4 weeks) and *House Mania* (2 weeks) and in cinemas that were mainstream cinema chains, not only arthouse cinemas catering for audiences with refined tastes. This was despite the film's low box office takings, particularly in northeast China where the film is set (Kam 2013). Although *The Piano in a Factory* falls short of being categorised as "arthouse", it has nonetheless been recognised as an "artistic" film by industry critics (Adams 2010), and hence *The Piano in a Factory*'s extended mainstream exhibition despite the film's weak commercial appeal and atypical mainstream production values is worthy of consideration within the context of China's cinema of class.

One sensitive to the nostalgia of China's past and the inequalities borne out of economic reforms may be inclined to understand *The Piano in a Factory*, as Tongyun Shi (2012: 105) claims, as a "man's film" that brings "dignity to the working class community, the film is an elegy for a glorious time past", and thus a "funny, lightweight comedy". Audiences receptive to *The Piano in a Factory* however, were privileged female urbanites, and their engagement with the film's narrative was lacking the warmth of nostalgia that Shi (2012) proposes. For these women, protagonist Chen Guilin's tale asserted that the human "quality" of China's population (*suzhi renkou*, 素质人口), or individual *suzhi* (素质), was lacking and this was the cause of China's backwardness. They took from the film's narrative that they needed to ensure that their children did not suffer a similar fate. For the privileged viewer's enjoyment, Chen Guilin's destitution became a spectacle of poverty from which to draw lessons. Accordingly, this chapter explores a number of ways in which *The Piano in a Factory* manifests notions of *suzhi* both in its narrative and among its audiences in their spectatorship. Among audiences, *suzhi* was exemplified through audiences' tastes with only privileged female audiences showing a preference for watching artistic cinema. Within the narrative, the single child became the site for *suzhi* cultivation through socially advantageous education; while Xiao Ju's request for a divorce as her "self-liberation" from the poverty-stricken matrimony with Chen Guilin aligned her acquisition of *suzhi* as her individual's right to social mobility – thereby ensuring that *suzhi* in *The Piano in a Factory* is portrayed as modern in its de-collectivised conceptualisation, as opposed to the collective (and backward) past.

At 199 minutes, *The Piano in a Factory* proved to be a demanding film-viewing experience for the majority of audiences. The dialogue is interspersed with sometimes

130 *The Piano in a Factory*

pregnant, sometimes hollow, silences, defying the classical editing practices typically employed in commercial Chinese films emulating the Hollywood format, yet necessarily lending to the melancholy of the characters the film portrays. This melancholic pace, however, is often unexpectedly interrupted by upbeat musical interludes which see protagonist Chen Guilin and his fellow colleagues break into dance and colour filling the screen in a stylistically obtuse fashion, only to revert without warning of transition to the lacklustre palette of the industrial landscape and pace of the abandoned cityscape. Although the musical interludes arguably are intended as black humour and an esoteric expression of the cultural starvation felt by these fictional retrenched workers in their forgotten corner of northeast China, they proved on the whole unappreciated by audiences from all classes. *The Piano in a Factory* stylistically, and visually, proved to be a film for an audience with an "acquired" taste, and thus an exercise in viewership as an audience member's *suzhi*.

Audiences and group discussions

The average age of an audience member for group discussions about *The Piano in a Factory* was 33 years of age; 24 members were male and 14 were female. Group discussions in Hangzhou and Nanjing consisted of rural migrant workers, and in Beijing, the group consisted of educated urban sophisticates employed in white collar labour. Two discussion groups were held in Lanzhou: one consisted of coal factory workers (G), and the second consisted of postgraduate students (H). In Taiyuan, the discussion group consisted of educated professionals and low to mid-level white collar workers. University students in Lanzhou and the majority of urban white collar workers in Taiyuan had heard of *The Piano in a Factory* prior to participating in the film screening. Only a couple of urban sophisticates with high levels of education in Beijing, however, had sought out the film to watch prior to participating.

The Piano in a Factory was awarded the Artistic Exploration Award at the Beijing University Student Film Festival and subsequently nominated in multiple categories, including Best Feature Film for the Golden Rooster Award (2011) offered by the China Film Association (*zhongguo dianyingjia xiehui*, 中国电影家协会), a sub-division of the China Federation of Literary and Art Circles (*zhongguo yixue shujie lianhe hui*, 中国文学艺术界联合会). Internationally, *The Piano in a Factory* circulated at film festivals in Miami, Tokyo, Taiwan and Hong Kong. As a result, SARFT awarded the production further substantial financial support for the film's post-production in South Korea. *The Piano in a Factory* subsequently obtained distribution internationally through film distributors *FilmMovement*. The international exposure and artistic acclaim *The Piano in a Factory* received from cultural leaders domestically and internationally was the most of any other film considered in this book. This acclaim, however, was far from mainstream appreciation, suggested not only because of the culturally elite circles within which the film was praised, but also because of the modest box office ticket sales.

In an interview, the producer of *The Piano in a Factory*, Jessica Kam, characterised the target audience for the film, as "a more sophisticated, urban audience that we knew would be sympathetic to the issues". As group discussions about *The Piano in a Factory* revealed, Jessica Kam's prediction that urban sophisticates would be the target audience for the film proved to be correct: as rural migrant worker PIAF21 in Nanjing succinctly confirmed, "That was *not* my taste in cinema." Similarly, Kam's prediction that the target audience would not only be "urban sophisticates", but urban sophisticates "sympathetic" to the issues portrayed in the film's narrative again proved correct. For the urban sophisticate who watches artistic films about the class other's poverty can only ever do so with a sympathetic, not an *empathetic*, gaze. Among audiences who could in fact empathise with the retrenched workers on screen, namely the factory workers in Lanzhou, frustration with the depressing depiction of retrenched workers' hardship was clearly evident in their short responses and body language during the group discussion. Sympathy is the privilege of an audience receptive to artistic commercial cinema about their class other. Empathy is the frustration, humiliation, and lack of privilege of the audiences of the class portrayed. In this case it was sympathy that allowed a lower classed character's poverty to become an entertainment spectacle.

The atmosphere at the conclusion of all film screenings of *The Piano in a Factory* was far from upbeat and optimistic. Rather, adjectives to describe audience moods as "solemn", "depressed", "defensive", "uncertain", "alienated" and even "bored" could be suitably applied. All rural migrant workers, factory workers and a proportion of urban privileged males agreed they would not recommend the film to their social networks. Professional men in Beijing and Taiyuan could see value in *The Piano in a Factory*'s ambitions, but explained they preferred watching action films or movies with optimistic outlooks. Perhaps also, the building of a piano, as opposed to the masculine nature of heavy machinery that steel is usually associated with, feminised for audiences *The Piano in a Factory*'s thematic relevance. Only postgraduate students in Lanzhou and three privileged males in Taiyuan and Beijing agreed that they would recommend the film to their social networks to signify their approval of the film's content and cultural value. If *The Piano in a Factory* is indicative of a filmgoer's preference for artistic cinema as having *suzhi*, such a distinction was restricted to a very minimal portion of these Chinese audiences, and was reflective of the exclusive nature and access to the internalised codes of cultural pedigree that *suzhi* embodies. As it was, audiences receptive to the artistic film consisted of educated females, experienced in overseas travel, study and business, and noticeably recipients of, or proponents for, music education – and where applicable, music education for their children (or planned children). While this is not to suggest that the film did not resonate with male audiences, it was women who were most passionate about the topics discussed and the value of the film in the group discussions. Watching artistic cinema was seemingly a female trait and confined to women of privilege. With women still the primary carers of children in China, the opportunities and advantages that are passed on to a child with a mother who is aware of the implications of *suzhi*, such as those who responded positively to *The Piano in a Factory*, should not be underestimated. Perhaps this is why the audience responses to the film showed such a gendered bias. As such, privileged female engagement with *The Piano in a*

132 *The Piano in a Factory*

Factory was of particular interest in the study of China's cinema of class, as real and future nurturers of *suzhi*, and by extension, propagators of the middle class values that cultivating *suzhi* aspires to achieve.

Suzhi and building Xiao Yuan's piano

The teaching and learning of the piano played a key role in the formation of the European middle class identity "to expropriate the cultural pretentions of the old aristocracy, and to raise itself above the working class" (Kraus 1989: 14). *The Piano in a Factory* links the cultivation of *suzhi* to middle class aspirations in the narrative through Chen Guilin's inability to afford his daughter's piano tuition. Chen Guilin does not build a piano because he believes that he and his colleagues' workmanship will be superior to that of a piano bought at a retail outlet. Rather, the piano is built because Chen Guilin does not have the financial means to purchase one, clarifying that the cultivation of *suzhi* and socially advantageous education is intrinsically related to economic advantage. *Suzhi* is not the privilege of all children in contemporary China, nor the privilege of all parents to cultivate it in their children. Thus by positioning one parent as poverty stricken and one parent as China's "new rich", both keen to see their daughter socially mobilise, *The Piano in a Factory* indicates the obligation parents with economic advantage have to invest in their child's cultivation of *suzhi*, because this is the end goal that all Chinese parents supposedly share.

The Piano in a Factory begins with Chen Guilin sneaking Xiao Yuan into the local school during the middle of the night with the assistance of his friend Wang Kangmei, employed as the school's night guard, to practise the piano. Once discovered, Wang Kangmei loses his job, and unable to sneak Xiao Yuan into the school anymore, Chen Guilin convinces his friends to help him steal the same piano from the school. Caught, Chen Guilin and his friends spend their night in the local police station. Resorting to creativity, Chen Guilin's next option is to construct a piano out of a slate of wood covered with a paper re-creation of a keyboard, and encourages Xiao Yuan to "hear the music with her heart" while play-acting her piano practise on the wood. Chen Guilin explains to his sometimes-girlfriend Shu Xian his reason behind his desperation for Xiao Yuan's piano education:

Shu Xian: 你看我给孩子选的这方向：书法。拿根笔弄点纸就完了。又省事又费钱就费点破报纸

Look what I've chosen for my kid – calligraphy. Just get her a brush and some paper, that's it. Hassle free and doesn't cost anything, except some old newspapers.

Chen Guilin: 我爹给我起这个名：陈桂林。就是希望我能像陈桂林山水一样甲天下。结果没甲了，弄夹生了。所以啊，我必须让小元学钢琴

My father gave me the name Chen Guilin, so I'd be like the scenery in Chen Guilin. The best in the world. But I didn't make it, just got half way. So, I must get her to learn piano.

The key to understanding this exchange lies in the ambiguity of what Chen Guilin refers to by "just got half way" (*jia sheng*, 夹生). Chen Guilin's comment could on the one hand be read as not being a wealthy man who can afford a piano for his daughter, or his self-reflection on being a brass instrument player. The latter conclusion is drawn from Richard Kraus's (1989: 210) observation that in rural China, "peasants appear to honor the urban middle class when they form brass bands." Chen Guilin, not having had the chance to play the "heroic voice of the concert virtuoso" (Menuhin and Davis 1979: 179), could believe that playing the piano was the height of self-accomplishment for his daughter from a musical standpoint. Rather, and more likely, Chen Guilin's comment may refer to the missed opportunities of the development of his *suzhi* in contrast to the accomplished technical skills he has acquired in the smelting factory. His lack of *suzhi* is now the labour discipline that obstructs his attempts to improve his own life circumstances. Accordingly, Xiao Yuan, as the soon-to-be middle class single child, becomes "fetishized as a site for the accumulation of the very dimensions of *suzhi* wanting in its 'other' " (Anagnost 2004: 190–194), in this case, her father Chen Guilin.

Xiao Yuan's piano and its audiences

With both of Xiao Yuan's parents deeply invested in her piano education, *The Piano in a Factory* suggests that the investment into cultivating a child's *suzhi* is a common desire among all Chinese parents – more specifically, desired by Chinese parents of all classes, suggesting that the cultural codes that *suzhi* has are universally understood and accessible. The film also presents these desires as common to parents of both genders. Indeed, scholarly literature about *suzhi* very rarely refers to the role that mothers specifically play as the distiller of *suzhi* for their children's benefit. Attitudes expressed by audiences, though, suggested that a universal understanding of the cultural codes of *suzhi* might not in fact be as accurate as the film suggests. Not only were few audiences adamant that their children required music education, but the audience members who were, were notably educated and privileged females. Privileged males and other audience members who were similarly classed to Chen Guilin appeared unconcerned whether or not their child learned how to play the piano.

This was most notable among rural migrant workers in Nanjing, Hangzhou, factory workers in Lanzhou and, to a lesser degree, urban low-level administrators who indicated a rural background in their demographic surveys, or that their parents worked in peasant labour. Only one factory worker (PIAF13) could recall learning an instrument when he was younger as a child living in a work unit. Apart from PIAF13, of the 38 audience members, only 5 others had studied an instrument when they were younger. These audience members had grown up in urban areas, had strong scholastic records, and had parents in professional occupations. An example is PIAF5 in Beijing, a female in her late 20s, who studied both European and Chinese instruments growing up, including the piano. She had completed a Master's degree in Australia and now worked in a Government

134 *The Piano in a Factory*

bureau in Beijing. PIAF5 was adamant that her children would also learn to play the piano like she had.

For rural migrant workers in Nanjing and Hangzhou and factory workers in Lanzhou, music education was perceived as a leisure time activity that privileged Chinese undertook because they had money to spare. Playing the piano was considered "good fun" (*hao wan'er*, 好玩儿) – not necessarily an investment in education that would advantage their children in their futures. "If you don't have money, you just don't learn the piano," PIAF12 in Hangzhou matter-of-factly explained as he shrugged his shoulders to indicate that nothing was amiss for a child by not learning how to play.

The building of a piano, an instrument no one in these three groups had learned to play or perceived that their child would play (unless they expressed firm desires for lessons), alienated lower classed audiences from the film's outset for what seemed like a frivolous ambition by Chen Guilin to build an instrument that they could not understand as being important. Chen Guilin's attempt to maintain custody of his child was perceived as highly admirable by these audiences, but his choice in building a piano to win his daughter's custody seemed farfetched and unconvincing. This was in stark contrast to the distinctly educated female audiences, whose children studied piano (Beijing and Taiyuan: approximately 35–40 years old, PIAF1; PIAF4; PIAF33; PIAF35). These women believed it was crucial for their children to study (i.e. it was not for the child's enjoyment) and enforced piano practice and lessons within their respective households. These households also owned a private piano. The mothers believed that learning to play the piano was important for their children in order to have a "unique skill" (PIAF4), or benefit their child's scholastic progress by enabling them to "think differently" (PIAF33). Despite *every* audience member agreeing that overall "education" was important for their children to get ahead in contemporary Chinese society, music education was only important for these four females. Male audiences furthermore, appeared unlikely to hold musical education in high esteem. Professional, educated males in Taiyuan, and male postgraduate students in Lanzhou, stated and then agreed with each other that their children's music education was (or would be) up to their wives to dictate. The fact that privileged females were the most vocal about their child's need to play the piano indicates the importance that mothers play in encouraging socially advantageous education for their children. Statistical data shows that prior to the introduction of compulsory schooling years in the early stages of economic reforms, a mother's level of education directly influenced the education levels of her children (Knight et al. 2013). In present-day China, the role of the mother clearly continues to play a significant role: now as the conduit to intergenerational exchange of *suzhi*.

For other female audiences in urban areas who were *not* the female advocates of music education, the most commonly heard response was: "if the child likes it or wants to learn, then I will agree to lessons." These offerings appeared, however, to be non-committal responses provided to indicate an openness to the concept of music education for their children, and sometimes what appeared to be the mother's desire to respond positively within a forum whereby "motherhood" was

The Piano in a Factory 135

being expressly linked to piano education by male and privileged female audiences alike. By admitting that they as mothers could not afford lessons for their children, or did not see the purpose for such education, these women arguably ran the risk of exposing their own level of *suzhi*, and by extension, their child's.

The mothers who saw music education of their children as a priority clearly had funds to provide what they saw as socially advantageous education for their children. As the family unit provides life chances for the next generation, the nurturing of certain developmental attributes in some children and not others has led to differences in cultural pedigree that is well formed by the time the child has become a young adult. Unlike what *The Piano in a Factory* may suggest in both Chen Guilin and Xiao Ju wanting their daughter to have piano lessons, the starting point from which advantageous education is perceived by a mother for her child must be recognised as conditioned by her own class positioning. Whereas advantageous education and acquisition of *suzhi* for a privileged mother may be judged as investing in her child's piano lessons, advantageous education for a mother who is employed as a factory worker may simply be expressed by her wish for her child to complete the middle years of schooling.[3] *The Piano in a Factory*'s narrative, therefore, could only ever be of value to an audience with similar class sensibilities and the privilege of access to the cultural codes that determine what socially advantageous education is for their children. *The Piano in a Factory*, therefore, distorts the realities of class-based desires for *suzhi* embodied in the protagonist, a male retrenched industrial worker, for the entertainment benefit of the privileged female audience member keen to nurture *suzhi* in her child.

Divorce and the assertion of individual needs

The struggle for Xiao Yuan's custody is resolved in the closing scenes of *The Piano in a Factory*. Xiao Yuan is brought to the factory by her mother Xiao Ju to play the "steel" piano her father and his friends have built for her as a gesture of goodwill between the divorcing parents. The piano is brought in on a pulley system, making a grand entrance as if descending from the industrial heavens of Liaoning, and placed on the open floor of the factory. To the symbolic "left" of the piano stands the collective of Chen Guilin and his former colleagues and to the symbolic "right" stands Xiao Ju, alone. Xiao Yuan asks Chen Guilin what she should play for him on the piano and he responds "something simple". Chen Guilin's somewhat ambiguous request is filled with a poignancy that alludes at once to conceding defeat over the custody battle; his deference to Xiao Yuan's generation that he and his colleagues can no longer maintain pace with; and in reference to her audience that consists of his former factory colleagues, who have a modest understanding of European classical music. As Xiao Yuan plays Beethoven's Bagatelle No. 25 in A minor: "Für Elise", the camera retreats slowly out of the factory, letting the closing frame linger so audiences may ponder how drastically China has changed within the space of a generation – as well as ponder the fate of the collective and the individual.

Divorce and the family unit is a moral issue, and audience responses towards the issue of Chen Guilin and Xiao Ju's divorce showed a very distinct polarisation

136   *The Piano in a Factory*

of opinions along class-based lines. This was exacerbated by the association that was made between Xiao Ju's request for a divorce to marry a man that Chen Guilin claims manufactures "fake medicine" and his accusations of Xiao Ju's desire for social mobility. Whether Chen Guilin's accusations are legitimate or not, the film-makers never provide Xiao Ju's character a chance to explain her motives, leaving audiences taking Chen Guilin's accusations as fact. *The Piano in a Factory*, therefore, establishes that Xiao Ju's opportunities for social mobility have come about by the assertion of her individual needs and wants first and foremost. Xiao Ju's individualistic needs and wants for social mobility are likewise linked to her ability to provide and afford Xiao Yuan's music education and *suzhi* cultivation. So, divorce in this film becomes a much broader moral dilemma for audiences than simply the misfortune of the breakdown of the family unit, or learning the piano. Divorce is packaged as the abandonment of the collective, for which social mobility, wealth acquisition and *suzhi* is the reward. Xiao Ju's newfound individualism is presented as key to her privilege and that which comes at the expense of Chen Guilin's demise as the head of the collective family unit. Conveniently, the audience never sees Xiao Ju with her new husband, although Chen Guilin's colleagues constantly surround him. Just as *The Piano in a Factory* depicts polarised attitudes between the privileged and lower classes through the issue of divorce, privileged and lower classed audiences mirrored this dichotomy in the moral conclusions they drew about the couple's divorce.

Audiences were asked whom they believed at the conclusion of the film Xiao Yuan should continue living with: Chen Guilin or Xiao Ju. Contrary to expectations that audiences would all agree with "Xiao Ju", irrespective of class position for the role that the mother assumes as primary carer for children and her financial advantage, rural migrant workers in Nanjing were steadfastly unanimous that the child should continue living with Chen Guilin. Audiences in Hangzhou and factory workers in Lanzhou, unprompted, came to a group consensus that Chen Guilin and Xiao Ju *should not* divorce. Only PIAF8 in Hangzhou, the most senior of the workers and recently married, believed Xiao Yuan should stay with Xiao Ju. Both in Hangzhou and Lanzhou audiences expressed clear dissatisfaction with the narrative's resolution for the couple's inability to resolve their marital problems. The consistency across Nanjing, Hangzhou and factory workers in Lanzhou to empathise with Chen Guilin and systematically overlook the benefits that the mother's new wealth could provide Xiao Yuan's future through education was striking. The uniformity of this perspective, regardless of the city in which the sentiments were expressed, suggested a class-based morality about how social mobility should be achieved. If Chen Guilin was to be poor, then Xiao Ju, as his wife, should also accept being poor, and Xiao Yuan by extension, should anticipate the same fate. At least this way, the collective family unit would stay together and this was the ideal solution.

Educated urbanites perceived the ideal solution as being the opposite. Although postgraduate student PIAF18 in Lanzhou was unable to choose between Chen Guilin and Xiao Ju, and four more audience members in Taiyuan and Beijing echoed PIAF18's indecision, in both cities their concern with Xiao Yuan living with Xiao

The Piano in a Factory 137

Ju was related to the fact that Xiao Ju's new husband-to-be sold fake medicine. These audiences were concerned about *the new husband's* moral character – not Xiao Ju's for wanting a divorce. Significantly, these indecisive audience members did not at any point consider that the couple should reunite. Arguably the depiction of Chen Guilin's poverty is what swayed them to not immediately respond with "Chen Guilin". Male audiences in Beijing, Lanzhou (postgraduate students) and Taiyuan answered confidently that Xiao Yuan should stay with Xiao Ju, as she was able to provide for the child financially – in Beijing and Taiyuan these were the same men who stipulated that their children's music education was a decision to be made by their wives. Privileged women in Beijing and Taiyuan likewise whose children were studying piano firmly agreed that the child should stay with Xiao Ju. They could understand the sacrifices that Xiao Ju was making in order to assist her child to succeed. To maintain family values would be to return to poverty and miss the opportunity for upward social mobility.

When these polarised responses towards Chen Guilin and Xiao Ju's divorce was presented to Jessica Kam, *The Piano in a Factory*'s producer, she was surprised that the issue of divorce had polarised audiences. "It is so common nowadays, I do not think divorce is provocative at all", she explained. Kam's response is not without reason. Statistics indicate that divorce in urban China is on the rise (Davis 2010). For the educated audiences in privileged social positions, the issue was as Kam believed and as statistics may indicate nothing provocative. They understood Xiao Ju's choice for a better life in order to provide for her daughter's future.

When asked whether audiences understood *The Piano in a Factory* to be about education or divorce, audiences in Hangzhou and Nanjing and factory workers in Lanzhou were unanimous that Chen Guilin and Xiao Ju's "divorce" was central to the narrative. Group opinion was evenly divided in Taiyuan and Beijing between those who believed the film was about "both divorce and education" and those who believed it was a film about "education". The four distinctly privileged women who were advocates of their children learning to play the piano (Beijing and Taiyuan) responded "education" – following with "especially to succeed in China". None of the postgraduate students, or audiences in Taiyuan and Beijing responded exclusively with "divorce" like their lower classed counterparts. Postgraduate students PIAF21 and PIAF22 in Lanzhou believed that "education" was the "explanatory variable", but the rest claimed "both". PIAF5 in Beijing was the only audience member who replied "neither", for he understood the themes of divorce and education to be metaphors for the breakup of the socialist system in general, not themes in their own right.

The morality of divorce in *The Piano in a Factory* served the purpose of providing the framework within which to portray two conflicting modes of social organisation facing Chinese society: that of the collective stability and that of the individual's needs. If the responses recorded here are anything to go by, Xiao Ju's individualism appears to be the key to her and her daughter's social mobility, and morality only privileged audiences were open to. On the one hand, the film's narrative alludes to collectivism as what obstructs the acquisition of *suzhi*, and on the other, it also suggests that collectivism results in

138   *The Piano in a Factory*

life stagnation and the intergenerational inheritance of poverty. To assert one's individual needs by sacrificing a poverty-stricken family unit for the sake of acquiring a greater *suzhi* could be, therefore, perceived as the liberation from backwardness.

Framing the retrenched industrial worker

The framing of the retrenched worker in *The Piano in a Factory* as backwards and stagnated in a "time warp" due to a pining for collective worker nostalgia is crucial to conceptualising social mobility and *suzhi* for privileged urban sophisticates who are likely to be attracted to this artistic film. *The Piano in a Factory* is set in China's so-called "rust belt" of Liaoning province, where the processes of restructuring the industrial sector and the work units that historically had provided universal welfare for housing, employment, education and health services affected the lives of millions of urban Chinese (Rocca 2003: 84). The transition into the market economy was not a smooth process for all work unit residents and as unemployment does not exist within the ideological framework of communism, retrenched workers suddenly found themselves leading precarious and ambiguous existences in China's new market labour economy with minimal transitional welfare protection from the Party-state. Rather than being unemployed, retrenched workers became people "of temporary non-working status" (ibid: 80). As such, many retrenched workers resorted to becoming individual business entities or sole traders (*getihu*, 个体户), which Phillip Huang describes as a "lowly and menial status" attached to the artisan and peddler-type nature of such service provision. Phillip Huang (2013: 353–358) provides figures of sole traders at anywhere between 65–90 million, who work "under terms and conditions of a second-class informal economy". These figures are not insignificant, and understanding these sole traders as an emerging petite bourgeoisie masks the reality of their self-subsistence labour and lack of entrepreneurial privilege compared with the Chinese who have acquired quick riches, and are the feature of China's booming economy narrative. Whereas cinema has depicted the rural migrant worker as morally superior, capable and optimistic in *Lost on Journey*, or even as wealthy landowners in *House Mania*, the retrenched worker in *The Piano in a Factory* is portrayed as unable to economically stabilise within the new market economy, torn by outmoded notions of a collective worker nostalgia and as a consequence, suffering under life stagnation. Their poverty is depicted as unexceptional, and as a result, a normalised condition by which they have come to be recognised.

Chen Guilin and his former colleagues are all sole traders making financial ends meet. Chen Guilin and Shu Xian have become buskers and wedding performers; Fathead gambles at Mahjong; Brother Ji runs a black-market racket in metals he steals from abandoned factories; Lightning Fingers trades as an individual locksmith at 2 cents a key cut – his shop a "hole in the wall"; Wang Kangmei works graveyard shifts as a night guard of a primary school; Big Liu is a butcher who rears his own animals to sell and whose wife controls their family accounts. Mr Wang, the educated engineer Chen Guilin engages to design the steel piano, is

The informality of Chen Guilin's labour status does not afford him the privilege of participating in China's contemporary consumer society. In the first invitation *The Piano in a Factory* makes to its audience to enter Chen Guilin's apartment, director Zhang Meng takes care to bring to the audience's attention the material possessions owned by Chen Guilin with deliberate camera close-up. Durables such as an old washing machine, an electric fan (not air conditioning), and even the time given by the camera to the computer game played by Xiao Yuan on a monitor dating back to the early 1990s (not an iPad or laptop): Nintendo's "Super Mario Bros World" (version 1–2), are all indicators of the economic capacity and enthusiasm to consume that the early years of China's economic reforms provided these workers. Conveniently, the dating of these durables also pinpoints the time in which these workers' employment statuses, and their economic capacities, stagnated.

Xiao Ju's improved economic advantage is indicated when she arrives to request her divorce from Chen Guilin. Xiao Ju wears a white jacket to distinguish herself from Chen Guilin and his colleagues wearing dark clothes to conceal the dirt of the industrial area that they cannot avoid. As audience feedback indicated, the stereotyping of the lowly classed rural migrant worker in *Lost on Journey* relied heavily on the connotation of dirty clothes, so Xiao Ju's character is consciously depicted as very clean in white to indicate her improved social status. Chen Guilin is often framed aimlessly meandering through the barren streets of the former bustling industrial town. The few retrenched workers who do remain in the former industrial city idle their time away gambling measly sums of money playing Mahjong and participating in community ballroom dance classes to occupy their days, a poignant desire for human touch to remind them that they are still alive. The opening of *The Piano in a Factory* frames the retrenched worker as destitute and isolated from modern China, and because of this, deeply bored and bordering on having empty souls. Of course, the ambiguous nature of Chen Guilin and his former colleagues' forms of employment is exactly what affords these characters the time to partake in the piano building project.

The framing of the retrenched workers' life stagnation is further exacerbated by Chen Guilin's frequent employment of revolutionary jargon and his search for collective solutions for problems in a manner that he and his colleagues became accustomed to in pre-reform times. By depicting Chen Guilin as straddling two ideologically different eras of China's modern history, Chen Guilin's attachment to collective ideals is also implied as being backwards and the reason for his life stagnation. As *suzhi jiaoyu* (education for persons of "quality") is essential to creating *suzhi renkou* (a "quality" population) in order to resolve China's backwardness on its path to development (Anagnost 2004), the multiple factors of

140   *The Piano in a Factory*

Chen Guilin's character, including his propensity for collective worker nostalgia, come to embody the very backwardness that the individuals who acquire *suzhi* by seeking life improvements should be rid of. Chen Guilin's colleagues, who may not necessarily straddle these ideological worlds but empathise with their comrades, likewise attract a similar value judgement through association with him. In Lanzhou, PIAF13 in no uncertain terms spoke of his dislike in watching the themes in *The Piano in a Factory*, because "all of this is in the past!" PIAF13 believed that life in contemporary China was much better than before, irrespective of the favourable nostalgia in the film Chen Guilin may express or try to stimulate. PIAF13 perceived himself (and by extension the group) to be as involved in China's modernity as the next person.

An example of Chen Guilin's attachment to the "past" is in his attempt to engage his sister to recruit her husband to partake in the piano building project. Chen Guilin visits his sister, who operates her own hairdressing stand in a hut on the sidewalk. His sister is concerned about her husband, who cannot seem to find work. Chen Guilin advises his sister that his brother-in-law needs to "liberate his thinking before liberating himself" in order to stop fearing the humiliation of failure in the new labour economy. Without patience for ideological rhetoric, Chen Guilin's sister dryly retorts, "Well hurry up and liberate him then", to which Chen Guilin responds, "I'll liberate him from head to toe!" Not amused, his sister continues cutting her customer's hair. As Chen Guilin pauses in the conversation, behind him outside the window, a piece of meat attached to a long stick can be seen to slowly move off screen. It is revealed to the audience that this is Chen Guilin's meat that was left tied to his bicycle. Upon discovering his meat has been stolen, Chen Guilin yells into the empty streets, "Is there nothing that you won't steal now?" – his reference to "now" indicates his understanding that in the past, theft was uncommon and that neighbourly trust was once reliable.

In another scene, a problem arises when the wood that has been collected to build the piano turns out to be unsuitable. Chen Guilin suggests that the piano is built entirely from steel. Reverting to former collective decision-making protocols of the socialist era, Chen Guilin calls for a group vote on the change in production design (Figure 7.2):

Chen Guilin:	咋们决定改成钢骨架的咋们举手表个态， 好不好
	Who's for changing over to a steel piano frame?
	[Chen Guilin raises his hand to indicate a vote]
Shu Xian:	你走那形式干吗啊？你说做啥样就做啥样的
	What's the point in voting? It's your project, what you say, goes.
	[Shu Xian tells Chen Guilin to ask Mr. Wang for his opinion]
Mr. Wang:	没有敢想敢干敢拼的精神那不是我们工人干的事儿！
	Ah, we workers can do anything if we put our minds to it!
	[Mr Wang's defiant language is met with silence and everyone avoids eye contact]

Figure 7.2 Chen Guilin seeks collective solutions

It is each man for himself in the new market economy, and Mr Wang's enthusiasm for Chen Guilin's ideological zeal for a group vote places Chen Guilin in a time warp that outdates his ageing durables at home to that of *pre-reformed* China. Even though Chen Guilin's ideological zeal is admirable, his and Mr Wang's optimism is in marked comparison to their peers, who appear deeply scarred by their experience shifting to the new labour economy. In contrast, Xiao Ju, who has completely discarded her collective ideals and has no interest in Chen Guilin's collective building project, is the only character that successfully improves her life standing by the plot's resolution. One cannot be surprised by the lower classed audiences of *The Piano in a Factory*'s instinct to create a distance between them and the character of Chen Guilin; in fact most of the characters that surround Chen Guilin are shown to want to as well.

In combination with the themes of divorce and Xiao Yuan's acquisition of a piano education, *The Piano in a Factory* reminds audiences that individual responsibility achieves social mobility: class struggle is not the solution. It is no surprise therefore that those who could empathise with the characters onscreen were disgruntled with the depiction. For the former industrial heroes, the film's depiction denies this group of fictional labourers' active inclusion in China's modernity narrative in its shift to a competitive market economy, improvements to their standards of living or *suzhi*, and labour opportunities. Furthermore, it downplays the importance of any camaraderie they may continue to feel. As the next section will show, exclusion from China's modernity narrative like this has very real consequences for the socialisation of China's class society.

142   *The Piano in a Factory*

Segmented labour force, segmented audience

If high and low *suzhi* are part of China's modernity and development narrative in the formal economy, exclusion from the modernity narrative portrayed in the characters of Chen Guilin and his colleagues effectively places retrenched workers-turned-self-subsistence labourers in the informal economy, or those still facing ambiguous unemployment, as having an indeterminable value. This indeterminable value is arguably even more limiting to an individual than having low *suzhi* within the formal economy. To highlight this, these closing remarks on audiences' inconsistencies in pinpointing when *The Piano in a Factory*'s narrative is set provides further consideration for how the film ensured that audience engagement was exclusive to an educated audience.

Only two audience members, PIAF2 in Beijing and PIAF21 in Lanzhou believed that the narrative was set in the 2000s. Both of these young males had travelled recently to northwest China and knew of places that the imagery of *The Piano in a Factory* resembled. Other than these two men, no one else had travelled to northeast China; so they placed the timing of the narrative as when they knew the industrial sector was restructured during the mid-1990s. As it is, Chen Guilin and his colleagues appeared well established in their new forms of employment or self-subsistence labour, suggesting that *The Piano in a Factory*'s narrative is set at a period of time since the 1990s and capturing the time warping that retrenched workers face. Listening to audiences mutter to each other when asked this question clarified that it was difficult for audiences other than the two who stated the 2000s to contemplate that Chinese people lived like this now. This is not so surprising given the attention by Zhang Meng to rest the camera's gaze on Chen Guilin's material possessions of a bygone era, and the general pervasiveness of China's modernity narrative of development that celebrates impressions of full employment.

Factory workers who had retained their employment in Lanzhou understood the film to be set in the 1990s, although PIAF14 noted that workers would not have had mobile phones at that time. In Taiyuan, PIAF36 noted that the brand of car in the final scene driven by Xiao Ju was only available in China during the last decade (i.e. mid-2000s), but as a group the agreement was *The Piano in a Factory* must be set in the 1990s. Younger audiences in Lanzhou (postgraduate students) and Beijing (25–35 year old professionals and white collar workers) did not pick up any specific material inconsistencies and understood the film to be set in the mid-1990s, which they agreed was accurately depicted in the film. Their conclusions could have been influenced by the general speed by which China has developed, taking for granted what they perceived now to be the norm, such as telephones and cars. None of these urbanites considered that Zhang Meng had placed these items within the film in order to portray contemporary visions of stagnant and normalised poverty in the present.

Among rural migrant workers in Nanjing and Hangzhou, the dating of the narrative's setting was particularly difficult. Audiences in Hangzhou hesitated to confirm the accuracy of the depiction until PIAF8 asserted that the representation was correct. What his peers thought can only be a point of speculation. Rural migrant workers in Nanjing, however, simply responded with a chorus of "do not know".

When probed further, Nanjing audiences conjectured that the film was perhaps set in the 1960s because, they reasoned, the character of Mr Wang wore a blue Mao suit. This was despite expressing surprise at what they deemed mistakes by the film-makers in the era's depiction, such as high-rise buildings, the use of mobile phones, and the visit to a karaoke centre, where one of the musical interludes is set. PIAF26 and PIAF27 chuckled between themselves at the filmmakers' oversights. It became evident that what contributed to audiences in Nanjing and Hangzhou finding *The Piano in a Factory*'s narrative intensely boring was that they were unfamiliar with China's urban industrial history and thus the narrative held little relevance to their immediate lives. This is not to discount PIAF11 in Hangzhou's claim that he would like to watch the film again for the reason that he found the film "informative". The general unfamiliarity of China's urban history denied audiences from rural origins the ability to engage with the film's narrative more deeply. Moreover, it certainly did not provide them the "spectacle" that privileged audiences had, or even the enjoyment of watching characters of a similar class defying the odds, as, say, the peasants in Lanzhou had enjoyed in watching the character Niugeng in *Lost on Journey*.

Alvin So calls China's labour force "segmented" (2007: 139) due to the perception of retrenched industrial workers, rural migrant workers and retained industrial workers (and arguably also low level service workers) that their industrial objectives and class disadvantage are not unifying concerns. So suggests that these workers understand themselves to be class competitors vying for similar jobs in urban China. Group discussions indicated that *The Piano in a Factory*'s audiences mirrored this phenomenon, proving to be likewise a segmented audience. Not only did audiences interpret the narrative to be a matter of the past, but also the unfamiliarity shown by rural migrant workers towards the experiences of China's proletariat industrial history lent credence to the argument that Chinese workers are more than just competitors within a segmented labour force. They are in fact historical and present-day class strangers. A prospect that can only call into question the unity of the hammer and sickle that sits so prominently on the wall behind numerous political gatherings of the historical and present Chinese Party-state.

As the cinema of class provides the conceptual insight for audiences to make sense of the world around them, audience engagement with *The Piano in a Factory* appeared to place the issues of re-entry into the labour force of retrenched workers, and poverty of Chinese urbanites, as an issue locked into China's past. Looking past the various intrusions into the film that would suggest a relevance to the present, pre-conditioned by the all-pervasive modernity narrative of development and *suzhi*, made those living on the periphery of the modernity narrative difficult to reconcile in the imagination of these audiences. The film's ambiguity of the time in which the narrative is set likewise assured that a rural audience member would not receive education about China's "present" through watching the film.

Making poverty acceptable

As a narrative for audience interrogation, *The Piano in a Factory* provided an opportunity to consider how artistic cinema fared in a popular cinema context.

144 *The Piano in a Factory*

That the filmmakers of *The Piano in a Factory* consciously employed a piano as the centrepiece of the film's narrative to divert audience's attentions from the plight of China's retrenched workers to that of the necessity of socially advantageous education for China's next generation is not very likely. Having said this, the fact that the narrative did not feature Chen Guilin or his friends' efforts to re-enter the labour market and focused the film rather on Chen Guilin's efforts to gain custody of his daughter in the face of an impending divorce by building a piano, leaves little room for surprise that audience attentions were directed to the role of the piano in the film and the impending divorce of Chen Guilin and Xiao Ju.

The inability of audiences to place the retrenched worker's disadvantage in the informal economy to a definite timeframe or in a context that provided a contemporary relevance also appeared to subordinate issues of the retrenched worker's disadvantage to that of a spectacle for privileged audiences, and issues "of the past" for factory workers. An argument could be made that the extended period of exhibition of *The Piano in a Factory* in mainstream cinemas, therefore, pandered more to sophisticated filmgoers' tastes than encouraged a call for concern for the class inequalities that retrenched workers face. If this is indeed the case, the extended exhibition of *The Piano in a Factory* in mainstream cinemas, while admirably providing a variety of cinema available to the Chinese public, must come with a degree of caution. Making poverty an acceptable issue to bypass or portray as the result of a collective nostalgia no longer applicable to contemporary China not only undermines any chances that China's urban poor have to form a closer or unified class identity with other workers and establish a narrative of a shared history, but also pits classes against one another. Exoticising poverty for the benefit of privileged Chinese audiences, who are in positions of cultural and political power, is likewise a potential breeding ground for legitimising prejudices expressed in previous chapters – not only for what this means in terms of the new moral standards that China now advocates, but also because it reduces the chances to improve the conditions that China's lower classes and those in the informal economy face on a daily basis.

If *Go Lala Go!* advocated for the retreat from the labour market by educated, professional women in order to perform their maternal duties, *The Piano in a Factory* confirmed what these maternal duties entail. In doing so, the film once more seemed to engage the "crisis of masculinity" presented in *House Mania*, to suggest that backward and underperforming men are responsible for holding women back from achieving these duties of cultivating intergenerational *suzhi*. Audiences of *The Piano in a Factory* confirmed that the cultural codes of *suzhi* are indeed exclusive, and *suzhi*'s exclusivity is why the futures of Chinese children can only ever be unequal.

Notes

1 Box office figure as of 31 January 2016 (Entgroup); approximate USD at historical exchange rate for 1 August 2011 (XE Currency); URL: http://www.cbooo.cn/m/592214/
2 Douban rating: 8.3/10 stars for 140, 915 reviews. URL: http://movie.douban.com/subject/4876722/ (last accessed: 16 July 2016).

The Piano in a Factory   145

3 PIAF17 shared with her focus group her dismay at her daughter's low school marks and her quitting school after completing only junior middle school. Her daughter now works seven days a week at a convenience store on the outskirts of Lanzhou.

References

Adams, Mark. 3 November 2010. The Piano in a Factory. *Screendaily*. URL: http://www.screendaily.com/reviews/latest-reviews/the-piano-in-a-factory/5020078.article. Accessed: 12 November 2013.

Anagnost, Ann. 2004. The Corporeal Politics of Quality (*Suzhi*). *Public Culture* 16 (2): 189–208.

Bordwell, David. 1979. The Art Cinema as a Mode of Art Practice. *Film Criticism* 4 (1): 56–64.

Davis, Deborah. 2010. Guess Who Gets the House? Renegotiating Property Rights in Post-Socialist Urban China. *Modern China* XX (X): 1–30.

Huang, Phillip. 2013. Misleading Chinese Legal and Statistical Categories: Labor, Individual Entities, and Private Enterprises. *Modern China* 39 (4): 347–379.

Kam, Jessica (producer). *The Piano in a Factory*. Interview: 24 April 2013.

Kraus, Richard C. 1989. *Pianos and Politics in China: Middle-class Ambitions and the Struggle over Western Music*. Oxford: Oxford University Press.

Menuhin, Yehudi, and Davis W. Curtis. 1979. *The Music of Man*. Toronto, New York, London and Sydney: Methuen.

Rocca, Jean-Louis. 2003. Old Working Class, New Working Class: Reforms, Labour Crisis and the Two Faces of Conflicts in Chinese Urban Areas. In *China Today: Economic Reforms, Social Cohesion and Collective Identities*, edited by Taciana Fisac and Leila Fernández-Stembridge, 77–104. London: RoutledgeCurzon.

Shi, Tongyun. 2012. Chinese Working-class Identity in the Piano in a Factory. *Intercultural Communication Studies* 21 (3): 93–107.

So, Alvin Y. 2007. The State and Labor Insurgency in Post-socialist China: Implication for Development. In *Challenges and Policy Programmes of China's New Leadership*, edited by Joseph Y. S. Cheng, 133–151. Kowloon: City University of Hong Kong Press.

8 Conclusion

Class, the film and the filmmaker

Screen-based storytelling is important to the sense we make of the world around us, while class dictates the quality of our lives, our and our children's chances and ultimately how disconnected we are from the realities and lived experiences of our fellow citizens. While this is evident in the comprehensions of big screen Chinese films that Chinese audiences from varying classes revealed in these discussion groups, they are not alone in this predicament; this is arguably a situation that audiences face wherever class exists. David E. James (1996, 1999) has been a vocal proponent for the relationship between class and film studies, and deeply critical of the American academe's repression of class theory in film studies due to the "zero-sum rules of academic identity politics" (1996: 1) that he believes diverted scholarly discourse in film and cultural studies away from class theory to discourses on gender and race. James argued that class theory shares commonalities with *both* gender and race movements and that the assault on the global working class brought about by "Reaganomics" in the 1980s was aided by the academe's intellectual shift. Paul W. Kingston's book published in 2000 titled *The Classless Society*, which forcefully claims that class no longer exists in America, suggests that the subordination of class discourse that James observed among American film and cultural theorists was part of a much broader trend across America's intelligentsia. As Hollywood's and China's film industries draw closer in alliance with the ambition of sharing audience markets and investment potential (and indeed Hollywood blockbusters have come to dominate the Chinese box office on a regular basis and commercial Chinese films now circulate North America's film market) – the alarm bells that rang for James about film theory studies in America should similarly be ringing for scholars focused on contemporary Chinese cinema. Especially in light of China's economic reforms that have seen China become one of the most unequal societies in the space of a single generation. That China's intellectuals might declare China is also a classless society, or underplay circumstances of class struggle as merely examples of provincial, ethnic or gendered differences in Chinese "culture", would be a sombre eventuality – not only for those currently severely disadvantaged by the present class structure in China, but for generations of Chinese to come.

The five films featured here are only a tiny fraction of the over 500 commercial films that were produced annually and approved for registration by SARFT (now

Conclusion 147

SAPPRFT) in the years these films screened in cinemas across mainland China during 2010–2011, or the thousands that have been produced since. One must probe further into the many stories being told to truly understand popular cinema's role in socialising the imaginations that underpin China's class society. The preliminary findings presented here in combination, though, indicate that China's cinema of class is a dynamic and complex hierarchy of ideas, prejudices and emotional and ideological manipulations. As the preceding chapters have shown, James was right to claim that class still has a place within film studies. Not only in the study of film narratives, but necessarily so the study of film audiences. The coordination of the film screenings indicated that both onscreen and off, class is well socialised into everyday understandings of inferiority and superiority among Chinese people.

Although interpretations sometimes correlated between differently classed audiences, often the pre-conditioning for sense making that brought the audiences to their conclusions was vastly different. Audiences on a whole believed that *Let the Bullets Fly* implied that the authoritarian rule of the Party-state was unchallengeable. For privileged audiences this was because they believed the Party-state had made political and economic progress, while China's subordinate classes indicated that acquiescing to the Party-state's rule was a means for self-preservation. Similarly, all audiences believed that homeownership was paramount to a man's marriageability after watching *House Mania*, yet audiences had different expectations for what the ideals of homeownership entailed. Privileged Chinese saw housing as a means of personal social distinction and would not recommend the film to their social network, as they believed that the houses presented in the film were pitched at lower classed audiences. In contrast, rural migrant workers perceived homeownership as a result of hard work, and a site where community and family could connect and thus looked for different characteristics in their domestic spaces to those of the aspirational classes – all the while unaware that this may reflect to the broader community their lower class status in an urban environment. For young adults in Beijing, homeownership appeared financially beyond their immediate realities and thus they were lukewarm about the film's glorification of property speculation and pragmatically reasoned that the houses portrayed in the film were liveable. Yet, these young adults would not trade their cosmopolitan lives in the nation's capital for that of their counterparts in Lanzhou with a more favourable property market, reflecting the regional divisions on life quality young Chinese adults have.

No matter whether urban or rural, privileged or underprivileged, all audiences believed that the representation of China's rural migrant workers in *Lost on Journey* and *House Mania* as ignorant of urban etiquette, dirty and uncivilised were true characterisations of China's subordinate classes. Again, though, while professionals and white collar workers believed this because characterisations affirmed the low *suzhi* of China's rural folk and their questionable moralities, audiences from what constitute the subordinate classes read into these same characterisations truthful representations of a shared class-based honesty, diligence and willingness to "work hard" and bear all hardships. None of these audiences showed sympathy for China's poverty stricken, though, such as the able-bodied beggar in *Lost on*

148 *Conclusion*

Journey or the sole traders in China's informal economy in *The Piano in a Factory*. But while audiences from the privileged classes would proactively avoid beggars and public displays of poverty in their everyday lives (staring being considered low *suzhi*), they were comfortable with poverty artistically portrayed for China's big screens. Conversely, the lower classes would happily crowd around to stare at poverty out of curiosity in reality, but were disinclined to enjoy watching portrayals of poverty they understood all too well on the big screen for entertainment purposes.

Strong family values, and the importance of friendships, communal living, honesty and "hard work" were repeated numerous times throughout focus group discussions with China's rural migrant workers and factory workers – even for films that they were unable to find much relevance to their own realities, such as *Go Lala Go!*. In contrast, privileged urbanites never once mentioned the phrase "hard work" as an explanation for benefits gained. Rather, these audiences perceived the divorce depicted in *The Piano in a Factory* as explainable and rational to rid one's self of poverty without working hard, and displayed few inhibitions in expressing their unfavourable prejudices towards China's lower classes – prejudices, it should be noted, that if acknowledged by lower classed audiences, were held without retaliation or excuse making, especially not in front of a foreign researcher – even if they had desired to do so.

While rural migrant audiences treated sense making of the films they watched a collective process and a process that seemed to echo hearsay of the hardworking underclasses' ability to "eat bitterness" (*chi ku*, 吃苦), privileged audiences found opportunities to contradict each other's film comprehension and understood this freedom of opinion as their entitlement as sense-making audiences. The socialised expectation to form and express opinions became a defining attribute of film consumption among China's audiences – aside from the glaringly obvious issue of decreased media literacy skills such as those which appeared in audience reception to *Let the Bullets Fly*. And just as notions of consumption, labour, wealth, power abuse and homeownership have become socialised in the fabric of the mainstream, so too has the socialisation of opinion making and the freedom by which opinions are expressed and articulated. While some Chinese have been pre-conditioned to sense-make as citizens with privilege, others have been pre-conditioned to sense-make within state-ordained paradigms that encourage acquiescence to the status quo, and seemingly to their detriment if we take how social distinction, political engagement and identity are now articulated through popular Chinese cinema.

Since the fieldwork on which this book has been based was undertaken, domestic blockbusters have continued to propagate narratives with similar themes. *Box Office Mojo* reports *Personal Tailor* (Feng Xiaogang: 2013) accrued USD 115.5 million at the box office – a film told in three vignettes. The first vignette features themes of political corruption and bribe taking; the second, China's inability to make "artistic" films – a taunt at highbrow and lowbrow film directors in China; and lastly, a tale about an impoverished woman who spends the day as a billionaire. Familiar themes of privileged women choosing romance and married bliss over careers also performed resoundingly well at the box office, starting with the *Tiny Times* series (Guo Jingming: 2013, 2014, 2015). The most recent instalments,

Tiny Times 3, accrued USD 82.32 million and *Tiny Times 4*, USD 77.75 million at the Chinese box office, while *Finding Mr. Right* (Xue Xiaolu: 2013) took in USD 82.68 million. *Let's Get Married* (Liu Jiang: 2015) sold USD 45.42 million in tickets, and the Chinese remake of Hollywood's *Bride Wars* (Tony Chan: 2015) accrued USD 27.7 million. In 2016, a further 42-part instalment of Lala's life featured in the tele-series 《我是杜拉拉》 *I am Lala* (Liu Junjie: 2016) broadcast on CCTV. The migrant worker of *Lost on Journey* was again "lost" in *Lost in Thailand* (Xu Zheng: 2012, USD 197.41 million); and *I Am Somebody* (Dereck Yee: 2015), while performing modestly with a box office total of USD 9.87 million, rehashed the myth of the rural underclasses reaching fame and glory in the big city – albeit this time in China's movie business itself. *The House* (Ma Jun: 2014), another modest earner circulating in China's online streaming platforms (which attracted 130,000 watchers in the 18 months since it was posted), set in Beijing, relays the story of a young man literally nicknamed "House" (*fangzi*, 房子) by his work colleagues. House is a mature-aged man who has failed to grow up and whose wife is perpetually disappointed in her continual competition with House's addiction to computer games. Stuck with House because a divorce would mean losing the capital in the apartment she has bought for them, a familiar theme shows itself when House's wife falls for the charm of House's successful, statuesque and wealthy (*wen-wu-chan*) boss. While the figures that *Box Office Mojo* report on its website are questionable and very likely include some degree of estimation in their calculations as Chinese box office data gathering methods are not necessarily reliable, Chinese filmmakers, both established and up and coming, should feel confident that continuing to produce narratives promoting the humorous side of China's new class society are welcomed by both the film circuit, film investors, and paying audiences alike – not to forget newly introduced commercial platforms such as online streaming.

The theoretical frameworks of class are, and always will be, contentious. Class in China cannot be excused from this contention. Efforts to create an olive shaped society while maintaining an overarching social harmony relies on a socialisation of new norms, emotions, perceptions of the self, the collective and how they relate to the Chinese leadership – norms that are vastly different from those aspired to in the nation's recent revolutionary past. Currently, this socialisation seems to be most apparent among Chinese of the aspirational middles classes as the future social gatekeepers between rich and poor, urban and rural – and the most likely cinema patrons. Commercial cinema is one forum within which narratives of class can construct meaning around new emotional responses to poverty, inequality and prejudice, and can either aid the writing of shared histories and commonalities between people or ensure segregation.

Chinese cinema, though, is not produced in a vacuum. The film industry relies on filmmakers, writers and actors, among many other cultural practitioners and investors, to bring to life the narratives of class that are subsequently watched on the big screens by China's audiences. Likewise, an academe and network of film critics that interrogate and validate the nuances of the cultural production to stimulate the exchange between filmmakers and audiences are required. Class theory

150 *Conclusion*

does not just exist in the cinematic text alone – China's cinema of class already starts at its very point of creative inception and production.

As it stands, this book has focused on how Chinese audiences consume commercial cinema narratives. The question remains, what role do cultural producers play in the socialisation process? How *conscious* are filmmakers of how Chinese audiences interpret their films and how their work contributes to broader class socialisation and formation? What the ambitions truly were of the directors for each of the films featured can only be speculative. One can only draw from audience responses how filmmakers *may* have been positioned in their creative process and their negotiations for approval with SAPPRFT for production and commercial exhibition. What can comfortably be assumed is that filmmakers are no longer expected to produce cinema that speaks to the peasants, workers, soldiers and cadres of the socialist era – or that filmmakers are required to rid themselves of their bourgeois tendencies that Mao Zedong demanded of his artists and writers in his 1942 talk at the Yan'an Forum on Literature and Art.

Today, China's film students possess the potential to join China's cultural elites, and the associated benefits that come with being privileged in contemporary China. Lin and Sun (2011) report that monthly salaries of graduates from the Central Academy of Drama and the Beijing Film Academy in 2007 were well within the top twenty highest of universities across China. The data Lin and Sun provide show that the graduate salaries from these two academies out-ranked graduate salaries from other prestigious Chinese universities such as Tsinghua University, Sun Yat-sen University, Renmin University of China and Peking University. The skill in producing film narratives that meet the Party-state's agenda for social reform is the environment within which hopeful Chinese filmmakers and their performers learn the trade of big screen entertainment. While one can show that China's audiences are not uniform and that, indeed, class plays a significant role in their film spectatorship and consumption, how China's filmmakers are positioned is still to be investigated.

Arguably, Chinese filmmakers, with their access to filmmaking education, capital, facilities and even the time for creativity, can only ever be of the privileged classes – or the "creative class" or "intelligentsia" as they may also be categorised. By simply *being* filmmakers, Chinese filmmakers produce from a position of privilege and socio-cultural capital unimaginable to China's subordinate classes such as the urban poor or the rural migrant workers and factory workers featured in this book. While these filmmakers may have had the great fortune to socially mobilise from lower class origins, they nonetheless now produce from a privileged position. In order to gain approval for commercial distribution of their films, filmmakers likewise engage and negotiate with peers who are also in positions of power and socio-cultural capital. Thus, no commercial Chinese filmmaker produces cinema from a position rooted in the lower classes, but within a social hierarchy that aligns their professionalism and skills closer to China's elites and aspirational classes than perhaps even the audiences who consume their films.

Further research is necessary to gauge exactly how conscious China's commercial filmmakers are of how their narratives and their presentation of these

Conclusion 151

narratives reach out to and touch the hearts and minds of Chinese audiences. While Mao declared in his 1942 lecture to artists and writers that their duty was to understand the audiences they produced for during the socialist era – peasants, workers, soldiers and cadres – the pendulum of artistic responsibility has swung firmly back to its starting point in economically reformed China. Now, hopeful commercial filmmakers target paying audiences, and with the economic stimulation the country has experienced in the last few decades, these audiences are more populous than ever before. These audiences search for ways to distinguish themselves in a society where the superficial now counts as important. How the perpetuation of a "*culture of inequality* and an *inequality of culture*" (Sun 2013: 27, author's emphasis) can be halted in light of this inevitability of privilege that Chinese filmmakers find themselves with seems unlikely to be resolved in the very near future. Indeed, this was the very crux of Mao's conundrum with creative practitioners during his leadership. Yet, the privileged position of the filmmaker is often very little discussed, and is overlooked by either Chinese film scholars or general advocates of the relationship between class theory and the study of cinema.

How much the varied worldviews that audiences brought to their readings of these five films reflect the worldviews of the filmmakers behind the narratives is anyone's guess. What can comfortably be agreed upon, though, is that China's commercially exhibited cinema succinctly reflects the socialisation of China's new class society among its domestic audiences – but that in the limited access that China's underclasses have to China's commercial film industry, the films can only ever be seen to pander to the worldviews of privileged audiences. Accordingly, we may *speculate* that the thoughts and imaginations of China's privileged filmmakers, the vanguard of China's cinema of class, are just as accurately reflected too in these very same productions. As China's film industry continues to grow year after year, and new projection screens are installed every other day, China's film industry is en route to becoming the world's largest commercial film industry. More significant, though, is China's film industry is en route to becoming the world's largest and most lucrative exercise in social engineering of a single people, both audiences and filmmakers alike: that is, China's Cinema of Class.

References

James, David E. 1996. Introduction: Is There Class in This Text? In *The Hidden Foundation: Cinema and the Question of Class*, edited by David E. James and Rick Berg, 1–25. Minneapolis and London: University of Minnesota Press.

——. 1999. Is There Class in This Text?: The Repression of Class in Film and Cultural Studies. In *A Companion to Film Theory*, edited by Toby Miller and Robert Stam, 182–201. Massachusetts and Oxford: Blackwell Publishers.

Kingston, Paul W. 2000. *The Classless Society*. Stanford, CA: Stanford University Press.

Lin, Jing, and Xiaoyan Sun. 2011. Higher Education Expansion and China's Middle Class. In *China's Emerging Middle Class: Beyond Economic Transformation*, edited by Cheng Li, 217–242. Washington, DC: Brookings Institute Press.

Sun, Wanning. 2013. Inequality and Culture: A New Pathway to Understanding Social Inequality. In *Unequal China: The Political Economy and Cultural Politics of Inequality*, edited by Wanning Sun and Yingjie Guo, 27–42. Oxon and New York: Routledge.

Films list

Chan, Tony. 2015. *Bride Wars*《新娘大作战》. Bona Film Group and Fox International Productions.

Feng, Xiaogang. 2013. *Personal Tailor* 《私人订制》. Emperor Film Productions and Huayi Brothers Media.

Guo, Jingming. 2013–2014. *Tiny Times* series 《小时代》. Le Vision Pictures (Tianjin) Co.

Huang, Yu-Shan. 1991. *Twin Bracelets* 《双手》. Cosmopolitan Film Productions.

Hughes, John. 1987. *Planes, Trains & Automobiles*. Paramount Pictures (presents) Hughes Entertainment.

Jiang, Wen. 2011. *Let the Bullets Fly* 《让子弹飞》. Dongyang Bu Yi Le Hu Film Company, China Film Group, Emperor Motion Pictures.

Liu, Jiang. 2015. *Let's Get Married*《我们结婚吧》. Perfect World (Beijing) Pictures Co., Heyi Film, and Taihe Film Investment Co. Ltd.

Liu, Junjie. 2016. *I Am Lala* 《我是杜拉拉》. Shanghai Haoju (好剧) Film Distribution Ltd.

Ma, Jun. 2014. *The House* 《房子》. 北京德泰影艺文化服务有限责任公司

Star, Darren. 1998. *Sex and the City*. Darren Star Productions, Home Box Office (HBO).

Sun, Da. 2011. *House Mania* 《房不剩防》. Beijing Shengshi Huarui Films Investment Co., Ltd., Haoxing Jieji (Beijing) International Media Co., Ltd., Jiuzhou Tiancheng Entertainment Co., Ltd.

Xie, Jin. 1961. *Red Detachment of Women* 《红色娘子军》. Tianma Film Studios.

Xu, Jinglei. 2010. *Go Lala Go!* 《杜拉拉升职记》. China Film Group Corporation, DMG Entertainment Group, Beijing Guoran Entertainment Co. Ltd.

Xu, Zheng. 2012. *Lost in Thailand*《人再囧途之泰囧》. Enlight Pictures.

Xue, Xiaolu. 2013. *Finding Mr. Right* 《北京遇上西雅图》. Edko Films.

Yee, Dereck. 2015. *I Am Somebody*《我是路人甲》. Jiangsu Bona Television Productions Ltd.

Yip, Raymond. 2010. *Lost on Journey* 《人在囧途》. Hubei Films Distribution Co. Ltd., Wuhan Hua Qi Film & TV Production Co., Ltd.

Zhang, Meng. 2011. *The Piano in a Factory* 《钢的琴》. Perfect World (Beijing) Film, Entertainment Co., Ltd., Dalian Hongyuan Entertainment Media Co., Ltd., Liaoning Film Studio.

Appendix
Group discussants

Let the Bullets Fly

- **Beijing:** White collar workers
  CCP membership: 5 out of 7 participants
  7 female participants: appendix references LBF1–LBF7
- **Lanzhou:** Master students (social sciences)
  CCP membership: 3 participants and 3 Youth League members
  2 male and 4 female participants: appendix references LBF8–LBF13
- **Nanjing:** Rural migrant workers, low levels of education and limited career mobility
  CCP membership: none
  1 male and 4 female participants: appendix references LBF14–LBF18
- **Taiyuan A:** Low-level administrators with rural backgrounds and some education
  CCP membership: 4 without membership and 1 with Youth League membership
  4 males and 1 female participant: appendix references LBF19–LBF24
- **Taiyuan B**: Workers in mixed levels of administration with some education, some chance of career progression
  CCP membership: 1 participant
  7 female participants: appendix references LBF25–LBF31
- **Taiyuan C:** Master students (Business)
  CCP membership: 3 out of 4 participants
  4 female participants: appendix references LBF32–LBF35

Beijing

Date: 23 September 2012
Participants: White collar workers
Location: Culture Yard, Dongcheng, Beijing

LBF1 (F)
Born: Jining, Inner Mongolia (内蒙古省集宁市); *Age:* 31; *Household registration:* Jining, Inner Mongolia; *Employment:* Environment and Energy Technology

Appendix: group discussants 155

company; *Family background*: Parents reside in Jining; *CCP membership in family*: Father has membership, LBF1 and mother do not; *Highest level of education*: Bachelor degree

LBF2 (F)

Born: Weifang, Shandong (山东省潍坊市); *Age*: 25; *Household registration*: Beijing, Xicheng (北京西城); *Employment*: Public relations and media; *Family background*: Parents reside in Qingdao, Shandong (山东省青岛市), LBF2 grew up in different cities in Shandong, parents are employed in part-time work; *CCP membership in family*: LBF2 has membership, her parents do not; *Highest level of education*: Master degree

LBF3 (F)

Born: Hubei (河北); *Age*: 26; *Household registration*: Hubei (河北); *Family background*: Parents reside in Hubei, parents are self-employed; *CCP membership in family*: LBF3 has membership, parents do not; *Highest level of education*: Bachelor degree

LBF4 (F)

Born: Weifang, Shandong (山东省潍坊市); *Age*: 26; *Household registration*: Weifang, Shandong; *Employment*: International exhibition centre; *Family background*: Parents reside in Weifang, father is a public servant in local government and mother is a housewife; *CCP membership in family*: LBF4 and her father have membership, mother does not; *Highest level of education*: Bachelor degree

LBF5 (F)

Born: Beijing (北京市); *Age*: 30; *Household registration*: Beijing; *Employment*: Public servant in local government; *Family background*: Parents reside in Beijing; *CCP membership in family*: LBF5 has membership, parents do not; *Highest level of education*: Master degree

LBF6 (F)

Born: Beijing (北京市); *Age*: 23; *Household registration*: Beijing; *Employment*: Studio manager in the entertainment industry; *Family background*: Parents reside in Beijing, father works in real estate and mother is a housewife; *CCP membership in family*: LBF6 is a member of the Youth League; *Highest level of education*: Bachelor degree

LBF7 (F)

Born: Beijing (北京市); *Age*: 32; *Household registration*: Beijing; *Employment*: Public servant; *Family background*: Parents reside in Beijing, father is a public servant and mother works in tourism; *CCP membership in family*: Parents have membership, LBF7 does not; *Highest level of education*: Bachelor degree

156   *Appendix: group discussants*

Lanzhou

Date: 1 June 2012
Participants: Postgraduate students
Location: Northwest Normal University

LBF8 (M)

Born: Huanxian, Qingyang, Gansu (甘肃省庆阳市环县); *Age*: 22; *Household registration*: Huanxian, Qingyang; *Employment*: Master student; *Family background*: Parents reside in Huanxian, father is a doctor and his mother is a peasant; *CCP membership in family*: LBF8 and his father have membership, his mother does not; *Highest level of education*: Master degree

LBF9 (F)

Born: Xifeng, Qingyang, Gansu (甘肃省庆阳市西峰); *Age*: 25; *Household registration*: Xifeng, Qingyang; *Employment*: Master student; *Family background*: Parents reside in Xifeng, father is a driver and mother is a housewife; *CCP membership in family*: LBF9 has membership, her parents do not; *Highest level of education*: Master degree

LBF10 (F)

Born: Wudu, Longnan, Gansu (甘肃省陇南市武都); *Age*: 23; *Household registration*: Wudu, Longnan; *Employment*: Master student; *Family background*: Parents reside in Wudu, father is a worker and mother is a housewife; *CCP membership in family*: Father has membership, mother does not; LBF10 is a member of the Youth League; *Highest level of education*: Master degree

LBF11 (F)

Born: Bangluozhen, Tongweixian, Dingxi, Gansu (甘肃省定西市通渭县榜罗镇); *Age*: 23; *Household registration*: Tongwei; *Employment*: Master student; *Family background*: Parents reside in Bangluozhen, father and mother are business people; *CCP membership in family*: Neither parent has membership, LBF11 is a member of the Youth League; *Highest level of education*: Master degree

LBF12 (M)

Born: Minqinxian, Wuwei, Gansu (甘肃省武威市民勤县); *Age*: 24; *Household registration*: Minqin, Wuwei; *Employment*: Master student; *Family background*: Parents reside in Minqin, father is a teacher and mother is a police officer; *CCP membership in family*: LBF12 and his parents have membership; *Highest level of education*: Master degree

LBF13 (F)

Born: Lanzhou, Gansu (甘肃省兰州市); *Age*: 24; *Household registration*: Lanzhou; *Employment*: Master student; *Family background*: Parents reside in Lanzhou, father works at a major national bank and mother is a housewife; *CCP membership in family*: Father has membership, her mother does not; LBF13 is a member of the Youth League; *Highest level of education*: Master degree

Appendix: group discussants   157

Nanjing

Date: 27 June 2012
Participants: Rural migrant workers
Location: Nanjing University

LBF14 (F)

Born: Sihongxian, Suqian, Jiangsu (江苏省宿迁市泗洪县); *Age*: 37; *Household registration*: Sihong, Suqian; *Employment*: University canteen worker; *Family background*: Parents reside in Sihong, parents are peasants; *CCP membership in family*: Parents have membership, LBF14 does not

LBF15 (M)

Born: Sihongxian, Suqian, Jiangsu (江苏省宿迁市泗洪县); *Age*: 37; *Household registration*: Sihong, Suqian; *Employment*: University campus security guard; *Family background*: Parents reside in Sihong, parents were peasants; *CCP membership in family*: None; *Highest level of education*: Junior middle school (初中)

LBF16 (F)

Born: Sihongxian, Suqian, Jiangsu (江苏省宿迁市泗洪县); *Age*: 37; *Household registration*: Sihong, Suqian; *Employment*: University canteen worker; *Family background*: Parents reside in Sihong, parents are peasants; *CCP membership in family*: Father has membership, LBF16 and her mother do not; *Highest level of education*: Primary school (小学)

LBF17 (F)

Born: Sihongxian, Suqian, Jiangsu (江苏省宿迁市泗洪县); *Age*: 38; *Household registration*: Sihong, Suqian; *Employment*: University canteen worker; *Family background*: Parents reside in Sihong, parents are peasants; *CCP membership in family*: None; *Highest level of education*: Primary School (小学)

LBF18 (F)

Born: Suzhou, Jiangsu (江苏省苏州市); *Age*: 23; *Household registration*: Suzhou; *Employment*: University canteen worker; *Family background*: Parents reside in Suzhou, parents are peasants; *CCP membership in family*: LBF18 was a member of the Youth League; *Highest level of education*: Junior middle school (初中)

Taiyuan A

Date: 1 September 2012
Participants: Low-level administration workers
Location: Office block, Taiyuan downtown

LBF19 (M)

Born: Dongtaipun, Taiyuan, Shanxi (山西省太原市东太堡村); *Age*: 37; *Household registration*: Dongtaipun, Taiyuan; *Employment*: Employed by manufacturers

158 *Appendix: group discussants*

of plastic piping company; *Family background*: Parents reside in Dongtaipun, father and mother are SOE factory workers; *CCP membership in family*: None; *Highest level of education*: Vocational training (大专)

LBF20 (M)

Born: Xiaoyi, Lüliang, Shanxi (山西省吕梁市孝义市); *Age*: 24; *Household registration*: Xiaoyi, Lüliang; *Employment*: Amway, China; *Family background*: Parents reside in Xiaoyi, parents are peasants; *CCP membership in family*: Parents do not have membership, LBF20 is a member of the Youth League; *Highest level of education*: Middle vocational training (中专)

LBF21 (M)

Born: Yuanping, Xinzhou, Shanxi (山西省忻州原平); *Age*: 30; *Household registration*: Yuanping; *Employment*: SOE coal producers; *Family background*: Parents reside in Yuanping, father is employed with a SOE electricity company and mother is a peasant; *CCP membership in family*: LBF21 has membership, his parents do not; *Highest level of education*: Bachelor degree

LBF22 (M)

Born: Taiyuan, Shanxi (山西省太原市); *Age*: 29; *Household registration*: Taiyuan; *Employment*: Employed in food exports; *Family background*: Parents reside in Taiyuan, father works in a private enterprise and mother works at a hospital; *CCP membership in family*: Father has membership, LBF22 and his mother do not, although LBF22 had Youth League membership; *Highest level of education*: Vocational training (大专)

LBF23 (F)

Born: Shanxi (山西省); *Age*: 25; *Household registration*: Shanxi; *Employment*: Amway, China; *Family background*: Parents reside in Taiyuan; *CCP membership in family*: None; *Highest level of education*: Vocational training (大专)

LBF24 (M)

Born: Xinzhou, Shanxi (山西省忻州); *Age*: 31; *Household registration*: Taiyuan (山西省太原市); *Employment*: Petroleum SOE; *Family background*: Parents reside in Xinzhou, parents are peasants; *CCP membership in family*: None; *Highest level of education*: Vocational training (大专)

Taiyuan B

> **Date:** 7 September 2012
> **Participants:** White collar workers
> **Location:** Office block, Taiyuan downtown

LBF25 (M)

Born: Yuanping, Xinzhou, Shanxi (山西省忻州市原平); *Age*: 36; *Household registration*: Wanbailin, Taiyuan, Shanxi (太原市万柏林区); *Employment*: Financial investment; *Family background*: Parents reside in Yuanping, parents are peasants; *CCP membership in family*: None; *Highest level of education*: Specialised vocational training (专科)

LBF26 (F)

Born: Xinghualing, Taiyuan, Shanxi (山西省太原市杏花岭); *Age*: 33; *Household registration*: Xinghualing, Taiyuan; *Employment*: Unemployed; *Family background*: Parents reside in Xinghualing, parents are workers; *CCP membership in family*: Father has membership, LBF26 and her mother do not; *Highest level of education*: Bachelor degree

LBF27 (F)

Born: Taiyuan, Shanxi (山西省太原市); *Age*: 52; *Household registration*: Taiyuan; *Employment*: Vegetable exports and sales; *Family background*: Parents reside in Taiyuan, father was a police officer and mother worked in customer service; *CCP membership in family*: Father has membership, LBF27 and her mother do not; *Highest level of education*: Regular secondary education (高中)

LBF28 (F)

Born: Sichuan (四川省); *Age*: 60; *Household registration*: Taiyuan (太原市); *Employment*: Design (architectural) institute; *Family background*: Parents live in Taiyuan, but LBF28 was brought up in Beijing during primary school and Tianjin during secondary school, father worked in the Ministry of Defence and mother was a medical practitioner; *CCP membership in family*: Parents had membership, but LBF28 does not; *Highest level of education*: Junior middle school (初中)

LBF29 (F)

Born: Xixian, Linfen, Shanxi (山西省临汾市隰县); *Age*: 23; *Household registration*: Xixian, Linfen; *Employment*: Marketing; *Family background*: Parents reside in Linfen, parents are peasants; *CCP membership in family*: None; *Highest level of education*: Middle vocational training (中专)

LBF30 (F)

Born: Huangpocun, Wanbolin Forest, Taiyuan, Shanxi (山西省太原市万柏林区黄坡村); *Age*: 45; *Household registration*: Huangpo, Wanbolin Forest; *Employment*: Hotel customer service; *Family background*: Parents reside in Huangpo, parents' jobs unspecified; *CCP membership in family*: None; *Highest level of education*: Regular secondary education (高中)

LBF31 (F)

Born: Yangquan, Shanxi (山西省阳泉市); *Age*: 56; *Employment*: Business (事业); *Family background*: Parents reside in Yangquan, parents are retired; *CCP membership in family*: LBF31 and her father have membership, her mother does not; *Highest level of education*: Specialised vocational training (本科)

160 *Appendix: group discussants*

Taiyuan C

> **Date:** 13 September 2012
> **Participants:** Postgraduate Business students
> **Location:** Office block, Taiyuan downtown

LBF32 (F)

Born: Linfen, Shanxi (山西省临汾市); *Age*: 23; *Household registration*: Linfen; *Employment*: Master student; *Family background*: Parents reside in Linfen, parents are teachers; *CCP membership in family*: Father has membership, mother does not, LBF32 is a member of the Youth League; *Highest level of education*: Master degree

LBF33 (F)

Born: Jincheng, Shanxi (山西省晋城市); *Age*: 24; *Household registration*: Taiyuan; *Employment*: Master student; *Family background*: Parents reside in Jincheng, parents are sole traders (个体); *CCP membership in family*: LBF33 has membership, her parents do not; *Highest level of education*: Master degree

LBF34 (F)

Born: Taiyuan, Shanxi (山西省太原市); *Age*: 25; *Household registration*: Taiyuan; *Employment*: Master student; *Family background*: Parents reside in Taiyuan, parents are business people; *CCP membership in family*: LBF34 and her father have membership, her mother does not; *Highest level of education*: Master degree

LBF35 (F)

Born: Yuncheng, Shanxi (山西省运城市); *Age*: 23; *Household registration*: Yuncheng; *Employment*: Master student; *Family background*: Parents reside in Yuncheng, father is a worker and mother is a nurse; *CCP membership in family*: Parents have membership, LBF34 does not; *Highest level of education*: Master degree

Lost on Journey

- **Lanzhou A:** Peasants
  5 male participants: appendix references LOJ1–LOJ5
- **Lanzhou B:** Undergraduate students (mixed disciplines)
  3 male and 5 female participants: appendix references LOJ6–LOJ13
- **Taiyuan D:** White collar professionals with higher levels of tertiary education
  3 male and 4 female participants: appendix references LOJ14–LOJ20
- **Taiyuan E:** A mix of white collar workers with low, moderate and high education levels and with career opportunities
  3 male and 4 female participants: appendix references LOJ21–LOJ27

Appendix: group discussants 161

- **Taiyuan F:** A mix of white collar workers with moderate to high levels of education and professional occupations, one participant with low level education and employment status
3 male and 5 female participants: appendix references LOJ28–LOJ36

Lanzhou A

Date: 12 June 2012
Participants: Peasants
Location: Chengguanzhen, Yuzhongxian, Lanzhou, Gansu (甘肃省兰州市榆中县城关镇)

LOJ1 (M)

Born: Dayingcun, Chengguanzhen, Yuzhonxian, Lanzhou, Gansu (甘肃省兰州市榆中县城关镇大营村); *Age*: 30; *Household registration*: Chengguan; *Employment*: Peasant; *Family background*: Parents reside in Dayingcun, parents are peasants; *CCP membership in family*: None; *Highest level of education*: Junior middle school (初中)

LOJ2 (M)

Born: Dayingcun, Chengguanzhen, Yuzhonxian, Lanzhou, Gansu (甘肃省兰州市榆中县城关镇大营村); *Age*: 31; *Household registration*: Chengguan; *Employment*: Peasant; *Family background*: Parents reside in Daying, parents are peasants; *CCP membership in family*: None; *Highest level of education*: Junior middle school (初中)

LOJ3 (M)

Born: Chengguanzhen, Yuzhonxian, Lanzhou, Gansu (甘肃省兰州市榆中县城关镇); *Age*: 45; *Household registration*: Chengguan; *Employment*: Peasant; *Family background*: Parents reside in Chengguan, parents are peasants; *CCP membership in family*: None; *Highest level of education*: Junior middle school (初中)

LOJ4 (M)

Born: Dayingcun, Chengguanzhen, Yuzhonxian, Lanzhou, Gansu (甘肃省兰州市榆中县城关镇大营村); *Age*: 58; *Household registration*: Chengguan; *Employment*: Peasant; *Family background*: Parents were peasants in Daying; *CCP membership in family*: LOJ4 has membership, his parents did not; *Highest level of education*: Junior middle school (初中)

LOJ5 (M)

Born: Dayingcun, Chengguanzhen, Yuzhonxian, Lanzhou, Gansu (甘肃省兰州市榆中县城关镇大营村); *Age*: 32; *Household registration*: Chengguan; *Employment*: Peasant; *Family background*: Parents reside in Daying, parents are peasants; *CCP membership in family*: Father has membership, LOJ5 and his mother do not; *Highest level of education*: Junior middle school (初中)

162 *Appendix: group discussants*

Lanzhou B

Date: 3 June 2012
Participants: Bachelor students
Location: Northwest Normal University

LOJ6 (F)

Born: Zhangye, Gansu (甘肃省张掖市); *Age*: 22; *Household registration*: Zhangye; *Employment*: Bachelor student; *Family background*: Parents reside in Zhangye, father is a driver and mother a business person; *CCP membership in family*: None; *Highest level of education*: Bachelor degree

LOJ7 (F)

Born: Chengguanzhen, Wushanxian, Tianshui, Gansu (甘肃省天水市武山县城关镇); *Age*: 21; *Employment*: Bachelor student; *Family background*: Parents reside in Chengguan, father is a public servant and mother is a peasant; *CCP membership in family*: Father has membership, LOJ7 and her mother do not; *Highest level of education*: Bachelor degree

LOJ8 (M)

Born: Jingzhou, Dunhuang, Jiuquan, Gansu (甘肃省酒泉敦煌泾州); *Age*: 22; *Employment*: Bachelor student; *Family background*: Parents reside in Dunhuang, parents are peasants; *CCP membership in family*: Parents do not have membership, LOJ8 is a member of the Youth League; *Highest level of education*: Bachelor degree

LOJ9 (F)

Born: Baiyin, Gansu (甘肃省白银市); *Age*: 22; *Employment*: Bachelor student; *Family background*: Parents reside in Baiyin, parents are workers; *CCP membership in family*: Parents do not have membership, LOJ9 is a member of the Youth League; *Highest level of education*: Bachelor degree

LOJ10 (M)

Born: Pingquanzhen, Zhenyuanxian, Qingyang, Gansu (甘肃省庆阳市镇原县平泉镇); *Age*: 24; *Employment*: Bachelor student; *Family background*: Parents reside in Pingquanzhen, parents are peasants; *CCP membership in family*: Parents do not have membership, LOJ10 is a member of the Youth League; *Highest level of education*: Bachelor degree

LOJ11 (F)

Born: Xuebaixiang, Minqinxian, Wuwei, Gansu (甘肃省武威市民勤县薛白乡); *Age*: 22; *Household registration*: Xuebaixiang; *Employment*: Bachelor student; *Family background*: Parents reside in Xuebaixiang, parents are peasants; *CCP membership in family*: Parents do not have membership, LOJ11 is a member of the Youth League; *Highest level of education*: Bachelor degree

Appendix: group discussants 163

LOJ12 (F)

Born: Zhouquxian, Gannanzhou, Gansu (甘肃省甘南州舟曲县); *Age*: 22; *Household registration*: Zhouquzhen; *Employment*: Bachelor student; *Family background*: Father is a teacher and mother does not work; *CCP membership in family*: Father has membership, mother does not, LOJ12 is a member of the Youth League; *Highest level of education*: Bachelor degree

LOJ13 (F)

Born: Minqinxian, Wuwei, Gansu (甘肃省武威市民勤县); *Age*: 22; *Household registration*: Minqinzhen, Wuwei; *Employment*: Bachelor student; *Family background*: Parents reside in Minqinzhen, parents are sole traders (个体); *CCP membership in family*: Parents do not have membership, LOJ13 is a member of the Youth League; *Highest level of education*: Bachelor degree

Taiyuan D

> **Date:** 2 September 2012
> **Participants:** White collar professionals
> **Location:** Office block, Taiyuan downtown

LOJ14 (F)

Born: Taiyuan, Shanxi (山西省太原市); *Age*: 42; *Household registration*: Taiyuan; *Employment*: University employee; *Family background*: Parents reside in Taiyuan, father is a teacher and mother works at a kindergarten; *CCP membership in family*: LOJ14 and her father have membership, her mother does not; *Highest level of education*: Vocational training (大专)

LOJ15 (F)

Born: Hunyuanxian, Datong, Shanxi (山西省大同市 浑源县); *Age*: 27; *Household registration*: Taiyuan (太原市); *Employment*: Dance teacher; *Family background*: Parents reside in Hunyuan, father works in the Datong tourist bureau and mother works in the Datong cultural office; *CCP membership in family*: LOJ15 and her parents have membership; *Highest level of education*: Vocational training (大专)

LOJ16 (F)

Born: Taiyuan, Shanxi (山西省太原市); *Age*: 44; *Household registration*: Taiyuan; *Employment*: Administration for plumbing and mechanical parts company; *Family background*: Parents reside in Taiyuan, father is a high school teacher and her mother is a worker; *CCP membership in family*: Father has membership, LOJ16 and her mother do not; *Highest level of education*: Vocational training (大专)

LOJ17 (M)

Born: Ruichengxian, Yuncheng, Shanxi (山西省芮城县); *Age*: 47; *Household registration*: Taiyuan, Shanxi (山西省太原市); *Employment*: University staff; *Family*

164 *Appendix: group discussants*

background: Parents reside in Pingyuan, his parents are peasants; *CCP membership in family*: None; *Highest level of education*: Bachelor degree

LOJ18 (M)

Born: Taiyuan, Shanxi (山西省太原市); *Age*: 43; *Household registration*: Taiyuan; *Employment*: University staff; *Family background*: Parents reside in Taiyuan, parents are retired teachers; *CCP membership in family*: None (LOJ19's membership undisclosed); *Highest level of education*: Bachelor degree

LOJ19 (M)

Born: Jiaochengxian, Lüliang, Shanxi (山西省吕梁市交城县); *Age*: 38; *Household registration*: Taiyuan (太原市); *Employment*: University staff; *Family background*: Parents reside in Jiaocheng, parents are workers; *CCP membership in family*: None; *Highest level of education*: Master degree

LOJ20 (F)

Born: Longquan, Taiyuan, Shanxi (山西太原市龙泉); *Age*: 44; *Household registration*: Longquan; *Employment*: High school teacher; *Family background*: Parents reside in Taiyuan, father is a cadre and her mother is a public officer; *CCP membership in family*: Father has membership, LOJ20 and her mother do not; *Highest level of education*: Bachelor degree

Taiyuan E

Date: 14 September 2012
Participants: Lower middle class white collar workers
Location: Office block, Taiyuan downtown

LOJ21 (M)

Born: Pingyaoxian, Jinzhong, Shanxi (山西省晋中市平遥县); *Age*: 28; *Household registration*: Taiyuan (太原市); *Employment*: Pharmaceutical company; *Family background*: Parents reside in Pingyao, parents are self-employed; *CCP membership in family*: None; *Highest level of education*: Bachelor degree

LOJ22 (F)

Born: Taiyuan, Shanxi (山西省太原市); *Age*: 35; *Household registration*: Taiyuan; *Employment*: Master student; *Family background*: Parents reside in Taiyuan, father is a worker and mother is a teacher; *CCP membership in family*: LOJ22 has membership, but her parents do not; *Highest level of education*: Master degree

LOJ23 (F)

Age: 46; *Household registration*: Taiyuan, Shanxi (山西省太原); *Family background*: Parents reside in Taiyuan, parents are self-employed; *CCP membership in family*: None; *Highest level of education*: Junior middle school (初中)

Appendix: group discussants   165

LOJ24 (F)

Born: Taiyuan, Shanxi (山西省太原市); *Age*: 49; *Household registration*: Taiyuan; *Employment*: Geology and engineering industry; *Family background*: Parents reside in Taiyuan, LOJ24 grew up in Puyang, Henan (河南省濮阳市), father is a technician and mother is unemployed; *CCP membership in family*: None; *Highest level of education*: Vocational training (大专)

LOJ25 (M)

Born: Pingcheng, Shanxi (山西省晋城市); *Age*: 32; *Household registration*: Pingcheng; *Employment*: Scientific research; *Family background*: Parents reside in Pingcheng, parents are workers; *CCP membership in family*: Parents do not have membership, LOJ25 was a member of the Youth League; *Highest level of education*: Bachelor degree

LOJ26 (M)

Born: Datong, Shanxi (山西省大同市); *Age*: 30; *Household registration*: Datong; *Employment*: Trade; *Family background*: Parents reside in Datong, father is a worker; *CCP membership in family*: None; *Highest level of education*: Bachelor degree

LOJ27 (F)

Born: Zuoyunxian, Datong, Shanxi (山西省大同市左云县); *Age*: 28; *Household registration*: Zuoyunzhen, Datong; *Employment*: Pharmaceutical sales; *Family background*: Parents reside in Zuoyun, parents are freelance workers; *CCP membership in family*: None; *Highest level of education*: Bachelor degree

Taiyuan F

Date: 7 September 2012
Participants: Mix of white collar workers, professionals and students
Location: Office block, Taiyuan downtown

LOJ28 (F)

Born: Taiyuan, Shanxi (山西省太原市); *Age*: 50; *Household registration*: Taiyuan; *Employment*: Heavy utilities trade; *Family background*: Parents reside in Taiyuan, parents are retired from the Shanxi Mining Bureau; *CCP membership in family*: Father has membership, LOJ28 and her mother do not; *Highest level of education*: Bachelor degree

LOJ29 (M)

Born: Taiyuan, Shanxi (山西省太原市); *Age*: 46; *Household registration*: Taiyuan; *Employment*: Real estate; *Family background*: Parents reside in Taiyuan; *CCP membership in family*: Father has membership, LOJ29 and his mother do not; *Highest level of education*: Regular secondary education (高中)

166 *Appendix: group discussants*

LOJ30 (F)

Born: Yunci, Pingzhong, Shanxi (山西省晋中市榆次); *Age*: 50; *Household registration*: Yunci, Pingzhong; *Employment*: Bureau of Textiles; *Family background*: Parents reside in Yunci, father worked at a timber company and mother worked at a textile factory; *CCP membership in family*: None; *Highest level of education*: Junior middle school (初中)

LOJ31 (M)

Born: Taiyuan, Shanxi (山西省太原市); *Age*: 52; *Household registration*: Taiyuan; *Employment*: Tobacco factory; *Family background*: Parents reside in Taiyuan, father works in a factory and mother works in a real estate agency; *CCP membership in family*: LOJ31 and his parents have membership; *Highest level of education*: Bachelor degree

LOJ32 (F)

Born: Hanjialoucun, Wuzhaixian, Xinzhou, Shanxi (山西省忻州市五寨县韩家楼村); *Age*: 20; *Household registration*: Hanjialoucun, Wuzhai; *Employment*: Bachelor student; *Family background*: Parents have moved to Fengbaohuayuan (佳泰花园), another district within Wuzhai, father is self-employed and mother works in marketing; *CCP membership in family*: None; *Highest level of education*: Vocational training (大专)

LOJ33 (F)

Born: Shuozhou, Shanxi (山西省朔州市); *Age*: 27; *Household registration*: Taiyuan (太原市); *Employment*: Doctor (undertaking medical internship for qualification); *Family background*: Parents reside in Shuozhou, parents are sole traders (个体); *CCP membership in family*: Parents have membership, LOJ33 does not; *Highest level of education*: Bachelor degree

LOJ34 (F)

Born: Wutaixian, Shanxi (山西省五台县); *Age*: 49; *Household registration*: Yunci, Pingzhong, Shanxi (山西省晋中市榆次); *Employment*: Administration; *Family background*: Parents reside in Yunci, but LOJ34 was brought up in Wutai; father is a teacher and mother is a retired worker from a tobacco factory; *CCP membership in family*: LOJ34 and her parents have membership; *Highest level of education*: Bachelor degree

LOJ35 (F)

Born: Linxian, Lüliang, Shanxi (山西省吕梁市临县); *Age*: 21; *Household registration*: Linxian, Lüliang; *Employment*: Real estate; *Family background*: Parents reside in Xiaowang (小王, nearby to Lüliang), LOJ35 grew up in Linxian, parents are business people; *CCP membership in family*: LOJ35 has membership, but her parents do not

LOJ36 (M)

Born: Yangquan, Shanxi (山西省阳泉市); *Age*: 59; *Household registration*: Taiyuan, Shanxi (山西省太原市); *Employment*: Medical practitioner; *Family*

background: Parents reside in Yangquan, father is a retired cadre; *CCP membership in family*: Father has membership, LOJ36 and his mother do not

Go Lala Go!

- **Beijing:** Highly educated and successful white collar workers and one younger administrator
  2 male and 2 female discussants: appendix references GLG1–GLG4
- **Hangzhou:** Rural migrant workers
  1 male and 3 female participants: appendix references GLG5–GLG8
- **Lanzhou C:** Middle–aged male supervisors at a coal factory and one female worker
  4 males and 1 female participant: appendix references GLG9–GLG13
- **Lanzhou D:** Master students (Humanities)
  1 male and 5 female participants: appendix references GLG14–GLG19
- **Nanjing:** Rural migrant workers
  3 male and 2 female participants: appendix references GLG20–GLG24
- **Taiyuan:** Bachelor students (Business) 4 male and 5 female participants: appendix references: GLG25–GLG33

Beijing

Date: 26 August 2012
Participants: White collar workers
Location: Culture Yard, Dongcheng, Beijing

GLG1 (F)

Born: Wuyishan, Nanping, Fujian (福建省南平市武夷山); *Age*: 22; *Household registration*: Wuyishan, Nanping; *Employment*: Administration for a cultural exchange centre; enrolled as a Bachelor student; *Family background*: Parents reside in Wuyishan, father is employed in the broadcasting services and mother is an engineer; *CCP membership in family*: None

GLG2 (F)

Born: Shenyang, Liaoning (辽宁省沈阳市); *Age*: 30; *Household registration*: Shenyang; *Employment*: Scriptwriter for SAPPRFT's Children's Studios (青年电影制片厂); *Family background*: Father is a worker and mother is a white collar worker; *CCP membership in family*: GLG2 and her mother have membership, her father does not; *Highest level of education*: Master by Research

GLG3 (M)

Born: Anhui (安徽); *Age*: 30; *Household registration*: Beijing (北京市); *Employment:* Academic with state research institute; *CCP membership in family*: GLG2 has membership, his parents do not; *Highest level of education*: PhD

168　*Appendix: group discussants*

GLG4 (M) Participant 4 (M)

Born: Shandong (山东); *Age*: 29; *Household registration*: Beijing (北京市); *Employment*: Business consultant (CEO of own company); *Family background*: Parents reside in Shandong, father is a retired worker and his mother was a peasant; *CCP membership in family*: GLG4 and his father have membership, his mother does not; *Highest level of education*: Master degree

Hangzhou

> **Date:** 10 July 2012
> **Participants:** Rural migrant workers
> **Location:** Zhejiang University campus dormitory rooms

GLG5 (M)

Born: Suqian, Jiangsu (江苏省宿迁市); *Age*: 29; *Household registration*: Suqian; *Employment*: Sole trader (个体); *Family background*: Parents reside in Suqian, parents are also sole traders (个体); *CCP membership in family*: None, although GLG5 was a member of the Youth League; *Highest level of education*: Regular secondary education (高中)

GLG6 (F)

Born: Lanxicun, Jinhua, Zhejiang (浙江省金华市兰溪村); *Age*: 29; *Household registration*: Lanxicun, Jinhua; *Employment*: KTV customer service supervisor; *Family background*: Parents reside in Lanxi village, parents are peasants; *CCP membership in family*: None; *Highest level of education*: Middle vocational training (中专)

GLG7 (F)

Born: Lin'an, Hangzhou, Zhejiang (浙江省杭州临安); *Age*: 35; *Employment*: Sole trader (个体); *Family background*: Parents reside in Lin'an, parents are workers in a SOE; *CCP membership in family*: None, but GLG7 was a member of the Youth League; *Highest level of education*: Regular secondary education (高中)

GLG8 (F)

Born: Chun'anxian (rural periphery), Hangzhou, Zhejiang (浙江省杭州市淳安县); *Age*: 33; *Family background*: Parents reside in Chun'an, parents are peasants; *CCP membership in family*: None; *Highest level of education*: Junior middle school (初中)

Lanzhou C

> **Date:** 11 June 2012
> **Participants:** Factory middle management/workers (coal industry)
> **Location:** Northwest Normal University

Appendix: group discussants 169

GLG9 (M)

Born: Lanzhou, Gansu (甘肃省兰州市); *Age*: 48; *Household registration*: Lanzhou; *Employment*: Middle management, coal company; *Family background*: Parents reside in Lanzhou, parents are now retired, but were employed in the coal industry too (兰煤公司); *CCP membership in family*: GLG8 and his father have membership, his mother does not; *Highest level of education*: Regular secondary education (高中)

GLG10 (F)

Born: Lanzhou, Gansu (甘肃省兰州市); *Age*: 22; *Household registration*: Lanzhou; *Employment*: Coal sales; *Family background*: Parents reside in Lanzhou, father is a worker and her mother are sole traders; *CCP membership in family*: None; *Highest level of education*: Vocational training (大专)

GLG11 (M)

Born: Lanzhou, Gansu (甘肃省兰州市); *Age*: 50; *Household registration*: Lanzhou; *Employment*: Middle management, coal company; *Family background*: Parents reside in Lanzhou; *CCP membership in family*: GLG10 and his (now passed away) father had membership, his mother does not; *Highest level of education*: Vocational training (大专)

GLG12 (M)

Born: Wuwei, Gansu (甘肃省武威市); *Age*: 44; *Household registration*: Lanzhou, Gansu (甘肃省兰州市); *Employment*: Team supervisor, coal company; *Family background*: Parents reside in Wuwei, father was employed at SOE coal factory prior to retiring, and his mother was a peasant; *CCP membership in family*: GLG11 has membership, his parents do not; *Highest level of education*: Middle vocational training (中专)

GLG13 (M)

Born: Lanzhou, Gansu (甘肃省兰州市); *Age*: 40; *Household registration*: Lanzhou; *Employment*: Team supervisor, coal company; *Family background*: Father was also employed at SOE coal factory prior to retiring, mother was a housewife; *CCP membership in family*: GLG13 and his father have membership, his mother does not; *Highest level of education*: Vocational training (大专)

Lanzhou D

> **Date:** 2 June 2012
> **Participants:** Master students
> **Location:** Northwest Normal University

GLG14 (M)

Born: Lanzhou, Gansu (甘肃省兰州市); *Age*: 24; *Household registration*: Lanzhou; *Employment*: Master student; *Family background*: Parents reside in Lanzhou,

170 *Appendix: group discussants*

father is a public servant and mother is a housewife; *CCP membership in family*: GLG14 and his father have membership, his mother does not; *Highest level of education*: Master degree

GLG15 (F)

Born: Qingyang, Gansu (甘肃省庆阳市); *Age*: 24; *Household registration*: Lanzhou, Gansu (student household registration) (甘肃兰州); *Employment*: Master student; *Family background*: Parents reside in Qingyang, father is a driver and mother is a housewife; *CCP membership in family*: GLG15 and her father have membership, her mother does not; *Highest level of education*: Master degree

GLG16 (F)

Born: Zhengningxian, Qingyang, Gansu (甘肃省庆阳市正宁县); *Age*: 24; *Household registration*: Zhengningzhen, Qingyang; *Employment*: Master student; *Family background*: Parents reside in Zhengning, father is a judge and mother is an accountant; *CCP membership in family*: Parents have membership and GLG16 is a member of the Youth League; *Highest level of education*: Master degree

GLG17 (F)

Born: Yongdengxian (rural, peripheral), Lanzhou, Gansu (甘肃省兰州市永登县); *Age*: 27; *Household registration*: Yongdengzhen, Lanzhou; *Employment*: Master student; *Family background*: Parents reside in Yongdengzhen, parents are retired private enterprise staff; *CCP membership in family*: Father has membership, her mother does not, GLG16 is member of the Youth League; *Highest level of education*: Master degree

GLG18 (F)

Born: Ningxia (宁夏); *Age*: 23; *Household registration*: Ningxia; *Employment*: Master student; *Family background*: Parents reside in Ningxia, father is a driver and mother is a housewife; *CCP membership in family*: Parents do not have membership, GLG18 is a member of the Youth League; *Highest level of education*: Master degree

GLG19 (F)

Born: Sanyuanxiang, Jingyuanxian, Baiyin, Gansu (甘肃省白银市靖远县三摊乡); *Age*: 25; *Household registration*: Sanyuanxiang, Jingyuanxian; *Employment*: Master student; *Family background*: Parents reside in Sanyuanxiang, parents are peasants; *CCP membership in family*: GLG19 and her father have membership, her mother does not; *Highest level of education*: Master degree

Nanjing

> **Date:** 26 June 2012
> **Participants:** Rural migrant workers
> **Location:** Nanjing University

Appendix: group discussants   171

GLG20 (M)

Born: Sihongxian, Suqian, Jiangsu (江苏省宿迁市泗洪县); *Age*: 36; *Household registration*: Sihongzhen, Suqian; *Employment*: University canteen worker; *Family background*: Parents reside in Sihong, father is a public counter and mother is a peasant; *CCP membership in family*: Father has membership, GLG20 and his mother do not; *Highest level of education*: Junior middle school (初中)

GLG21 (M)

Born: Sihongxian, Suqian, Jiangsu (江苏省宿迁市泗洪县); *Age*: 38; *Household registration*: Sihongzhen, Suqian; *Employment*: University canteen worker; *Family background*: Parents reside in Sihong, father is a retired teacher and mother is a peasant; *CCP membership in family*: Father has membership, GLG21 and his mother do not; *Highest level of education*: Junior middle school (初中)

GLG22 (F)

Born: Suiningxian, Xuzhou, Jiangsu (江苏省徐州市睢宁县); *Age*: 31; *Household registration*: Suining, Xuzhou; *Employment*: University canteen worker; *Family background*: Parents reside in Suining, parents are peasants; *CCP membership in family*: None; *Highest level of education*: Junior middle school (初中)

GLG23 (M)

Born: Lixinxian, Bozhou, Anhui (安徽省亳州市利辛县); *Age*: 20; *Household registration*: Lixin, Bozhou; *Employment*: University canteen worker; *Family background*: Parents reside in Lixin, parents are peasants; *CCP membership in family*: None; *Highest level of education*: Junior middle school (初中)

GLG24 (F)

Born: Xuyixian, Huai'an, Jiangsu (江苏省淮安市盱眙县); *Age*: 33; *Household registration*: Xuyi, Huai'an; *Employment*: University canteen worker; *Family background*: Parents reside in Xuyi, parents are peasants; *CCP membership in family*: Father has membership, GLG24 and her mother do not; *Highest level of education*: Regular secondary education (高中)

Taiyuan

Date: 5 September 2012
Participants: Bachelor of Business students
Location: Office block, Taiyuan downtown

GLG25 (M)

Born: Xiaoyi, Lüliang, Shanxi (山西省吕梁市孝义市); *Age*: 21; *Household registration*: Xiaoyi, Lüliang; *Employment*: Bachelor student; *Family background*: Parents reside in Xiaoyi, parents are peasants; *CCP membership in family*: Parents do not have membership, GLG25 is a member of the Youth League; *Highest education level*: Bachelor degree

172 *Appendix: group discussants*

GLG26 (M)

Born: Caizhuangzhen, Weishixian, Kaifeng, Henan (河南省开封市尉氏县蔡庄); *Age*: 23; *Household registration*: Caizhuangzhen, Weishixian; *Employment*: Bachelor student; *Family background*: Parents reside in Caizhuangzhen, father is a sole trader and mother is peasant; *CCP membership in family*: Parents do not have membership, GLG26 is a member of the Youth League; *Highest education level*: Regular secondary education (高中)

GLG27 (M)

Born: Jincheng, Shanxi (山西省晋城市); *Age*: 21; *Household registration*: Jincheng; *Employment*: Bachelor student; *Family background*: Parents reside in Jincheng, parents are workers; *CCP membership in family*: Parents do not have membership, GLG27 is a member of the Youth League; *Highest level of education*: Bachelor degree

GLG28 (F)

Born: Gucheng, Dingxingxian, Baoding, Hubei (河北省保定市定兴县固城); *Age*: 23; *Household registration*: Gucheng, Dingxingxian; *Employment*: Bachelor student; *Family background*: Parents reside in Hubei, parents are peasants; *CCP membership in family*: Parents do not have membership, GLG28 is a member of the Youth League; *Highest level of education*: Bachelor degree

GLG29 (F)

Born: Xinjiang (新疆); *Age*: 21; *Household registration*: Xinjiang; *Employment*: Bachelor student; *Family background*: Parents reside in Xinjiang, parents are peasants; *CCP membership in family*: Parents do not have membership, GLG29 is a member of the Youth League; *Highest level of education*: Bachelor degree

GLG30 (F)

Born: Shaoyang, Hunan (湖南省邵阳市); *Age*: 20; *Household registration*: Shaoyang; *Employment*: Bachelor student; *Family background*: Parents reside in Shaoyang, parents are peasants; *CCP membership in family*: Parents do not have membership, GLG30 is a member of the Youth league; *Highest level of education*: Bachelor degree

GLG31 (M)

Born: Ganzhou, Jiangxi (江西省赣州市); *Age*: 21; *Household registration*: Ganzhou; *Employment*: Bachelor student; *Family background*: Parents reside in Ganzhou, parents are peasants; *CCP membership in family*: Parents do not have membership, GLG31 is a member of the Youth League; *Highest level of education*: Bachelor degree

GLG32 (F)

Born: Hutunzhen, Feichengxian, Tai'an, Shandong (山东省泰安市肥城县湖屯镇); *Age*: 22; *Household registration*: Hutunzhen, Feichengxian; *Employment*: Bachelor student; *Family background*: Parents still reside in Hutuzhen, parents are peasants; *CCP membership in family*: Parents do not have membership, GLG32 is a member of the Youth League; *Highest level of education*: Bachelor degree

GLG33 (F)

Born: Jincheng, Shanxi (山西省晋城市); *Age*: 20; *Household registration*: Jincheng; *Employment*: Bachelor student; *Family background*: Parents reside in Jincheng, father is a worker and mother is a peasant; *CCP membership in family*: Parents do not have membership, GLG33 is a member of the Youth League; *Highest level of education*: Bachelor degree

House Mania

- **Beijing:** Young urbanites on modest incomes, but educated and consumers of foreign media and involved with expat community
  3 males and 3 female participants *(one home owner)* HM1–HM6
- **Hangzhou:** Rural migrant workers
  3 males and 1 female participant
  (3 with family access to land in the village they come from) HM7–HM10
- **Lanzhou E:** Bachelor students (Humanities)
  2 male and 3 female participants *(no homeowners)* HM11–HM15
- **Lanzhou F:** University professors (Social sciences)
  5 male and 1 female participant *(4 homeowners)* HM16–HM21
- **Taiyuan:** Mid level white collar workers and established professionals
  7 male and 5 female participants *(9 homeowners)* HM22–HM26
- **Nanjing:** Rural migrant workers
  2 males and 3 female participants *(no homeowners)* HM27–HM38

Beijing

Date: 24 August 2012
Participants: Beijing low-income youth (but educated)
Location: Culture Yard, Dongcheng, Beijing

HM1 (M)

Born: Beijing (北京); *Age*: 24; *Household registration*: Beijing; *Employment*: Media industry (public relations); *Family background*: Parents reside in Beijing; *CCP membership in family*: None; *Highest education level*: Vocational training (大专)

HM2 (F)

Born: Beijing (北京); *Age*: 27; *Household registration*: Beijing; *Employment*: Accountant; *Family background*: Parents reside in Beijing, father is a driver and mother is an accountant; *CCP membership in family*: Parents have membership, HM2 does not; *Highest education level*: Master degree (obtained in Australia)

174 *Appendix: group discussants*

HM3 (F)

Born: Mudanjiang, Heilongjiang (黑龙江牡丹江); *Age*: 25; *Household registration*: Mudanjiang; *Employment*: Art gallery employee; *Family background*: Parents reside in Mudanjiang, father is a gardener and mother works for a private corporation; *CCP membership in family*: HM3 has membership, her parents do not; *Highest level of education*: Bachelor degree

HM4 (F)

Born: Beijing (北京); *Age*: 23; *Household registration*: Beijing; *Employment*: Receptionist at foreign language magazine; *Family background*: Parents reside in Beijing, parents work in SOEs; *CCP membership in family*: Parents have membership, HM4 does not; *Highest level of education*: Bachelor degree

HM5 (M)

Born: Beijing (北京); *Age*: 28; *Household registration*: Beijing; *Employment*: Videographer; *Family background*: Parents reside in Beijing, father works for a newspaper corporation and mother is retired; *CCP membership in family*: None; *Highest level of education*: Vocational training (大专)

HM6 (M)

Born: Beijing (北京); *Age*: 24; *Household registration*: Beijing; *Employment*: Apprentice videographer; *Family background*: Parents reside in Beijing; *CCP membership in family*: None; *Highest level of education*: Vocational training (大专)

Hangzhou

> **Date:** 11 July 2012
> **Participants:** Rural migrant workers
> **Location:** Zhejiang University campus dormitory rooms

HM7 (M)

Born: Tangbian, Qingzhen, Changshanxian, Quzhou, Zhejiang (浙江省衢州市常山县青镇塘边); *Age*: 23; *Household registration*: Tangbian, Qingzhen; *Employment*: KTV customer service; *Family background*: Parents reside in Tangbian; father is an engineer and mother is a nurse; *CCP membership in family*: None; *Highest level of education*: Regular secondary education (高中)

HM8 (M)

Born: Chendian, Xincaixian, Zhumadian, Henan (河南省驻马店市新蔡县陈店镇); *Age*: 24; *Household registration*: Chendianzhen, Xincaixian; *Employment*: KTV customer service; *Family background*: Parents reside in Chendianzhen, parents are peasants; *CCP membership in family*: Father has membership, HM7 and his mother do not; *Highest level of education*: Junior middle school (初中)

Appendix: group discussants   175

HM9 (M)

Born: Fujian (福建); *Age*: 24; *Household registration*: Fujian; *Employment*: KTV customer service; *Family background*: Parents are peasants; *CCP membership in family*: Parents do not have membership, HM8 was a member of the Youth League; *Highest level of education*: Regular secondary education (高中)

HM10 (F)

Born: Linan, Hangzhou, Zhejiang (浙江省临安市); *Age*: 21; *Household registration*: Linan; *Employment*: Unemployed; *Family background*: Parents reside in Linan, parents are workers; *CCP membership in family*: Parents do not have membership, HM9 was a member of the Youth League

Lanzhou E

Date: 2 June 2012
Participants: Undergraduate students
Location: Northwest Normal University

HM11 (F)

Born: Feicheng, Tai'an, Shandong (山东省泰安市肥城市); *Age*: 24; *Household registration*: Tai'an, Feichang; *Employment*: Bachelor student; *Family background*: Parents reside in Tai'an, parents are "skilled workers"; *CCP membership in family*: Parents do not have membership, HM10 is a member of the Youth League; *Highest level of education*: Bachelor degree

HM12 (M)

Born: Shaozhaixiang, Lingtai, Pingliang, Gansu (甘肃省灵台县邵寨乡); *Age*: 23; *Household registration*: Shaozhaixiang, Lingtai; *Employment*: Bachelor student; *Family background*: Parents reside in Shaozhaixiang, parents are peasants; *CCP membership in family*: Parents do not have membership, HM11 is a member of the Youth League; *Highest level of education*: Bachelor degree

HM13 (F)

Born: Zhailizhen, Laicheng, Laiwu, Shandong (山东省莱芜市莱城寨里镇); *Age*: 23; *Household registration*: Laicheng; *Employment*: Bachelor student; *Family background*: Parents reside in Zhailizhen, parents are peasants; *CCP membership in family*: Parents do not have membership, HM12 is a member of the Youth League; *Highest level of education*: Bachelor degree

HM14 (F)

Born: Pingdu, Qingdao, Shandong (平度青岛山东); *Age*: 25; *Household registration*: Pingdu, Qingdao; *Employment*: Bachelor student; *Family background*: Parents reside in Pingdu, parents are administrators of an agricultural market; *CCP membership in family*: Parents do not have membership, HM13 is a member of the Youth League; *Highest level of education*: Bachelor degree

176   *Appendix: group discussants*

HM15 (M)

Born: Juanchengxian, Heze, Shandong (山东省菏泽市鄄城县); *Age*: 24; *Household registration*: Juancheng, Heze; *Employment*: Bachelor student; *Family Background*: Parents reside in Juancheng, father is a public servant and her mother is a business woman; *CCP membership in family*: Father has membership, mother does not, HM15 is a member of the Youth League; *Highest level of education*: Bachelor degree

Lanzhou F

> **Date:** 4 June 2012
> **Participants:** University lecturers/professors
> **Location:** Northwest Normal University

HM16 (M)

Born: Zhenyuanxian, Qingyang, Gansu (甘肃省庆阳市镇原县); Age: 38; *Household registration*: Lanzhou, Gansu (甘肃省兰州市); *Employment*: Social science academic; *Family background*: Parents reside in Zhenyuanxian, parents are peasants; *CCP membership in family*: HM16 and his father have membership, his mother does not; *Highest level of education*: PhD

HM17 (M)

Born: Zhangye, Gansu (甘肃省张掖市); Age: 33; *Household registration*: Lanzhou, Gansu (甘肃省兰州市); *Employment*: Social science academic; *Family background*: Parents reside in Zhangye, father's employment undisclosed, mother is a housewife; *CCP membership in family*: HM16 and his father have membership, his mother does not; *Highest level of education*: Master degree

HM18 (M)

Born: Qingyang, Gansu (甘肃省庆阳市); *Age*: 36; *Household registration*: Lanzhou, Gansu (甘肃省兰州市); *Employment*: Education studies academic; *Family background*: Parents reside in Qingyang, his father was a teacher and his mother was a peasant; *CCP membership in family*: HM17 and his father have membership, his mother does not; *Highest level of education*: PhD

HM19 (M)

Born: Huachixian, Qingyang, Gansu (甘肃省庆阳市华池县); *Age*: 38; *Household registration*: Lanzhou, Gansu (甘肃省兰州市); *Employment*: Lecturer; *Family background*: Parents reside now in Lanzhou too, parents were peasants; *CCP membership in family*: HM19 has membership, but his parents do not; *Highest level of education*: Master degree

HM20 (M)

Born: Huanxian, Qingyang, Gansu (甘肃省庆阳市环县); *Age*: 41; *Household registration*: Lanzhou, Gansu (甘肃省兰州市); *Employment*: Professor; *Family background*: Parents reside in Huanxian, his parents were employed in agricultural management; *CCP membership in family*: HM20 has membership, his parents do not; *Highest level of education*: PhD

Appendix: group discussants 177

HM21 (F)

Born: Weifang, Shandong (山东省潍坊市); *Age*: 32; *Household registration*: Lanzhou, Gansu (甘肃兰州); *Employment*: Academic; *Family background*: Parents reside in Weifang, father is retired and mother is a business woman; *CCP membership in family*: HM21 and her parents have membership; *Highest level of education*: PhD

Nanjing

Date: 30 June 2012
Participants: Rural migrant workers
Location: Nanjing University

HM22 (F)

Born: Zhongxingzhen, Siyang, Suqian, Jiangsu (江苏省泗阳县众兴镇); *Age*: 27; *Household registration*: Zhongxingzhen, Siyang; *Employment*: Unemployed; *Family background*: Parents reside in Zhongxingzhen, parents' employment unspecified; *CCP membership in family*: None; *Highest level of education*: Middle school (中学)

HM23 (M)

Born: Dongkanzhen, Binhaixian, Yancheng, Jiangsu (江苏省盐城市滨海县东坎镇); *Age*: 42; *Household registration*: Dongkanzhen, Binhaixian; *Employment*: Tradesmen with electricity and water bureau; *Family background*: Parents reside in Dongkanzhen, father is employed with Binghai water board, mother is a peasant; *CCP membership in family*: None; *Highest level of education*: Regular secondary education (高中)

HM24 (F)

Born: Gangnancun/Xingangxiang, Binhaixian, Yancheng, Jiangsu (江苏省盐城市滨海县新港乡/胜利村); *Age*: 43; *Household registration*: Gangnancun, Binhai; *Employment*: Nanjing University car park attendant; *Family background*: Parents reside in Gangnancun, parents are peasants; *CCP membership in family*: None; *Highest level of education*: Junior middle school (初中)

HM25 (M)

Born: Huaiyinxian, Huai'an, Jiangsu (江苏省淮安市淮阴县); *Age*: 26; *Household registration*: Huaiyinxian, Huai'an; *Employment*: University canteen worker; *Family background*: Parents reside in Huaiyinxian, father is an electrician for the Huaiyin city rail, mother is a peasant; *CCP membership in family*: Father has membership, HM25 and his mother do not

HM26 (F)

Born: Xuyixian, Huai'an, Jiangsu (江苏省淮安市盱眙县); *Age*: 34; *Household registration*: Xuyi, Huai'an; *Employment*: University canteen worker; *Family background*: Parents reside in Xuyi, parents are livestock peasants; *CCP membership in family*: None; *Highest level of education*: Middle school (中学)

178 *Appendix: group discussants*

Taiyuan

Date: 8 September 2012
Participants: White collar workers (all levels)
Location: Office block, downtown Taiyuan

HM27 (M)

Born: Xiaodian, Taiyuan, Shanxi (山西省太原市小店); *Age*: 41; *Household registration*: Xiaodian, Taiyuan; *Employment*: Plastics factory; *Family background*: Parents reside in Xiaodian; *CCP membership in family*: None; *Highest level of education*: Junior middle school (初中)

HM28 (F)

Born: Jishan, Yuncheng, Shanxi (山西省运城市稷山县); *Age*: 27; *Household registration*: Jishan, Yuncheng; *Employment*: Private operator; *Family background*: Parents reside in Houma, Linfen, Shanxi (山西省临汾市侯马), parents are private operators; *CCP membership in family*: None; *Highest level of education*: Vocational training (大专)

HM29 (F)

Born: Jiancaoping, Taiyuan, Shanxi (山西省太原市尖草坪); *Age*: 51; *Household registration*: Wenmiaoxian, Taiyuan, Shanxi (山西省太原市文庙县); *Employment*: Fashion industry; *Family background*: Parents reside in Jiancaoping, father was a doctor in the military hospital and mother was a factory worker; *CCP membership in family*: None; *Highest level of education*: Regular secondary education (高中)

HM30 (M)

Born: Zhangqingxiang, Yuci, Jinzhong, Shanxi (山西省晋中市榆次市张庆乡); *Age*: 58; *Household registration*: Zhangqingxiang, Yuci; *Employment*: Manager of a university canteen; *Family background*: Parents reside in Zhangqingxiang, Yuci, mother was a peasant, father's occupation undisclosed; *CCP membership in family*: None; *Highest level of education*: Junior middle school (初中)

HM31 (M)

Born: Xinzhou, Shanxi (山西省忻州市); *Age*: 49; *Household registration*: Taiyuan, Shanxi (山西省太原市); *Employment*: School teacher; *Family background*: Parents reside in Xinzhou, father was a businessman, mother was a housewife; *CCP membership in family*: HM31 has membership, his parents do not; *Highest level of education*: Regular secondary education (高中)

HM32 (F)

Born: Taiyuan, Shanxi (山西省太原市); *Age*: 34; *Household registration*: Taiyuan; *Employment*: Office administrator; *Family background*: Parents reside in Taiyuan, parents are retired workers; *CCP membership in family*: Both parents have membership, HM32 was a member of the Youth League; *Highest level of education*: Vocational training (大专)

Appendix: group discussants 179

HM33 (M)

Born: Jinan, Shandong (山东省济南市); *Age*: 63; *Household registration*: Taiyuan, Shanxi (山西省太原市); *Employment*: Editor, publishing company; *Family background*: Parents live in Taiyuan, parents were cadres; *CCP membership in family*: HM33 and his father have membership, his mother did not; *Highest level of education*: Master degree

HM34 (F)

Born: Wuhan, Hubei (湖北省武汉市); *Age*: 58; *Household registration*: Taiyuan, Shanxi (山西省太原市); *Employment*: Editor, publishing company; HM34 grew up in various places throughout China, parents have settled in Taiyuan, father was an officer in the army and mother was a secretary; *CCP membership in family*: Parents have membership, HM31 does not

HM35 (M)

Born: Shanyinxian, Shuozhou, Shanxi (山西省朔州市山阴县); *Age*: 56; *Household registration*: Shanyin, Shuozhou; *Employment*: Education bureau of Shanyin; *Family background*: Parents reside in Shanyin, parents were peasants; *CCP membership in family*: HM35 and his father have membership, his mother does not; *Highest level of education*: Vocational training (大专)

HM36 (F)

Born: Taiyuan, Shanxi (山西省太原市); *Age*: 50; *Household registration*: Taiyuan; *Employment*: Steel factory worker, HM36's parents were employed at the same factory; *CCP membership in family*: Father has membership, HM36 and her mother do not; *Highest level of education*: Middle vocational training (中专)

HM37 (M)

Born: Xinghualing, Taiyuan, Shanxi (山西省太原市杏花岭); *Age*: 51; *Household registration*: Xinghualing, Taiyuan; *Employment*: Computer salesmen; *Family background*: Parents reside in Xinghualing, father was employed in Taiyuan's business chambers, mother is unemployed; *CCP membership in family*: None; *Highest level of education*: Middle vocational training (中专)

HM38 (M)

Born: Taiyuan, Shanxi (山西省太原市); *Age*: 52; *Household registration*: Taiyuan; *Employment*: Plant nursery; *Family background*: Parents reside in Taiyuan, father was a mechanic; *CCP membership in family*: Father has membership, HM38 and his mother do not; *Highest level of education*: Junior middle school (初中)

The Piano in a Factory

- **Beijing:** Educated urbanites employed in white collar labour
  3 males and 4 female participants: appendix references PIAF1–PIAF7
- **Hangzhou:** Rural migrant workers employed in a fire alarm business
  5 male participants: appendix references PIAF8–PIAF12

180 *Appendix: group discussants*

- **Lanzhou G:** Coal factory workers with low levels of education
  4 males and 1 female participant: appendix references PIAF13–PIAF17
- **Lanzhou H:** Master students (social sciences)
  3 males and 2 female participants: appendix references PIAF18–PIAF22
- **Nanjing:** Rural migrant workers employed in a university canteen and the campus security unit
  2 males and 3 female participants: appendix references PIAF23–PIAF27
- **Taiyuan:** Educated professionals of a mature age and low to mid-level white collar workers
  7 males and 4 female participants: appendix references PIAF28–PIAF38

Beijing

Date: 15 September 2014
Participants: White collar workers
Location: Culture Yard, Dongcheng, Beijing

PIAF1 (F)
Born: Yancheng, Jiangsu (江苏省盐城市); *Age*: 35; *Household registration*: Beijing (北京); *Employment*: Electrical power industry; *Family background*: Parents reside in Yancheng, father is a public servant and mother is a teacher; *CCP membership in family*: Father has membership, PIAF1 and her mother do not; *Highest level of education*: Vocational training (大专)

PIAF2 (M)
Born: Shangqiu, Henan (河南省商丘市); *Age*: 28; *Household registration*: Shangqiu; *Employment*: Journalist for a finance magazine; *Family background*: Parents reside in Shangqiu, parents are peasants; *CCP membership in family*: None; *Highest level of education*: Master degree

PIAF3 (M)
Born: Chongqing, Sichuan (四川省重庆市); *Age*: 25; *Household registration*: Beijing (北京); *Employment*: PhD student; *Family background*: Parents reside in Chongqing, parents are technicians; *CCP membership in family*: Mother has membership, father does not, PIAF3 is a Youth League member; *Highest level of education*: PhD

PIAF4 (F)
Born: Meixian, Baoji, Shaanxi (陕西省宝鸡市眉县); *Age*: 35; *Household registration*: Meixian; *Employment*: Employed by a software company; *Family background*: Parents reside in Meixian, both parents are peasants; *CCP membership in family*: Parents do not have membership, but PIAF4 was a member of the Youth League; *Highest level of education*: Bachelor degree

PIAF5 (F)
Born: Jiangshan, Quzhou, Zhejiang (浙江省衢州江山市); *Age*: 29; *Household registration*: Beijing (北京); *Employment*: Asset management company; *Family*

background: Parents reside in Jiangshan, father works at a major national bank and mother used to work in a food production factory; *CCP membership in family*: PIAF5 and his father have membership, his mother does not; *Highest level of education*: Master degree

PIAF6 (M)

Born: Lanlingzhen, Cangshanxian, Linyi, Shandong (山东省苍山县临沂兰陵镇); *Age*: 28; *Household registration*: Lanlingzhen, Cangshan; *Employment*: Freelance; *Family background*: Parents reside in Lanlingzhen, both parents are peasants; *CCP membership in family*: Parents do not have membership, but PIAF6 is a Youth League member; *Highest level of education*: Vocational training (大专)

PIAF7 (F)

Born: Xinxiang, Henan (河南省新乡市); *Age*: 33; *Household registration*: Xinxiang; *Employment*: Customer service at a book shop; *Family background*: Parents reside in Xinxiang, father works at a plastic material factory and mother is a primary school teacher; *CCP membership in family*: Father has membership, her mother does not, PIAF7 was a member of the Youth league; *Highest level of education*: Vocational training (大专)

Hangzhou

Date: 12 July 2012
Participants: Rural migrant workers
Location: Offices of a fire alarm installation company in the outskirts of Hangzhou

PIAF8 (M)

Born: Jinhua, Zhejiang (浙江省金华市); *Age*: 30; *Household registration*: Jinhua; *Employment*: Fire protection worker; *Family background*: Parents reside in Jinhua, father is a customer service worker, mother is a peasant; *CCP membership in family*: None; *Highest level of education*: Middle vocational training (中专)

PIAF9 (M)

Born: Lanxi, Jinhua, Zhejiang (浙江省金华市兰溪村); *Age*: 22; *Household registration*: Lanxi; *Employment*: Fire protection worker; *Family background*: Parents reside in Lanxi, parents are self-employed; *CCP membership in family*: None; *Highest level of education*: Regular secondary education (高中)

PIAF10 (M)

Born: Hunan (湖南); *Age*: 27; *Household registration*: Hunan; *Employment*: Fire protection worker; *Family background*: Parents are retrenched workers; *CCP membership in family*: Parents do not have membership, PIAF10 was a member of the Youth League; *Highest level of education*: Regular secondary education (高中)

182　*Appendix: group discussants*

PIAF11 (M)

Born: Lanxi, Jinhua, Zhejiang (浙江省金华市兰溪村); *Age*: 29; *Household registration*: Lanxi, Jinhua; *Employment*: Fire protection worker; *Family background*: Parents reside in Lanxi, parents are peasants; *CCP membership in family*: Parents do not have membership, PIAF11 was a member of the Youth League; *Highest level of education*: Vocational training (大专)

PIAF12 (M)

Born: Lanxi, Jinhua, Zhejiang (浙江金华市兰溪村); *Age*: 27; *Household registration*: Lanxi, Jinhua; *Employment*: KTV customer service; *Family background*: Parents reside in Zhejiang, but work in a different city to Lanxi, parents are workers; *CCP membership in family*: Father has membership, mother does not, PIAF12 was a member of the Youth League; *Highest level of education*: Specialised trade school (职高)

Lanzhou G

Date: 5 June 2012
Participants: Factory workers
Location: Northwest Normal University

PIAF13 (M)
Born: Lanzhou, Gansu (甘肃省兰州市); *Age*: 55; *Household registration*: Lanzhou; *Employment*: Coal factory worker; *Family background*: PIAF13 grew up in Lanzhou, his father was an accountant and mother was a business woman; *CCP membership in family*: Father had membership, PIAF13 and his mother do not; *Highest level of education*: Middle vocational training (中专)

PIAF14 (M)

Born: Chengguan, Lanzhou, Gansu (甘肃省兰州市城关); *Age*: 52; *Household registration*: Chengguan, Lanzhou; *Employment*: Service provider at a coal factory; *Family background*: Parents are no longer alive, father was a worker and mother was a peasant; *CCP membership in family*: None; *Highest level of education*: Regular secondary education (高中)

PIAF15 (M)

Born: Qilihe, Lanzhou, Gansu (甘肃省兰州市七里河); *Age*: 42; *Household registration*: Qilihe, Lanzhou; *Employment*: Cashier at a coal factory; *Family background*: PIAF15's parents reside in Chengguan, Lanzhou (甘肃省兰州市城关) where PIAF15 grew up, father was a driver and mother was a housewife; *CCP membership in family*: Father has membership, PIAF15 and his mother do not; *Highest level of education*: Junior middle school (初中)

PIAF16 (M)

Born: Lanzhou, Gansu (甘肃省兰州市); *Age*: 40; *Household registration*: Lanzhou; *Employment*: Employee at a coal factory; *Family background*: Parents reside in

Lanzhou, parents are peasants; *CCP membership in family*: PIAF16 has membership, his parents do not; *Highest level of education*: Regular secondary education (高中)

PIAF17 (F)

Born: Lanzhou, Gansu (甘肃省兰州市); *Age*: 39; *Household registration*: Chengguan, Lanzhou (兰州市城关); *Employment*: Coal factory worker; *Family background*: Parents reside in Lanzhou, father worked for a former SOE coal factory, and mother was a housewife; *CCP membership in family*: Father has membership, mother does not, PIAF17 was a member of the Youth League; *Highest level of education*: Regular secondary education (高中) (she notes she did not complete)

Lanzhou H

Date: 6 June 2012
Participants: Postgraduate students
Location: Northwest Normal University

PIAF18 (F)

Born: Baiyin, Gansu (甘肃白银市); *Age*: 23; *Household registration*: Baiyin; *Employment*: Postgraduate student; *Family background*: Parents reside in Baiyin, father is self-employed and mother is unemployed; *CCP membership in family*: Parents do not have membership, PIAF18 is a member of the Youth League; *Highest level of education*: Master degree

PIAF19 (M)

Born: Pingluozhen, Kangxian, Longnan, Gansu (甘肃省陇南市康县平洛镇); *Age*: 21; *Household registration*: Lanzhou (兰州); *Employment*: Postgraduate student; *Family background*: Parents reside in Pingluozhen, parents are peasants; *CCP membership in family*: Parents do not have membership, PIAF18 is a member of the Youth League; *Highest level of education*: Master degree

PIAF20 (F)

Born: Wuwei, Gansu (甘肃省武威市); *Age*: 23; *Household registration*: Wuwei; *Employment*: Postgraduate student; *Family background*: Parents reside in Wuwei, father is a construction engineer and mother is a housewife; *CCP membership in family*: Parents do not have membership, PIAF18 is a member of the Youth League; *Highest level of education*: Master degree

PIAF21 (M)

Born: Jingtaixian, Baiyin, Gansu (甘肃省白银市景泰县); *Age*: 24; *Household registration*: Jingtaixian, Baiyin; *Employment*: Postgraduate student; *Family background*: Parents reside in Jingtai, father works at the Broadcasting and TV Bureau and mother is a housewife; *CCP membership in family*: PIAF18 and his father have membership, his mother does not; *Highest level of education*: Master degree

184 *Appendix: group discussants*

PIAF22 (M)

Born: Huiningxian, Baiyin, Gansu (甘肃省白银市会宁县); *Age*: 23; *Household registration*: Huining, Baiyin; *Employment*: Postgraduate student; *Family background*: Parents reside in Huining, parents are peasants; *CCP membership in family*: Parents do not have membership, PIAF19 is preparing his membership; *Highest level of education*: Master degree

Nanjing

Date: 29 June 2012
Participants: Rural migrant workers
Location: Nanjing University

PIAF23 (F)
Born: Pizhou, Xuzhou, Jiangsu (江苏省徐州市邳州); *Age*: 29; *Household registration*: Pizhou, Xuzhou; *Employment*: University canteen worker; *Family background*: Parents are peasants; *CCP membership in family*: Parents do not have membership, PIAF20 was a member of the Youth League; *Highest level of education*: Regular secondary education (高中)

PIAF24 (F)
Born: Caoqiaocun, Xinyi, Xuzhou, Jiangsu (江苏省徐州市新沂市草桥村); *Age*: 25; *Household registration*: Caoqiaocun, Xinyi; *Employment*: University canteen worker; *Family background*: Parents are peasants; *CCP membership in family*: None; *Highest level of education*: Junior middle school (初中)

PIAF25 (M)

Born: Suiningxian, Xuzhou, Jiangsu (江苏徐州市睢宁县); *Age*: 27; *Household registration*: Tangshanzhen, Jiangning, Nanjing, Jiangsu (江苏南京市江宁汤山镇); *Employment*: University canteen worker; *Family background*: Parents reside in Suiningxian, parents are peasants; *CCP membership in family*: None; *Highest level of education*: Junior middle school (初中)

PIAF26 (M)

Born: Xuzhou, Jiangsu (江苏省徐州市); *Age*: 22; *Household registration*: Xuzhou; *Employment*: University canteen worker; *Family background*: Parents reside in Xuzhou, parents are peasants; *CCP membership in family*: Parents do not have membership, PIAF23 is a Youth League member; *Highest level of education*: Vocational training (大专)

PIAF27 (M)

Born: Jiangning, Nanjing, Jiangsu (江苏省南京市江宁); *Age*: 31; *Household registration*: Jiangning, Nanjing; *Employment*: University canteen worker; *Family background*: Parents reside in Jiangning, parents are peasants; *CCP membership in family*: Parents do not have membership, PIAF24 was a member of the Youth League; *Highest level of education*: Vocational training (大专)

Taiyuan

Date: 10 September 2012
Participants: Professionals and white collar workers
Location: Office block, Taiyuan downtown

PIAF28 (M)

Born: Zuoyunxian, Datong, Shanxi (山西省大同市左云县); *Age*: 28; *Household registration*: Zuoyunxian, Datong; *Employment*: Pharmaceutical sales; *Family background*: Parents reside in Zuoyun, Datong, parents are self-employed; *CCP membership in family*: None; *Highest level of education*: Bachelor degree

PIAF29 (M)

Born: Yangquan, Shanxi (山西省阳泉市); *Age*: 56; *Household registration*: Wanbailin, Taiyuan, Shanxi (山西省太原市万柏林); *Employment*: Social welfare institution; *Family background*: Parents reside in Yangquan, parents are unemployed; *CCP membership in family*: PIAF29 and his father have membership, his mother does not; *Highest level of education*: Bachelor degree

PIAF30 (M)

Born: Taiyuan, Shanxi (山西省太原市); *Age*: 50; *Household registration*; Wanbailin, Taiyuan, Shanxi (太原市万柏林区); *Employment*: State-owned coal company; *Family background*: Parents reside in Taiyuan, PIAF30's parents were employed at the same SOE; *CCP membership in family*: PIAF30 and his father have membership, his mother does not; *Highest level of education*: Vocational training (大专)

PIAF31 (M)

Born: Taiyuan, Shanxi (山西省太原市); *Age*: 59; *Household registration*: Taiyuan; *Employment*: Employed at Taiyuan's central furnace plant; *Family background*: Parents reside in Taiyuan, parents are deceased; *CCP membership in family*: Parents did not have membership, PIAF31 does; *Highest level of education*: Vocational training (大专)

PIAF32 (M)

Born: Taiyuan, Shanxi (山西省太原市); *Age*: 40; *Household registration*: Laojungong, Taiyuan (山西省太原市老军营); *Employment*: Service provider in the cafeteria of Shanxi Hotel; *Family background*: Parents reside in Taiyuan city centre, parents are employed at a construction materials company; *CCP membership in family*: None; *Highest level of education*: Vocational training (大专)

PIAF33 (F)

Born: Taiyuan, Shanxi (山西省太原市); *Age*: 37; *Household registration*: Taiyuan; *Employment*: Employed at a training school; *Family background*: Parents reside in Taiyuan, father is a worker and mother is a peasant; *CCP membership in family*: Father has membership, PIAF33 and her mother do not; *Highest level of education*: Master degree

186   *Appendix: group discussants*

PIAF34 (F)

Born: Jincheng, Shanxi (山西省晋城市); *Age*: 23; *Household registration*: Taiyuan, Shanxi (山西省太原市); *Employment*: Postgraduate student; *Family background*: Parents reside in Jincheng, father is a teacher and mother is a financial manager; *CCP membership in family*: None; *Highest level of education*: Master degree

PIAF35 (F)

Born: Wanrongxian, Yuncheng, Shanxi (山西省运城市万荣县); *Age*: 50; *Household registration*: Taiyuan, Shanxi (山西省太原市); *Employment*: Employed in the publication and media industry; *Family background*: Parents reside in Wanrongxian, father is a teacher and mother is a peasant; *CCP membership in family*: PIAF35 and her father have membership, her mother does not; *Highest level of education*: Master degree

PIAF36 (M)

Born: Xinzhou, Shanxi (山西省忻州); *Age*: 49; *Household registration*: Taiyuan, Shanxi (山西省太原市); *Employment*: Taiyuan Work Safety Bureau; *Family background*: Parents reside in Xinzhou, parents work at a hospital; *CCP membership in family*: PIAF36 and his parents have membership; *Highest level of education*: Vocational training (大专)

PIAF37 (F)

Born: Taiyuan, Shanxi (山西省太原市); *Age*: 31; *Household registration*: Taiyuan; *Employment*: Taiyuan City Bureau of Gardening; *Family background*: Parents reside in Taiyuan, father is employed in the Propaganda Department of Municipal Party Council and mother employed by Taiyuan City Bureau of Gardening; *CCP membership in family*: PIAF32 and his father have membership, his mother does not; *Highest level of education*: Bachelor degree

PIAF38 (M)

Born: Taiyuan, Shanxi (山西省太原市); *Age*: 55; *Household registration*: Taiyuan; *Employment*: Manual labourer at a school; *Family background*: Parents reside in Taiyuan, parents are peasants; *CCP membership in family*: PIAF32 has membership, his parents do not

Index

access to cinema: class and 15–17; of privileged class 26; of working class 23–4

affirmative prejudice 52, 70

Allen, Michael Patrick 9

Artistic Exploration Award 130

audience, Chinese: access and class of 15–17; "buddy road movie" and 58–64; class and 2–3; entertainment sensibilities of 2–3; exclusion and class of 15–17; of *Go Lala Go!* 16, 76–9, 148; of *House Mania* 16, 103–5, 147; of *Let the Bullets Fly* 16, 30–1, 38–9, 45–6, 147; of *Lost on Journey* 52–4, 147–8; male 86–7, 137; marketing to 15–17; nation's cinema and 26; of *Piano in a Factory, The* 16, 130–2, 148; pre-conditioning 5–6, 22–6, 146; preferences of 10; segmented 142–3; sense making and 4–6, 26, 147–8; social engineering of 32, 151; of *Twin Bracelets* 5; UK audience versus 5; understanding 18; world views of 151; *see also* female audience; group discussants

background information on films: *Go Lala Go!* 74–6; *House Mania* 101–3; *Let the Bullets Fly* 29–30; *Lost on Journey* 51–2; *Piano in a Factory, The* 128–9

Barnett, Lisa A. 9

Berry, Chris 75–6

bias *see* prejudice; stereotyping

binge consumption 93–5

Bourdieu, Pierre 9

Braester, Yomi 2–3, 115

Bride Wars (film) 149

"buddy road movie" 58–64

CCP policy 5

Chan, Anita 8

chauvinism 13

China: class in 1–2, 8–9, 29, 51, 149; classless society in 2; collective incidents in 8; commercial cinema in 1–2; education policy in 7; film consumption in 15; film spectatorship in 2; flask-shaped society in 9; home ownership in 102, 119–20; housing reforms in 101; labour force in 142–3; leadership in 17, 29, 32–5, 39, 43, 46; legal system in 37, 39; masculinity in 105–6; media in 44–5; middle class in 6–7; peasant mobilisation in 41; popular culture in 58; power in 17, 32–5, 39, 43; property market in 102, 110, 123–4; social harmony in 2, 6–9, 29, 71; social organisation in, conflicting modes of 137; *suzhi* in 7; wealth accumulation in, assumptions about 34; *see also* China's cinema of class; Chinese films and film industry

China Central Television (CCTV) 24

China Film Group Corporation (CFGC) 29

China Household Income Project (CHIP) data 119–20

China's cinema of class: audience access and exclusion and 15–17; class consciousness as shared histories and 14–15; defining cinema of class and 1; filmmaker in 18, 146–51; films analyzed and 1, 9–10, 153; films list and 153; gender and class and 12–13; group discussions and 10–12; narrative resolutions in 17; new 26; prejudice and 52; prejudice and class and 13–14; shared histories and 14–15; socialised understanding of class and 12, 16–17, 151; studying 9; *suzhi* and class and 12–13; Western histories and 15; *see also specific film*

Chinese audience *see* audience

188 *Index*

Chinese films and film industry: access to 15–17; annual production by 146–7; blockbusters in, domestic 148; commercialisation of 3–4; consciousness of narratives and 150–1; globalization and 18; goals of 3; growth of 29, 151; landlord characters in 101; new research trends in 4; past research on 3; players in 149–50; political narratives in 29; privileged class and 150; social engineering of people and 151; women and, general portrayal of 75–6; *see also specific film*

CHIP data 119–20

Chuang, Tzu-i 80

Clark, Paul 2

class: access to cinema and 15–17; audience and, Chinese 2–3; of characters in film 12–13; in China 1–2, 8–9, 29, 51, 149; consciousness as shared histories 14–15; as exclusion to cinema 15–17; factors affecting positioning and 2–3; frameworks of, theoretical 149; gender and 13; *Go Lala Go!* and 10, 76; home ownership and 123; *House Mania* and 10; *Let the Bullets Fly* and 10, 32; *Lost on Journey* and 10, 50–2, 54, 58–9; middle 6–7, 9; *Piano in a Factory, The,* and 10, 141; prejudice and 13–14, 51–2, 54–8, 67, 70, 122; socialised understanding of 12; socialising 1–2, 9, 32, 141, 149, 151; social mobility and 67–70; stereotyping 13–14, 54–8, 67; structures 29; as *suzhi* 12–13; theory 149–50; tolerance based on 70–1; in United States 146; *see also* privileged class; working class

Classless Society, The (Kingston) 146

collective incidents in China 8

collective stability 137

computer graphic imagery (CGI) 9–10, 30

consumption: binge 93–5; in China 15; as female behavior 90, 92–5; of film in China 15; media 4–5; product placement and 90–1, *91*

corruption: in *Let the Bullets Fly* 34–5, 39; power 17, 32–5, 39; in property market 13, 102, 110–11, 118

"cultural authority" 8

"cuteness" performance: hierarchies and, navigating 80–3, *80*; social mobility and 83–5

deception 112, *112–14*

dialogue: in *Let the Bullets Fly* 30, 45; in *Piano in a Factory, The* 129–30

Dickson, Bruce 7–8, 34

discussion groups *see* group discussions

divorce 129, 135–8

Douban (social forum) 52

Dovidio, John F. 56

exclusion of power 34

family: divorce and 135–6; *Lost on Journey* and 68–9; *suzhi* of 7; white collar woman and 79

Farquhar, Mary 75–6

female audience: *Go Lala Go!* and 78–9, 94–5; *Let the Bullets Fly* and 38–9, 44; *Piano in a Factory, The*, and 129, 134–5

"female infantilization" 80; *see also* gender, stereotyping

Field, Patricia 90

film literacy 17, 30–1, 45

Friedman, Sara 5

Fudan University 4–5

gender: class and 12–13; professional sacrifice for white collar romances and 85–9; *shengnü* and 18, 75, 80, 89, 96, 102; stereotyping 75, 77, 79–85, 90, 92–5; *suzhi* and 12–13; *see also* female audience; masculinity

Go Lala Go! (film): audience of 16, 76–9, 148; background information about 74–6; class and 10, 76; female audience and 78–9, 94–5; gender stereotyping in 75, 77, 80–5; group discussants for 167–73; group discussions of 76–9, 84–6; hierarchies and, "cuteness" in navigating 80–3, *80*; Lala as an idol for a vanguard generation and 79–80; male audiences and 86–7; marriageability and 75; maternal duties and 144; mixed messages of 95–6; premise of 75; privileged class and, view of 77–8, 90, 93, 95–6; production values of 76; product placement in 76, 90, *91*; professional sacrifice for white collar romances and 85–9; promotional poster of *73*; selection of for study 9; sexual enticement in 89; *shengnü* and 18, 75, 80, 89, 96, 102; shopping as female behavior and 90, 92–5; social mobility in 74–5, 80–5; synopsis of 74; white

Index   189

collar women and 79–80, 96; white color romances and 85–9; working class and, view of 77–8, 88–9, 93, 95–6
Golden Rooster Award 130
Goodman, David 7–8, 11, 117
group discussants: compensation for 23, 25; *Go Lala Go!* 167–73; *House Mania* 173–9; *Let the Bullets Fly* 154–60; *Lost on Journey* 160–7; overview 11–12; *Piano in a Factory, The* 180–6; *see also* audience, Chinese; group discussions; privileged class; working class
group discussions: China's cinema of class and 10–12; Chinese versus US and Japanese films and 26; of *Go Lala Go!* 76–9, 84–6; of *House Mania* 103–12, 115–16, 121–2; length of time of 24–5; of *Let the Bullets Fly* 30–1, 34–5, 38–9, 42–6; of *Lost on Journey* 52–8, 64–71; methodology 12; of *Piano in a Factory, The* 130–7, 142–3; with privileged class 24–6; purposes of 10–11; with working class 22–4; *see also* group discussants; privileged class; working class
Guo, Yingjie 34

Hark, Ina Rae 58, 60
Hawes, Colin 37
Hendrischke, Hans 7
hierarchy *see* class
home ownership: in China 102, 119–20; in *House Mania* 18, 105–9, 114, 123
House Mania (film): audience of 16, 103–5, 147; background information about 101–3; box office revenue of 102–3; class and 10; deception in 112, *112–14*; destiny of 122; exhibition time of 9; group discussants for 173–9; group discussions of 103–12, 115–16, 121–2; home ownership and 18, 105–9, 114, 123; humor of 103; location of 103; marriageability and 102, 105–9; masculinity and 18, 105–9, 120; privileged class and, view of 103–5, 108–11, 114–15, 118, 121; privilege and, rethinking 117–18; production values of 103; promotional poster of *99*; property market and 102, 110–12, 114–15, 123–4; purpose of 118; residence choice and 115–17; rural investors in property and 122–4; rural to urban investment and 119–22, *120*; selection of for study 9; *siheyuan*

and 101, 115–16; synopsis of 100–1; working class and, view of 103–8, 114, 117–18, 123
House, The (film) 149
Hsing, You-Tien 110
Huang, Phillip 7, 138
Hu Jintao 6

I am Lala (film) 149
I am Somebody (film) 149
inclusion of power 34
individual needs, assertion of 135–8
industrial heroes 138–41
investment in housing, rural to urban 119–22, *120*

James, David E. 146
Jinglei, Xu 80
Jinhua, Dai 80
Jin, Xie 41
Johnson, Matthew 4

Kam, Jessica 130–1, 137
Kingston, Paul W. 146
Kraus, Richard 133

labour force in China 142–3; *see also* working class
landlord characters in Chinese film 101
leadership in China 17, 29, 32–5, 39, 43, 46; *see also* power
legal system: in China 37, 39; in *Let the Bullets Fly* 35–9
Let the Bullets Fly (film): ambiguity of plot conclusion in 31–2; audience of 16, 30–1, 38–9, 45–6, 147; background information about 29–30; box office revenue of 29; class and 10, 29, 32; collusion in, portrayal of 33–4; computer graphics imaging in 30; corruption in 34–5, 39; costumes in 30; criticism without political change and 45–6; dialogue in 30, 45; exhibition time of 9, 29; female audience's view of 38–9, 44; film literacy and 30; final scenes of 41–2, *42*; group discussants for 154–60; group discussions of 30–1, 34–5, 38–9, 42–6; irony in 38; legal system in 35–9; narrative conclusion of 31–2, 42; political narrative of 29; poor as masses in 40–5, *42*; power of 45; power and, socialising assumptions about 17, 32–5, 39, 43; privileged class view of 44–5; promotional poster

190   *Index*

for *27*; purpose of 32; selection of for study 9; setting of 34; status quo and, acquiescence to 29–30, 45–6; synopsis of 28–9; teahouse as "real magistracy" in 38; working class view of 30–1, 43–4
Let's Get Married (film) 149
Li, Lianjiang 8
Lin, Jing 150
Liu, Jieyu 86
Lost on Journey (film): affirmative prejudice and 52, 70; audience of 52–4, 147–8; background information about 51–2; beggar and, impression of 64–7, *65*; box office revenue of 52, 70; class and 10, 50–2, 54, 58–9; family and 68–9; group discussants for 160–7; group discussions of 52–8, 64–71; humor of 70; industrial juxtaposition in 54–5, *55*; in-groups versus out-groups and 54–8; location of 52; narrative conclusion of 62–4, 67–8; *Planes, Trains and Automobiles* and, narrative juxtaposition of 18, 58–64; prejudices about class and 17–18, 51, 64–7, *65*; privileged class and, view of 54–8, 66, 68–71; promotional poster of *49*; review of, number of positive 52; selection of for study 9; social mobility in 67–70; stereotyping class and 54–8, 67; synopsis of 50–1; tolerance and, class-based 70–1; working class and, view of 53–8, 66, 68–9
Lost in Thailand (film) 149
Louie, Kam 105
Lu, Xiaoning 101–2

male audience 86–7, 137
Mao Zedong 2, 150
marketing to audience 15–17
marriageability 75, 102, 105–9
masculinity: in China 105–6; in *House Mania* 18, 105–9, 120; in *Piano in a Factory, The* 144
maternal duties 144
media: in China 44–5; consumption 4–5
Meng, Zhang 142
middle class 6–7, 9

narratives: Chinese filmmakers consciousness of 150–1; commercial filmmakers and 5; juxtaposition of 18; political 29; resolutions of 17
negative pedagogy, theory of 101–2

O'Brien, Kevin J. 8

Painting the City Red (Braester) 115
Palmer, Augusta 120–1
peasants 41, *41*, 119–22; *see also* working class
People's Republic of China *see* China
Personal Trailer (film) 148
Piano in a Factory, The (film): as "acquired taste" 130; audience of 16, 130–2, 148; awards and recognition of 129–30; background information about 128–9; box office revenue of 129; class and 10, 141; dialogue in 129–30; distribution of, international 129–30; divorce and 129, 135–8; exhibition time of 129, 144; female audience and 129, 134–5; group discussants for 180–6; group discussions of 130–7, 142–3; individual needs and, asserting 135–8; industrial heroes and 138–41; male audience and 137; masculinity and 144; maternal duties and 144; mood of audience after 131–2; musical interludes in 130; poor and, socialising 143–4; privileged class and, view of 133, 136–7, 142; production value of 129; promotional poster of *127*; retrenched worker and 10, 129–31, 138–41, *141*, 144; segmented labour force and audience and 142–3; selection of for study 9; setting of, dating 142–3; social mobility and 141; *suzhi* and, cultivating 18, 129, 132–3, 144; synopsis of 128; working class and, view of 129, 133–4, 137, 144; Xiao Yuan's piano and 132–5
Planes, Trains and Automobiles (film) 18, 58–64
polarisation, socialised 96
political narratives 29
poor: beggar in *Lost on Journey* and, impression of 64–7, *65*; in *Let the Bullets Fly* 40–5, *42*; as masses 40–5, *42*; in *Piano in a Factory, The* 143–4; prejudice against 64–7, *65*; socialising 143–4
power: corruption 17, 32–5, 39; exclusion of 34; inclusion of 34; socialising assumptions about 17, 32–5, 39
pre-conditioning Chinese audiences 5–6, 22–6, 146

prejudice: affirmative 52, 70; China's cinema of class and 52; class 13–14, 51–2, 54–8, 67, 70, 122; connotation of 52; gender 77; against poor 64–7, *65*; rural to urban investments and 122; social action and 51

privileged class: access to cinema and 26; Chinese films and film industry and 150; compensation for 25; *Go Lala Go!* and, view of 77–8, 90, 93, 95–6; group discussions with 24–6; *House Mania* and, view of 103–5, 108–11, 114–15, 118, 121; length of discussions with 25; *Let the Bullets Fly* and, view of 44–5; *Lost on Journey* and, view of 54–8, 66, 68–71; *Piano in a Factory, The,* and, view of 133, 136–7, 142; political benefactors and 7–8; social humiliation of working class by 24–5

privilege, rethinking 117–18

product awareness 93

product placement in film 76, 90, *91*

property market: in China 102, 110, 123–4; corruption in 13, 102, 110–11, 118; *House Mania* and 102, 110–12, 114–15, 123–4

Qiang, Chen 101–2

Red Detachment of Women (film) 41, *41*, 101

Reicher, Stephen 51

Ren, Hai 6–7

Research Centre for Information and Communication Studies 4–5

retail therapy as female attribute 90, 92–5; *see also* consumption

retrenched workers 8, 10, 129–31, 138–41, *141*, 144; *see also* working class

rural migrant workers 43, 51–2, 77–8, 116–17, 148; *see also* working class

SARFT (now SAPPRFT) 29, 129, 146–7

screen-based storytelling, importance of 146

sense making of films 4–6, 26, 147–8

sexism 13

sexual enticement 89

shared class 14–15

shared histories 14–15

shengnü 18, 75, 80, 89, 96, 102

Shi, Tongyun 129

shopping as female behavior 90, 92–5; *see also* consumption

siheyuan 101, 115–16

Siu, Kaxton 8

So, Alvin 143

social engineering of audience and people 32, 151

social harmony in China 2, 6–9, 29, 71

social mobility: class and 67–70; "cuteness" performance and 83–5; in *Go Lala Go!* 74–5, 80–5; in *Lost on Journey* 67–70; in *Piano in a Factory, The* 141

social organization in China, conflicting modes of 137

social structure *see* class

State Administration of Press, Publications, Film, Radio and Television (SAPPRFT) 2–4

stereotyping: class 14, 54–8, 67; gender 77, 79–85, 90, 92–5

Stockman, Norman 33

subordinate class 8, 14; *see also* working class

Sun, Wanning 6, 54

Sun, Xiaoyan 150

Su, Xiaobu 6, 9

suzhi: of characters in film 12–13; in China 7; class as 12–13; defining 7; of family 7; gender and 12–13; *Piano in a Factory, The,* and, cultivating 18, 129, 132–3, 144; power and wealth and 7; prejudging and 13; socialising class and 9; working class and 16

Tiny Times series 148–9

tolerance, class-based 70–1

Tomba, Luigi 105

Twin Bracelets (film) 5

United Kingdom's audience research 5

United States 26, 146

Wen, Jiang 29, 45

Western histories 15

white collar romances 85–9

white collar women 79–80, 96

White-Haired Girl, The (film) 101

women, general portrayal in Chinese films 75–6

working class: access to cinema and 23–4; China's leadership and 43; compensation for 22–3; *Go Lala Go!*

192 *Index*

and, view of 77–8, 88–9, 93, 95–6; group discussions with 22–4; *House Mania* and, view of 103–8, 114, 117–18, 123; *Let the Bullets Fly* and, view of 30–1, 43–4; *Lost on Journey* and, view of 53–8, 66, 68–9; *Piano in a Factory, The,* and, view of 129, 133–4, 137, 144; social humiliation of 24–5; social unrest and 8; *suzhi* and 16; time of discussions with 24; work schedules of 22–4

xiagang gongren 8, 10, 129–31, 138–41, *141*, 144
Xu, Guiquan 5, 81

Yan Zhu 88
Yantao, Yang 75
Yip, Raymond 70

Zang, Xiaowei 8
Zhang, Yingjin 5, 29
Zhu, Ying 3–4